Threat Exposure Management

Risk | Resilience | Change

Andrew D. Banasiewicz, Ph.D.

with contribution by

Dave Weidman

Published by Erudite Analytics
Bristol, Rhode Island
USA

For information, contact Andrew Banasiewicz, P.O Box 951, Bristol, RI 02809, USA.

ISBN-13: 978-0-9815690-6-2
ISBN-10: 0-9815690-6-4

ERUDITE ANALYTICS

To my wife Carol, my daughters Alana and Katrina, and my son Adam.

Foreword

It is hard to think of an instinct that is more fundamental than the desire to survive. Not only does it cut across all lifeforms – it also permeates the metaphysical realm of our existence, as it inspires us to search for a deeper meaning of life. It seems reasonable to assert that we are programmed to want to survive, both in physical as well as existential sense.

Organizations exhibit many of the same human-like characteristics, which is not at all surprising given that at their core organizations are nothing more than collections of individuals joined in pursued of shared goals. Within a business firm context, this 'survival directive' takes the form of the so-called 'going concern' provision, which is an assumption that a particular business interest functions without the threat of liquidation for the foreseeable future. A direct, though rarely expressly acknowledged consequence of that assumption is that survival assurance is the most fundamental organizational goal. Winning customers, earning profit, growing market share are all subsumed under the going concern directive, much like esteem or self-actualization needs can be fulfilled only after the more fundamental physiological and safety needs. Why, then, is the broadly defined risk management function often the least sophisticated part of organizational governance and control systems?

One could propose numerous explanations for that – let's start with some easy ones: At least some of the descriptive labels commonly used to characterize organizational efforts aimed at threat identification and mitigation are a part of the problem, as exemplified by the widely used term 'risk management'. Considering that (as detailed later in this text) the majority of risks confronting an organization could be categorized as external and uncontrollable, isn't the term 'risk management' paradoxical? It is clear that acts of nature, such as storms or earthquakes cannot be 'managed'; moreover, from the standpoint of an organization, many manmade phenomena, such as macroeconomic or geopolitical trends, are equally unmanageable. What is manageable, however, about those and other potentially disruptive events is the degree of *exposure.* Locating in areas less susceptible to natural disasters or investing in appropriately engineered physical structure designs are two common examples of mitigating the degree of exposure to storms and other recurring disruptive events. Merely replacing 'management' with 'exposure' might seem to just be a trivial matter of labeling, but as shown throughout this book, it can have material impact on how organizations approach responding to threats.

The second and far more tangible and systemic reason behind the comparative lack of sophistication of organizational threat abatement mechanisms is what I call *scope myopia*. By and large, business organizations tend to rely on multiple planning, control and response mechanisms, which operate as stand alone, self-focused business functions. To that end, most larger firms have formal 'risk management' function, many have formal 'business continuity' and 'emergency management' capabilities, and some even have somewhat formalized 'change management' capabilities – however, in almost no cases, as far as I can tell, are those functions 'tied together' by a single 'total threat abatement' control and coordination system. Imagine if another, more mature organizational function, such as marketing, existed as a collection of independent, self-focused endeavors, such as 'advertising', 'direct mail', 'customer loyalty', etc. How efficient and effective would be the resultant marketing efforts geared at, let us say, new customer acquisition or current customer retention? It does not take a great deal of imagination – or marketing expertise – to see how inefficient, and likely ineffective such self-centric efforts would turn out to be. Although it might be somewhat less obvious, the very same rationale holds true to organizational efforts geared toward threat protection: It is imperative for business firms to develop all-threat-encompassing strategies and mechanisms to direct and coordinate systematic and sound *threat abatement* efforts. The Threat Exposure Management, or TEM for short, framework described here is intended to serve as a conceptual and methodological blueprint for organizations wishing to not only establish better risk protection mechanisms, but also to create a new source of competitive advantage.

Andrew D. Banasiewicz

Contents

Threat Exposure Management

Risk | Resilience | Change

1

Expecting the Unexpected

At the tail end of 2007, the United States and, to a somewhat lesser degree, the world economy became engulfed in a financial crisis, the likes of which has not been seen since the Great Depression. The Great Recession contributed to the loss of trillions of dollars of consumer wealth and a sharp decline in economic activity; even more startlingly, the crisis precipitated failures or near-failures of key financial organizations[1], which were unable to sustain the staggering losses[2] they brought upon themselves. In addition, far-reaching efforts of monetary authorities in the U.S. and abroad, aimed at preventing an outright collapse of the financial system, resulted in substantial fiscal commitments incurred by governments.

Crises of that magnitude can only happen because of system-wide, structural problems. Looking back, the financial near-catastrophe of 2007 appears to have been a direct consequence of excessive risk taking, itself a product of the gradual deregulation of the financial system. A closer look at the U.S banking industry illustrates that point.

---

[1] For instance, 140 banks failed in the U.S. in 2009 alone (compared to 25 failures the year before), leaving in their wake more than $34 billion in losses sustained by the Federal Deposit Insurance Corporation. It marked the highest rate of bank failure since the savings and loan crisis of the 1980s and early 1990s, during which time 747 savings and loan associations failed at a combined cost of more than $160 billion.

[2] A 2010 estimate by the Organization for Economic Cooperation and Development linked $1.23 trillion in banks' losses to the financial crisis of 2007/2008.

The Genesis of the Crisis

Until the early 1980s, commercial banks were restricted, for the most part, to financial intermediation – deposit taking and lending – to the exclusion of more speculative (i.e., risky) financial activities, such as underwriting of corporate securities. Furthermore, banks were also geographically constrained – in general, they were not permitted to expand beyond their home states. Under those conditions, the systemic risk – which is the vulnerability of the entire banking system – was relatively low, the assessment of banks' risk exposure fairly straightforward, and the failure of a single bank unlikely to threaten the stability of the entire financial system. At the same time, however, both the growth and the profitability of banks were, according to the proponents of free markets and self-regulation, 'artificially constrained'.

All of that began to change in the early 1980s with the onset of broad deregulation ushered in by the U.S President Reagan's administration. By the mid to late 1980s, essentially all key banking restrictions have been lifted, which freed banks to expand both in terms of geography as well as the scope of operation (see the U.S Banking and Financial Amendments in the Financial Services Competitiveness and Regulatory Relief Act). As evidenced by the rapid growth of financial derivatives, or instruments which derive their value from underlying assets, the banks' risk appetite grew by leaps and bounds. Now largely uninhibited in their pursuit of potentially riskier investment strategies, financial intermediaries embraced ever more speculative and complicated investment vehicles, such as collateralized debt obligations, or CDOs[3]. Some of those vehicles were in fact so complex that their true riskiness was practically indeterminate[4] which, oddly, did not seem to concern the executives investing in them, or the rating agencies evaluating their investment-worthiness (or, for that matter, regulatory agencies, such as the U.S Securities Exchange Commission).

---

[3] Collateralized debt obligations, or CDOs, are a type of structured asset-backed security whose value and payments are derived from a portfolio of underlying fixed-income assets. CDO securities are split into different risk classes, or tranches, whereby senior tranches are considered the safest securities. Interest and principal payments are made in order of seniority, so that junior tranches offer higher coupon payments (and interest rates) or lower prices to compensate for additional default risk. The first CDO was issued in 1987 by the now-defunct Drexel Burnham Lambert Inc.

[4] This is a retrospective conclusion; the Gaussian copula function, discussed later in this section, was at the time thought capable of yielding a reliable, if not deterministic, assessment of the underlying riskiness of investment derivatives.

In the end, the aggressive deregulation of the U.S. financial services industry created an environment where banks had the means, in the form of large deposit pools, and the motives, in the form of potentially high yields, to commit billions of dollars to increasingly more speculative investments. Ultimately, the unchecked demand for exotic (an industry euphemism for 'unintelligible risk') securities infused substantial amounts of systemic risk into the financial system, thus effectively creating a potential for a large scale financial disaster...Yet on paper, trillions of dollars of wealth were created.

The lion's share of the multi-trillion dollars, systemic risk-dressed-as-wealth bonanza was a speculative pyramid, a proverbial house of cards. Its foundation was a combination of housing market-based financial derivatives and the widely held belief in the improbability of a systemic housing price collapse (the belief held by most was that the housing market was primarily driven by regional economic forces, meaning that prices in one region moved independently of other regions' prices). In the end, presumably sophisticated financial intermediaries exposed themselves, their shareholders, and most importantly, those whose assets they managed to unacceptable amounts of risk. For that reason alone, we should view the 2007/2008 financial meltdown as nothing less than one of the farthest-reaching failures of executive risk management of the modern era.

The Culprits

As tends to be the case with just about any man-made catastrophe, the financial crisis of 2007/2008 led to many revelations and even more accusations. Fingers were pointed at executives of the financial giants teetering on the edge of collapse, regulatory and rating agencies, and of course, risk analytical tools that became the staple of financial risk management. Undoubtedly, much of the criticism is quite on point and warranted – still, some of the commentaries reflect a lack of deeper understanding of the underlying mechanisms, most notably, those attributing the responsibility for the financial collapse to quantitative risk measurement and management systems. Let us take a closer look.

It is clear that risk management models did not foresee the coming of a catastrophe. That said, the reasons are considerably more complex than what tends to be discussed by media pundits. In the most general sense, the roots of risk management models can be traced to multiple factors, perhaps the most visible of which is the normalcy of the patterns embedded in the available data. Simply put, contemplating an event which has not been observed, at least not within a reasonably recent history, is beyond the capabilities of risk assessment tools, or more specifically, mathematical models used to estimate the probability and the severity of adverse events. Stated differently, model-derived projections that comprise the core of risk quantification systems are essentially extrapolations (more or less) of patterns contained in historical data, which effectively define the limits of what a given model can anticipate. It means that if a particular outcome has not occurred within the time horizon covered by the data used in the analysis, the resultant mathematical projections will not 'foresee' it, which is to say that no numeric chances of that outcome materializing[5] will be generated.

Of course, one can create scenarios that look beyond the available data, but the probabilities associated with such scenarios will lack the requisite empirical rigor, which is usually necessary to establish the credibility of any model-based projections. In other words, without the foundation of hard data, catastrophe-prophesying forecasts are nothing more than speculative guesses, which rarely have behavior-changing impact. And in the case of most risk management models, the available data was simply not indicative of the events that materialized in 2007 and 2008, and if anyone was indeed pursuing speculative doomsday scenarios, that work did not get much attention, at least not among the vast majority of the key decision makers...More on that in the next section.

The relative normalcy of historical trends, however, was only one of the factors that contributed to the inefficacy of risk models. The other major trouble spots were the data analytic methodologies and data analytic assumptions – both of which further 'stacked the cards' against those tools' chances of forecasting the perfect storm of undesirable conditions. An in-depth discussion of those considerations falls outside the scope of this overview, but

---

[5] The ideas expressed here touch upon differences separating deterministic algorithms and the Monte Carlo simulation method. The former are often referred to in business as predictive analytics, which most commonly take the form of mathematical functions, where pre-determined inputs are related to an outcome of interest and where a particular set of inputs always produces the same output. The latter rely on repeated computation of random or pseudo-random numbers and are used for modeling phenomenon characterized by significant uncertainty of inputs. The common misconception surrounding the Monte Carlo method is that it can be used to model unknown outcomes, where in fact the (Monte Carlo) method-generated data requires the specification of a probability distribution (from which the data is generated in a random fashion). In other words, Monte Carlo method will not yield worthwhile results without some basic knowledge regarding the phenomenon of interest.

let it suffice to say that broadly defined statistical analyses (a collection of mathematical techniques for analysis of data) and analytical assumptions were both geared – as it is usually the case – toward forecasting likely, not aberrant outcomes. Stated differently, the inner structure of risk estimation tools has been designed with the goal of identifying events that could occur within a reasonable event and/or time horizon. Focusing on likely rather than aberrant outcomes may be viewed by some as a nearsighted choice, but in fact, it is a natural consequence of the scientific method, the philosophical and analytic bedrock of modern science. The key precepts of the scientific method entail the gathering of observable (i.e., measurable) evidence subject to specific principles of reasoning, which in turn supports the derivation of generalizable knowledge claims; most of what we refer to as empirical knowledge is a product of the broadly defined scientific method. As it relates to the analysis of risk, scientific method-derived outcomes, such as specific risk estimates, are not only more computationally manageable, but are also empirically verifiable – clearly, an important aspect of fostering the believability of numeric estimates. However, it all comes at a cost, which in this case is the aforementioned focus on likely, rather than aberrant outcomes.

Still, the roots of inefficiency in risk assessment tools run deeper than the nature of probabilistic projections. Even the most enlightened knowledge creation processes cannot overcome fundamental data deficiencies or compensate for the lack of data. And therein lies the rub: The focal risk projections were based on *proxies*, rather than outcome-specific data, because of the scarcity of direct behavioral data.

That was precisely the case with credit default swaps, or CDSs[6]. In the world of commercial transactions, the actual credit defaults are relatively rare, which means data paucity, which in turn impedes the estimation of (future) default probabilities[7]. At the same time, default swap price data, which tracks third party credit risk insurance (called 'swaps' for reasons discussed later) premium prices, is readily available. Taking a seemingly small leap of faith of

---

[6] A type of financial derivative product, a *credit default swap* is a transaction where the buyer of the swap receives credit protection, while the seller guarantees the credit worthiness of the product. In general, it is a means of transferring the credit exposure of fixed income products between parties.

[7] In order to be projectable and representative, statistically derived estimates require adequately large sample sizes, which translates into adequately high historical default rates (what constitutes adequate sample size is subject to numerous technical considerations which fall beyond the scope of this book, though they are detailed in most basic statistics texts).

assuming that the market prices individual risks correctly, an idea itself inspired by the *efficient market hypothesis*, CDS price spreads can then be interpreted as risk differentials. Add to that an ingenious application of a long-standing mathematical formula bearing the esoteric name of *Gaussian copula function* (named after its creator, a prodigal 18th//19th century mathematician C. F. Gauss) and the result is an elegantly simple solution to the previously intractable problem of quantifying default probabilities of bundled securities. In essence, the application of the Gaussian copula function to CDSs' prices reduced a conceptually complex and computationally messy task of estimating joint default probabilities to a relatively simple measure of bundled risk, expressed in the form of a single correlation estimate.[8] It did not matter how large or diverse the underlying asset pool was – if the overall credit default swap price correlation was low, the bundle of securities was deemed to be low risk. It was indeed a powerfully compelling idea, and essentially every major financial institution, from Wall Street to Main Street, embraced it.

The result was that just about anything that could be packaged into attractive investment pools – consumer mortgages, corporate bonds, bank loans – was indeed packaged, with the resultant market becoming known as collateralized debt obligations, or CDOs mentioned earlier. The wide-spread reliance on – and belief in – the Gaussian copula function-based risk measurement was the engine that propelled the CDO market to a spectacular growth, expanding from about $275 billion in 2000 to more than $4.7 trillion in 2006 – a 17-fold increase in just six or so years. The credit default swap market, which provided default insurance for the CDOs, grew right along with it. Aided by the absence of a natural ceiling on a number of swaps that could be sold against a single borrower, the CDS market grew to enormous

---

[8] In statistics, *copula function* is a general method of formulating multivariate distribution in such a way that variable interdependencies can be captured; the Gaussian function is one of many different types of copula functions. The appeal of this approach stemmed from the fact that by employing simple transformations (which themselves make use of an established methodology, known as the Sklar's theorem) otherwise disparate default rates could be expressed in terms of a uniform distribution, which in turn would make it possible for a bundle of risks to be expressed as a multivariate distribution of marginally random default rates. All of this means that Gaussian copula enabled financial intermediaries to quantify the combined risk of bundles of otherwise dissimilar securities as a single number, the inter-item correlation among component risks. The lower the correlation – the lower the risk, since the correlation measures the degree to which the component securities' credit default prices tend to move, or vary together.

proportions – from little more than $900 billion at the tail end of 2001, to its peak of more than $62 trillion at the end of 2007. It is a staggering amount of financial obligations, to say the least – to put it into perspective, the 2008 gross domestic product (GDP) of the United States was about $14.4 trillion; the combined GDP of all countries of the world was about $60.9 trillion.[9] In other words, the peak value of the CDS market was greater than the combined economic output of the entire world! A speculative bubble of truly epic proportions.

And last but not least: Even though, as mentioned above, credit default swaps were essentially a form of insurance, they were not treated as such – i.e., the obligations were not subject to insurance-like regulatory or reserving requirements.[10] Betting on the steadily increasing home values and the improbability of systemic defaults, the underwriters, such as the now-defunct Lehman Brothers and Bear Sterns as well as nearly-defunct AIG, were issuing billions upon billions of IOUs, making hefty profits at the time of issuance, while setting aside precariously little in reserves to cover future obligations…

What does all of that tell us about risk management? For one, it points to the conclusion that the failure to anticipate and manage the exposure of organizations to large scale risks was correlated with – but not caused by – risk estimation tools failing their users. The true cause of the meltdown was the users' failure to take the models for what they were – estimates that were subject to data and methodological limitations.

Those who continue to point to the inadequacy of risk quantification methodologies as the primary culprit of the financial meltdown seem to have lost sight of the obvious – namely, that the goal of mathematical models is to extract meaningful insights out of otherwise prohibitively large amounts of disaggregated data, not to make decisions, per se. In that sense, risk models provide decision makers with information pertinent to the decision at hand, but always subject to data and methodological limitations. The making of the actual decision almost always entails a combination of multiple data-derived projections or estimates and the decision maker's subjective knowledge and experience. All considered, mathematical models always have been – and as far

---

[9] According to the International Monetary Fund's *World Economic Outlook* database, October 2009.

[10] A reserve, from an insurance standpoint, is a sum of money that is set aside to meet some future obligation; its purpose is to make sure that the policy issuer is able to meet its obligations with regard to individual policies. Reserves are classified as liabilities on the company's balance sheet, which is one of the principal reasons the issuers of CDSs avoided classifying their product as insurance.

as I can tell – always will be subject to data limitations and computational assumptions, while the decision making process will (hopefully) remain to be a uniquely human endeavor. And so will the responsibility for errors in judgment – hiding behind data support systems' inadequacy amounts to nothing less than a remarkable abdication of decision makers' responsibilities.

What If?

In the earlier discussion of the nature of quantitative risk models, I mentioned that if anyone was indeed pursuing speculative doomsday scenarios, that work did not get much attention (among decision makers). This statement touches upon an important consideration, one that I would like to explore further: What if the failed and nearly failed organizations' risk management models did indeed forecast the very scenario we watched unfold in the latter part of 2007 and beyond? Would enough of the decision makers have believe those forecasts and acted accordingly?

Naturally, it is a lot easier to point out faulty reasoning looking back than looking ahead, yet at the same time, singling out the mistakes of the past is an important aspect of learning for the future. However, it is not as simple as just describing the chain of events that precipitated the event of interest or detailing the overt circumstances surrounding it. In general, the majority of economically catastrophic events are circumstantially dissimilar, which means that the uniqueness of each man-made catastrophe may greatly outweigh any cross-event commonalities. Stated differently, studying the root causes of the financial meltdown of 2007/2008 may help relatively little in preventing another crisis from occurring in the future, just as lessons learned from the Great Depression (late 1920s – early 1930s), the Black Friday stock market crash of 1987, the European Sovereign Debt Crisis and other severe economic downturns did little to help forecasters foresee the looming crash. A more instructive approach –at least insofar as economic crisis-like events are concerned – is to evaluate the event of interest in the context of the fundamental nature of human behavior, the key aspects of which capture the more generalizable and enduring qualities likely to shape the future.

In business, as well as a number of other contexts, human behavior is driven primarily by the balance between reward and punishment – the larger the disparity between these two elements, the more the heavier-weighted of the two will influence behavioral outcomes. That means that, if the upside (i.e., reward) of risk taking is significantly greater than its downside (i.e., punishment), the propensity of individuals to take on greater amount of risk will increase, which in aggregate will lead to the heightening of systemic risk. With that in mind, let us consider the character of (broadly defined) financial intermediation. As it relates to the balance between reward and punishment, financial intermediation is primarily institutional in nature (i.e., the ultimate risk takers are the shareholders of organizations, not the individual decision makers within organizations), but the reward structure favors the individual decision makers over the shareholders as a group, as evidenced by Wall Street bonuses awarded to individual decision makers being generally higher than gains realized by Wall Street firms' shareholders. Hence when big bets lead to big losses, it is typically the shareholders who suffer the consequences (as the value of their equity holdings declines) – yet, when big bets lead to big gains, it is the individual decision makers who reap the greatest benefits, typically through large cash bonuses (the share prices of their organizations may not necessarily increase – even if they do, the gains will typically be comparatively modest). In short, there are ample examples where the decision makers' upside of risk taking greatly outweighs its downside. Under those circumstances, risk taking tends to not be a zero sum (where reward and punishment are proportional), but rather a positive sum (where reward is significantly greater than the punishment) game, which manifests itself in a heightened propensity to take risks.

Given the above outlined reasoning, let us go back to the original question: What if the failed and nearly failed organizations' risk management models did indeed forecast the very scenario we watched unfold in the latter part of 2007 and beyond? Would enough decision makers believe those forecasts and act accordingly?

In my view not likely, simply because the reasons for dismissing doomsday forecasts (i.e., the potential rewards) were much more enticing than the reasons to accept those forecasts were threatening (i.e., the potential punishment). Stated differently, given the reward—punishment asymmetry, there are good reasons to believe that the majority of institutional investors would have looked past doomsday projections, even if such forecasts were readily available. In a more general sense, we could say that so long as it is possible (at least for some) to engage in high risk—high potential payoff activities with relative impunity (i.e., little-to-no punishment), even clairvoyant risk assessment models will be of little help in averting disasters...

Risk Management Myopia & the Way Forward

Let us take the idea of informational adequacy a step further and imagine for a moment that the reward—punishment asymmetry is corrected: Would the current risk management structures provide an acceptable risk measurement and response mechanism, at least for most organizations, most of the time?

Clearly, this is a very broad question and the answer will, to a large degree, vary across industries and organizations. For instance, financial companies are typically quite proficient at managing credit risk because they are in the business of lending money; industrial companies, on the other hand, tend to excel in operational risk management, such as workplace safety, as exemplified by DuPont, long a standard-bearer in workplace safety, tracing its proficiency to the company's heritage as an explosives manufacturer. However, risk type-specific proficiencies usually do not translate into overall risk management excellence for three fundamental reasons: 1. skill, data and methodological differences across different types of threats; 2. different levels of importance implicitly or explicitly assigned to different risks; 3. myopic risk management practices. The implications of the first two contributors are intuitively obvious – the third one, however, requires a more in-depth explanation.

To be carried out effectively, the task of managing risk needs to be approached as a system of interconnected decisions that jointly determine the organization's performance rather than as a series of largely unconnected tasks, which is essentially the idea behind enterprise risk management, or ERM. However, even the state-of-the-art ERM approaches are ultimately focused on known risks with well-defined mathematical properties, which renders those approaches ineffective for anticipating and responding to Great Recession-like events. Furthermore, to understand and manage the organization's aggregate risk exposure, one must consider not just individual risks – such as natural disasters, labor disputes, product liability or securities litigation – but must also develop a robust understanding of system-level interdependencies among the individual components of the entire risk management system, which is not expressly contemplated by leading enterprise risk management frameworks, namely COSO and ISO 3100. In short, to effectively manage the *totality* of threats confronting them, organizations need to look beyond current ERM frameworks that emphasize estimation-friendly known risks.

A word of clarification: I am not suggesting that effective management of risk is contingent on the development of some type of a complex supermodel encompassing all aspects of the organization and reducing complex systems to a set of deceitfully simple indicators. Quite to the contrary, I believe that such a mindset can lead to over-reliance on poorly understood and, quite possibly, unreliable decision guides, such as the Gaussian copula function discussed earlier. More specifically, risk managers should embrace purposeful and coordinated mining of the available data – and – should use the resultant insights as guides to reducing chances of selecting disadvantageous (to the organization) courses of action. However, rather than blindly depending on complex model-generated predictions of future states, managers would be well-advised to make use of data analytical techniques that 'fit' the quality and reliability of the available data, which could be simple measures of association or tests of difference yielding analytically simpler, but nonetheless more reliable insights. Stated differently, risk management should be approached as an empirical process, or one focused on revealing objectively verifiable causal interdependencies, but the use of the available data needs to reflect data's quality (accuracy, completeness, representativeness, etc.) as well as the projectability of historical trends.

Almost running counter to the aforementioned over-reliance on 'black box' mathematical models is the invariance in the use of the available data across different decision contexts. In some situations, such as credit risk assessment, data is used routinely to support decision making processes, while in other contexts, such as cultural, political or competitive risks, hardly at all. The reasons for that are both tangible (i.e., the availability of data) as well as intangible, the latter captured in the idea of behavioral inertia.

Nearly a century has passed since the pioneering work of F. W. Taylor (considered by many the father of *scientific management*) and more often than not, management is still viewed (and more importantly, practiced) as art, rather than science. We tend to favor our subjective 'gut feelings' over objective evidence, a phenomenon attributed, by cognitive psychologists and brain researchers alike, to our evolutionary development. Obviously, intuition and experience-based decision-making worked remarkably well within the confines of grand evolutionary processes – why couldn't it work equally well in business? Indeed, there are times when our instincts can and do work quite well, so long as the economic climate is calm and stable (as was the case through much of the 1990s). However, there are reasons to believe that the future might be considerably less unwavering. Even looking past the myriad social and security related flashpoints, there is emerging evidence suggesting that the economy is growing more turbulent; in fact, some of the leading management strategists now believe that turbulence is not an aberration, but the new face of normal. What does this mean for management decision making? The frequency with which many decisions will need to be made will rapidly increase, which means that effective risk management in the 21st century and beyond will have to be considerably more information-intensive. Intuition alone simply will not suffice.

It is not to say, however, that it will become less demanding of human problem solving. Quite to the contrary—the demands on decision makers will increase, most notably in terms of decision lead time and decision-making frequency. As suggested earlier, experience and intuition alone, though always of value, will be insufficient if not aided by robust, objective informational infrastructure. Incidentally, business landscape is becoming more and more permeated by database systems and complex data crunching algorithms, a trend which contributes to the growing automation of various aspects of operational decision-making. Unfortunately, it is a mixture of good and bad. On the plus side, it helps to translate (and thus, utilize) the vast quantities of data available to most organizations into more usable decision-aiding knowledge. Yet (and that is the negative), the resultant knowledge is not always consumed in the most beneficial manner, or not consumed – in the sense of being used in the decision process – at all. Using objectively derived insights as a decision linchpin is slowly gaining grounds, but old habits are, once again, proving themselves to be hard to break...

Lastly, it is important to not lose sight of the fact that the goal of automated information processing is to reduce or altogether eliminate tedious, non-thinking, and non-creative tasks and by doing so, free up time and resources for a more constructive use. The goal is not to replace creative problem solving with 'check-the-box approaches. Yet, that is not always the case in risk management, where there is a tendency to use decision support systems as an excuse not to think, as opposed to a reason to think and look deeper. In a very basic way this type of risk management automation was probably a strong contributor to the financial community's willingness to accept collateralized debt obligations and other convoluted investment instruments with structures so complex that they required Nobel-track scientists to set up, and dozens of pages of contractual documents to describe.

No One Approach Does It All

The notion of 'risk', as used in everyday business vernacular, communicates the possibility of adverse or otherwise undesirable events. Given the desirability of proactively addressing potential adversities, business organizations rely on structured, systemic processes to manage their exposure to risk. Known as risk management, those processes typically entail numerous activities that can be grouped into identification of distinct risks, assessment of each identifiable risk and selection of appropriate risk-specific responses.

Given its long history (see Figure 1.1 below), it is not surprising that the notion of 'risk management', as a subject of theoretical research and practical applications alike, can take on different, context-shaped meanings. For instance, business organizations routinely manage already-known risks, prepare for not-yet-known threats, attempt to adapt to changing trends, and seek to take advantage of emerging business opportunities. Although all of those activities entail protecting organizational assets, in practice only some fall within the scope of organizational risk management efforts, while others are treated as stand-alone activities. In the last twenty or so years the overall threat abatement efforts began to coalesce around three distinct disciplines of 1. *risk management*, which is focused on minimizing the impact of known risks; 2. *organizational resilience*, which addresses reducing vulnerability to unknown (i.e., not estimable) threats; and 3. *change management*, which is primarily concerned with maximizing the benefits of self-imposed change.

Figure 1.1

Distinct Disciplines Focused on Organizational Exposure Management

Management activities that aim to bring about minimization of the impact of known risks are built around reduction, mitigation and transfer of those risks; those aiming to reduce vulnerabilities to unknown threats are built around training, contingency planning and response infrastructure development; lastly, activities that support self-mandated and self-guided transformations are focused on balancing the dangers and the benefits of strategic and tactical transformations.

Does the three-pronged approach to managing the totality of organizational exposures, graphically illustrated in Figure 1, fulfill the promise of enterprise-wide risk management advocated by academic researchers[11], industry associations (e.g., CAS, COSO), ratings and standards organizations (International Organization for Standardization, Standard & Poor's), and business organizations themselves? Can the pursuit of the three-pronged organizational adversities management strategy give rise to competitive advantage? The goal of the ensuing analysis is to address these important questions and make forward-looking recommendations, starting with a brief outline of the genesis and the scope of each of the three organizational adversity abatement focused disciplines.

Risk Management

The efforts of manage risk in commercial setting have a long and distinguished history, going as far back as 2,000 BC. However, as graphically depicted in Figure 1.2, it was not until the 17th century that the contemporary notions of speculative risk transfer and risk pooling began to emerge, ultimately giving rise to insurance marketplace and alternative risk financing mechanisms. The modern practice of *risk management* began to take shape around the same time; originally focused on sea shipping, the management of risk expanded to property following the Great London Fire and then onto other aspects of commercial endeavor. Today, the theory and practice of risk management extend into natural disasters, man-made crises and liability, as well as endeavors, such as healthcare, banking and finance, security and crisis management, outdoor recreation, project management, information

[11] e.g., Duckert, G. H. (2011), *Practical Enterprise Risk Management: A Business Process Approach,* Wiley, Hoboken, NJ; Lam, J. (2014), *Enterprise Risk Management: From Incentives to Controls,* 2nd ed., Wiley, Hoboken, NJ; Marchetti, A. M. (2012), *Enterprise Risk Management: Best Practices from Assessment to Ongoing Compliance,* Wiley, Hoboken, NJ.

infrastructure maintenance, communication, and numerous others. It is also not surprising that, from the standpoint of organizational risk management, the management of multiplicity of risks can be approached holistically, a practice that has come to be known as *enterprise risk management* (ERM).

Figure 1.2
Risk Management Timeline

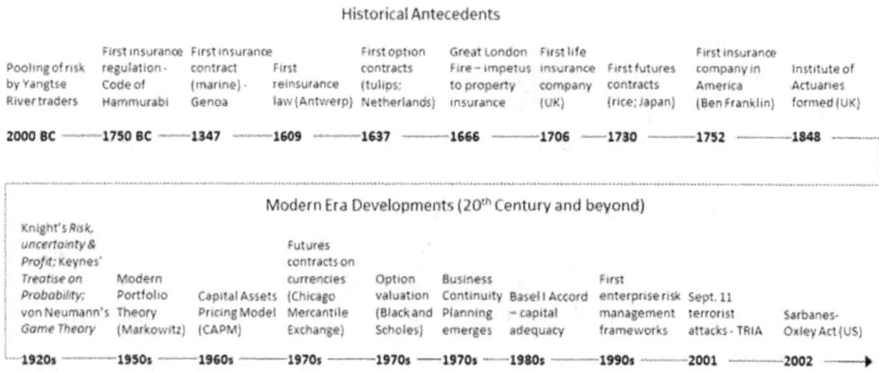

Historically, business organizations approached the management of risk as an expense minimization function, aiming to secure the greatest amount of risk protection for the lowest possible cost. In fact, even the state-of-the-art ERM practices are still primarily focused on risk economics, which is best evidenced by leading ERM frameworks' (i.e., COSO and ISO 31000) emphasis of reduction, mitigation and transfer of known risks. Although it is difficult to dispute the rationale of seeking cost savings, in the age of ever-greater volatility and rapidly proliferating risks, such mindset may ultimately diminish firms' competitiveness as it overemphasizes known downside risks, while largely sidestepping unknown threats and upside risks.

As the 'gold standard' in contemporary organizational risk management, ERM is built around a standard, stepwise process of identification, estimation, mapping and response, and it aims to enhance the efficiency and the efficacy of risk management decisioning through coordination of the management of multiple, diverse threats confronting the organization. However, as a subject of theoretical research, enterprise risk management is still in its infancy: Its earliest formal conceptualizations only date back to 1990s (AS/NZS 4360 Risk Management Standard, first published in 1995), though the bulk of the formative work took place in the first decade of 2000s (e.g., the 2003 CAS, the 2004 COSO, or the 2010 ISO 31000 frameworks). Hence the very conception of ERM continues to evolve – some influential sources define risk independently of firm objectives (for example, Standard & Poor's, 2012), while others define it as a byproduct of firm objectives (for example, COSO, 2004). Overall, as recently pointed out by Bromiley and his colleagues, the past decade of ERM-focused research is starting to yield some consensus, namely:

1. ERM assumes that managing a portfolio of risks is more efficient than managing each risk individually – it is like managing one's stock portfolio, where the goal is to maximize the total return on the overall portfolio;
2. ERM incorporates (traditionally) known risks, such as accidents or product liability, and unknown risks, such as product obsolescence or competitor actions; also, it encompasses downside as well as upside threats;
3. The goal of risk management is to exploit downside threats as well as upside threats and opportunities in a manner that makes positive contribution to the firm's competitiveness;

Still, in spite of its all-inclusive sounding label, the application of enterprise risk management has been limited to known risks with well-defined statistical properties, which leads to a systematic exclusion of a wide array of hard to quantify and emerging threats. Picking up the 'slack' created by risk management's selective focus, the disciplines of organizational resilience and change management emerged to help organizations deal with adversities that are not expressly included in the 'traditional' approach to risk management.

Organizational Resilience

Another, though largely separate set of efforts addressing potential organizational adversities is the emerging discipline of *organizational resilience* (OR). The general notion of 'resilience' has its roots in ecology, where it is defined as the capacity of an ecosystem to respond to a disturbance by resisting damage and by recovering quickly. Hence in contrast to risk management, which focuses on shielding organizations from known, undesirable events, organizational resilience is focused on developing capacity to absorb and 'bounce back' from adverse events. Stated differently, as graphically illustrated in Figure 1.1 above, OR is primarily concerned with reducing organizational vulnerability to largely unknown – in the sense of estimability – threats, primarily natural and man-made crises, disasters and emergencies.

In contrast to risk management, which as discussed earlier evolved over multiple centuries, organizational resilience, as a research and applied area, is comparatively new. In fact, the discipline can be seen as an evolutionary amalgamation of two previously distinct disciplines of *disaster risk reduction* (DRR) (which also includes emergency management) and *business continuity planning* (BCP). Consider figures 1.3a and 1.3b, which show a high development timeline of DRR and BCP, respectively.

Figure 1.3a
Organizational Resilience Timeline: DRR Dimension

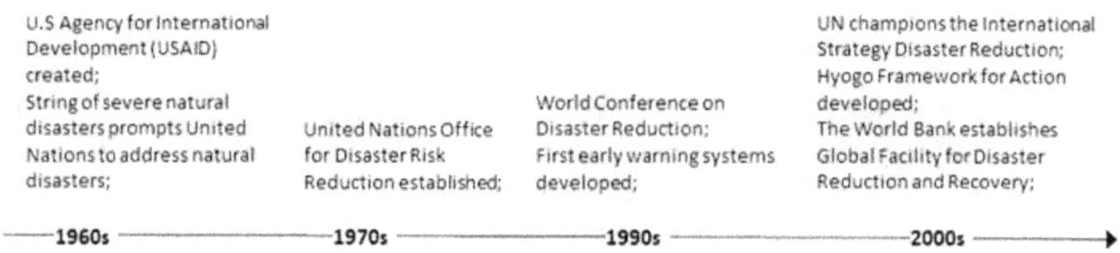

Figure 1.3b
Organizational Resilience Timeline: BCP Dimension

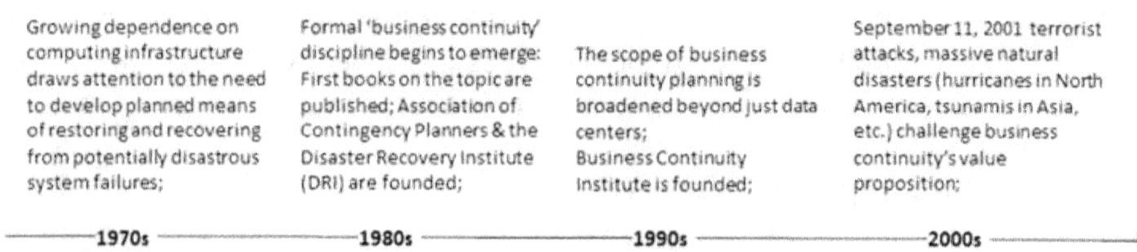

While disaster risk reduction, as a somewhat organized endeavor, emerged a few years prior to business continuity planning, both DRR and BCP essentially came of age in the course of the past four decades. As suggested by figures 1.3a and 1.3b, the impetus for disaster risk reduction came out of the rise of global efforts to mitigate the impact of disasters and catastrophes, while the growing dependence of businesses and governments on electronic communication and data infrastructure provided the motivation for business continuity planning.

Change Management

A still more recent discipline that addresses yet another dimension of managing organizational adversities is *change management* (CM), which first emerged in the 1980s as a consulting service helping large (typically, Fortune 50) companies realize cost savings through more efficient implementation of new programs and technologies. Since then, the initially applied notion blossomed into an extensive body of intellectual work addressing a spectrum of topics dealing with the management of change in an organizational setting. The resultant theoretical work can be grouped into how-to comprehensive guides, conceptual overviews, case illustrations, impact assessment and new approaches and techniques.

Endemic to the essence of managing change is that unlike risk management and organizational resilience, both of which are focused on diminishing the impact of undesirable events, the goal of change management is to maximize benefits presented by emerging or evolving trends and innovations (see Figure 1). Focused on intentional and directed organizational transformations, and considered a source of opportunity (rather than threat), CM is often considered tangential, but distinct from the traditionally defined risk management efforts. However, considering that, under most circumstances self-imposed transformation disturbs organizational status quo, the impact of such transformation or change is conceptually similar to that of a crisis or a disaster. Thus although change can be ultimately beneficial to the organization, it also poses significant threats which need to be managed like all other organizational adversities, which suggests that change management should be a part of a larger organizational danger abatement process.

Putting it All Together: The TEM Framework

More than two decades passed since the idea of jointly managing the totality of risks confronting organizations began to be implemented by forward-thinking business organizations; nowadays the compelling logic of enterprise-wide risk management is widely accepted by practitioners and theoreticians alike. That being the case, how does one explain the emergence and growth of three distinct disciplines focused on different aspects of organizational adversity: risk management, organizational resilience and change management? Even more importantly, is the embrace of such a three-pronged approach conducive to business organizations transforming their broadly defined adversity abatement efforts into a source of competitive advantage?

First and foremost, all three disciplines described here are ultimately focused on assuring the well-being of organizational assets; however, each of the disciplines plays a noticeably different role in that overall effort. Risk management, including ERM, is focused on identifiable and estimable events that can adversely impact organizational assets or its well-being; as shown in Figure 1, its goal is to choose a response option that will minimize the impact of those events. Within that context, the idea of enterprise-wide risk management is thus effectively limited to events that exhibit mathematically sufficient recurrence and impact characteristics. Organizational resilience, on the other hand, is focused on identifying and remedying vulnerabilities to events that are principally unknown, or highly uncertain, in the sense of likelihood of occurrence and/or the severity of impact. Thus although risk management and organizational resilience both can be conceptualized as mechanisms for protecting organizational assets against potentially adverse, speculative events, the role of the former is to act as a 'shield' that can deflect undesirable consequences, while the role of the latter is to create a 'buffer' capable of absorbing potential shocks, as graphically shown in Figure 1.4.

Figure 1.4
Threat Exposure Management: Roles and Responsibilities of Component Disciplines

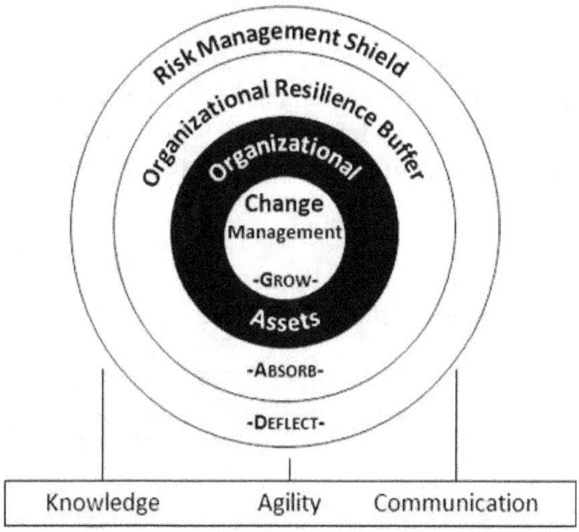

The role of the last of the three organizational adversity-focused disciplines – change management – is noticeably different in terms of its end objectives (although it shares the same core objective of assuring organizational well-being). To use sports analogy, to the degree to which risk management and organizational resilience can be seen as 'defensive' endeavors, change management can be seen as an 'offensive' function. That is because the driving force behind self-imposed organizational transformations, which are the typical focal points of change management efforts, is the desire to realize cost savings and/or revenue gains through adaption of innovative practices and technologies. At the same time, however, organizational transformations disturb the structure and the inner-workings of organizations, creating potential for adverse consequences, not unlike natural disasters or man-made crises. All considered, to manage the *totality* of potentially adverse events and developments in the manner contemplated, though not yet fully delivered by enterprise-wide risk management efforts organizations need to amalgamate the three prongs of their asset-protecting efforts, depicted in Figure 1.4, into a singular *Threat Exposure Management* framework. Doing so will enable firms to coordinate their adversity-abatement efforts to more effectively and efficiently respond to know risks, prepare to absorb the impact of unknown threats and better manage self-mandated organizational transformations.

An Evolutionary Perspective

The rationale underlying the Threat Exposure Management (TEM) conceptualization described here can be seen as an evolutionary consequence of the successively broader and progressively more interconnected sets of activities focused on protecting organizational well-being, graphically depicted in Figure 1.5.

Figure 1.5
Threat Exposure Management: The Evolutionary Perspective

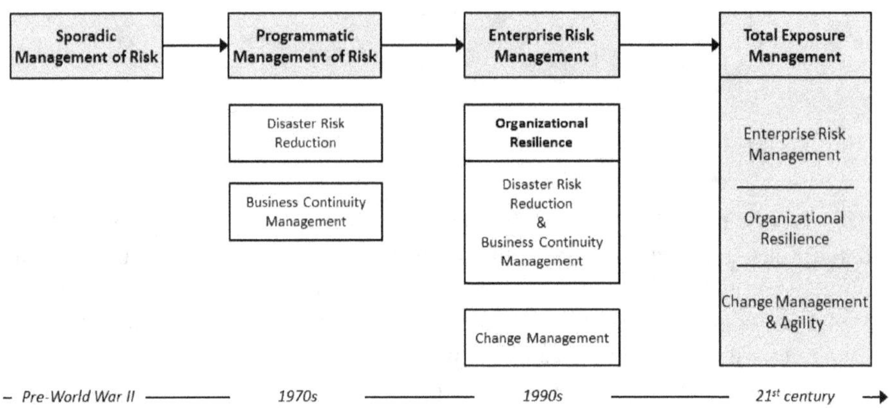

From the standpoint of a 'typical' business organization, the period before, and immediately following World War II was characterized by sporadic risk management activities, where some risks were managed on as-needed basis. The growing realization of the importance of protecting at least the key organizational assets resulted in the shift to programmatic management of risk, along with the emergence of two new disciplines of DRR and BCP. Realizing the inefficiency of silo-minder risk management yielded the next evolutionary changes: the emergence of ERM, the amalgamation of DRR and BCP into a broader, organizational resilience framework, and the emergence of yet another, organizational well-being focused discipline: change management. The next step in this evolutionary march is that of combining of enterprise risk management, organizational resilience and change management into a single framework of Threat Exposure Management, proposed in this research.

The Three Foundations

The implementation of the Threat Exposure Management (TEM) framework hinges on three distinct but complementary sets of activities: 1. the development of robust and reliable 'what' (threat identification and assessment) and 'how' (threat response) knowledge, 2. Effective communication of information, i.e., the 'right' information conveyed in the 'right' manner at the 'right' time, and 3. Dynamic capability or agility, or the organizational capability to muster and deploy resources. Each of those broad areas entails the development of enabling processes, acquisition and/or refinement of requisite skills, and securing of resources, all conceived and executed in an organizational context.

Knowledge

In the 'age of data' the rate at which new information is created continues to accelerate, largely due to the ever-expanding volume, variety, velocity and veracity of data. That, however, does not necessarily translate into a proportional increase in decision guiding insights for all business organizations – in fact, it is common for business organizations to self-characterize as being data-rich, but knowledge-poor. Hence, while the dizzying growth of volume and diversity of data available to businesses certainly contributes to the decision making, especially in the areas of marketing (e.g., customer experience, sentiment and churn analytics, marketing campaign management or search engine optimization), risk management (e.g., fraud detection, catastrophe modeling) or electronic commerce (e.g., network monitoring and security), overall, the impact of objective data on fundamental decision making processes can be best described as spotty. While the rapid advances in data storage, retrieval and processing greatly simplified and sped up the challenge of translating raw *data* into more refined and summative *information*, taking the next step, which is that of extracting decision-guiding *knowledge* continues to be a challenge…Thus while decades worth of systematic research detailed many biases that permeate subjective human information processing[12], decision makers' intuition still plays far greater role in business decisioning than data.

Communication

Within the confines of the broadly defined domain of organizational threat management, which includes the sub-domains of risk, business continuity and disaster management, the importance of sharing of threat reducing or abating plans, processes and measures with internal stakeholders is generally well understood and emphasized. Somewhat less prominent and less understood, however, is the external stakeholder focused crisis communication strategy. It is common for otherwise well thought out and implemented threat response plans to devote little-to-no attention to managing interactions with organizational outsiders, which may include customers, the press, regulators or shareholders, to name just a few. Hence, an essential part of the TEM framework is a two-pronged communication strategy: 1. A proactive, preparedness- and training-minded dissemination of procedural knowledge, focused primarily on key internal stakeholders, and 2. A responsive (to an organizational crisis, or other adverse developments), situational adaptiveness-minded plan of, primarily, outside stakeholders focused informational management.

Agility

The ultimate goal of the Threat Exposure Management framework is to compel decisive threat abatement actions to bring about meaningful reduction in the likelihood and the severity of adverse events. Keeping in mind the breadth of the framework's scope: risk management, organizational resilience (business continuity planning, disaster risk reduction and emergency management) and change management, effective management of the totality of threats demands *agility*. When considered within the confines of threat abatement, an agile organization is one that is capable of mustering and deploying whatever resources are necessary to respond to the ever-changing mix of threats. Further contributing to the difficulty of managing the totality of the organization's threat exposure is the need to bring those diverse knowledge bases under a single organizational control structure, which in turn imposes significant cross-learning requirements. For example, 'risk assessment' is a

---

[12] For a comprehensive review, see Kahneman, D. (2011), *Thinking, Fast and Slow,* Farrar, Strauss and Giroux, New York, NY.

core part of both risk management and business continuity planning, though there are substantial (as discussed later in this book) methodological differences between the two dimensions of threat abatement. In a similar vein, considerable means-related difference separate risk management, business continuity, emergency management and change management – for instance, risk management relies heavily on insurance-based risk transfer and related risk financing mechanisms, business continuity planning makes extensive use of table-top simulations, emergency management necessitates the establishment of control and response teams and protocols, while change management makes extensive use of structured process diagraming.

About this Book

The overall goal of this book is to offer an overview of a comprehensive approach to managing the totality of threats confronting business and other organizations. The approach for doing so is presented as a management framework, termed Threat Exposure Management or TEM – it is envisioned as the first, to the best of my knowledge, attempt at amalgamating the traditionally distinct disciplines of risk management, business continuity planning, disaster risk reduction and change management. The organizational structure of this book follows the rationale encompassed in the earlier discussed three foundations of the TEM framework: knowledge, communication and action.

The ensuing two chapters: Chapter 2: The Science of Knowing, and Chapter 3: The Art of Communication, offer an in-depth exploration of knowledge and communication, respectively, while the remaining chapters address the heart of the TEM framework – methods and means. The detailed discussion is built around three distinct components of the TEM framework: *risk management* (Chapter 4: Understanding Risk, Chapter 5: Measuring Risk, and Chapter 6: Risk Profiling of Organizations), *organizational resilience* (Chapter 7: Business Continuity Planning, and Chapter 8: Emergency Management), and *change management* (Chapter 9: Mastering Self-Imposed Change). Lastly, an overview of organizational and organizational actors' *compliance* related considerations (Chapter 10: Resilience and Compliance) is also offered as an important dimension of the overall threat abatement efforts.

Threat Abatement vs. Risk Management

The TEM framework aims to encapsulate the true totality of threats confronting business organizations, which necessitates careful selection of labels to convey TEM-wide threat 'totality'. Ideally, 'enterprise risk management' (ERM) could provide such label, but unfortunately as detailed in Chapter 4, neither the leading ERM conceptual frameworks nor the practical ERM applications encompass business continuity, emergency or change management. Furthermore, the conventional use of the term 'risk management' is closely tied to the widely accepted risk response mechanisms (accept, reduce, mitigate and transfer, also discussed in Chapter 4), which only account for some of the threats falling within the scope of the Threat Exposure Management framework. In addition, the term 'risk management' is also somewhat troubling from the epistemological point of view: Although there are numerous risks that can be managed many others are inherently unmanageable (think of hurricanes or actions of competitors), which renders the notion of risk management logically inconsistent. For those reasons the TEM framework calls for an alternative descriptor to convey the totality of threats confronting an organization.

Threat abatement is the term that both encompasses the very broad scope of the TEM framework, while at the same time appears to exhibit the necessary epistemic consistency. The notion of 'abatement' refers to a lessening, diminution or moderation – it can be used in a wide array of contexts, for instance, abatement of debts, noise, pollution, nuisance; hence its meaning is in alignment with the spirit of TEM. The notion is 'threat' is also more appropriate than 'risk' because it denotes a more general state of 'warning', whereas 'risk' communicates a more specific meaning of 'chance'. Thus while in the comparatively narrow context of identifying, estimating and responding to known or knowable dangers the term 'risk management' correctly communicates the target and the scope of impact-lessening activities the notion of 'threat abatement' better captures the far broader scope of managing the totality of organizational exposures to known and knowable risks, as well as planning for not knowable but potentially catastrophic events and managing self-imposed organizational change.

2

The Science of Knowing

There are some very hard to believe facts associated with folding an ordinary sheet of notebook paper. First, regardless of the size of a sheet, no one has been able to fold a sheet of paper more than twelve times[1]. However, what is even more extraordinary about paper folding is the height of the resultant stack. Starting with an appropriately sized sheet of ordinary notebook paper, folding it seven times (the number of folds once believed to constitute the upper limit) will result in a stack approximately equal in height to the thickness of an average notebook. Extra three folds will result in the stack height about the width of a hand (thumb included), and additional four (for a total of fourteen folds) would push the height of our stack to be roughly that of an average person. If we were to continue to fold our sheet of paper, the expected results become very hard to believe: Seventeen-fold would produce a stack the height of an average two story house; extra three folds (for a total of twenty) would yield a stack reaching approximately a quarter of the way up the Chicago's Sears (recently renamed Willis) Tower. If folded over thirty times, the resultant stack would reach past the outer limits of

[1] The 12-fold threshold was reached using a very long stretch of thin paper, resembling toilet paper, using what is known as "single direction folding." A number of people, however, questioned the validity of this mark, believing that a "proper" folding approach entailed folding a sheet in half, turning it 90° and then folding it again. Using the "proper" folding method, it has been shown that a single sheet of thin paper can be folded 11 times, with the first eight folds accomplished manually and the remaining three with the help of mechanical equipment (a steamroller and a forklift).

Earth's atmosphere, and lastly, our ordinarily thin, albeit extraordinarily large in terms of area (to allow a large number of folds) sheet would produce a stack of paper reaching…all the way to the Sun. That is roughly 94 million miles!

For most of us, years of schooling imprinted our minds with a variety of abstract notions, while also conditioning our psyche to accept a considerable amount of intangible truths. So long as those scientific and other truths do not come in conflict with our "common sense" of reality, most of us are generally willing to accept even somewhat far-fetched claims. However, when that is not the case—that is, when a particular claim violates what we consider to be reasonable, the result is cognitive dissonance. We just cannot accept a particular fact or a claim as being true. Even if the underlying rationale and the empirical method both seem acceptable and correct, it can be still very, very hard to believe a conclusion that does not make intuitive sense. That is precisely the case with the paper folding exercise. It is an example of exponential growth, which is a phenomenon where the rate of growth rapidly increases as the quantity (e.g., the above stack of paper) gets larger. Since it is a well-defined mathematical property we can compute its values without the need for physical measurements, which is the reason we are able to estimate the height of the stack of paper, even though we are not physically able to fold a sheet of paper fifty times. I am going to venture to say that those of us who at some point in our educational journey were exposed to the notion of exponential growth found it to be intuitively clear and reasonable; furthermore, once properly explained, the computational steps also made sense, which is to say their logic does not clash with our view of the world. Yet when put to a bit of an extreme test, that otherwise acceptable concept can yield unacceptable conclusions. Folding a thin sheet of paper a relatively small number of times simply cannot result in such a staggeringly high stack…

This example underscores both the value and the challenge associated with using data analysis derived knowledge as the basis decision making. It is very easy to accept the findings which fall in line with our existing beliefs, though it could be argued that little incremental value comes out of such 'discoveries'. It is altogether a different story when findings contradict our a priori beliefs—Is there a problem with the data? Is the approach flawed? Are there any errors…? To be fair, data can be corrupted, an approach can be flawed and we all certainly make mistakes. At the same time, however, none of that could be the case—what then? Oftentimes, doubts linger and what could have become an inspiration for a competitively advantageous decision joins the repository of many other research initiatives, all dutifully written up, but never acted on.

Yet taking the leap of faith and acting in accordance with objectively validated insights can be quite beneficial. Much of information technology that permeates our professional and personal lives is "powered" by quantum mechanical predictions; in fact, quantum theory is, in terms of the accuracy of its predictions, the most accurate scientific theory ever constructed[2]. At the same time, it is among the most bizarre, hard to believe frameworks in terms of its postulates. In quantum theoretical world objects can exist in two states or places simultaneously (a condition known as 'superposition'), in addition to which, objects are also instantaneously "aware" of distant other objects (an effect known as 'quantum teleportation'). It is akin to saying that a person can be simultaneously alive and dead and furthermore, that a person's physical existence is entangled with consciousness of others. What then determines whether someone is alive or dead? The act of looking, stipulates quantum mechanics. In other words, perception creates physical reality. Does that sound believable?

To Einstein these were 'spooky interactions' which is a term he coined deriding the quantum theory. In fact, the great scientist spent more time trying to disprove the quantum theory than he did crafting his own theories of general and special relativity. But in the end, he failed. As much as it is hard to intuitively come to terms with the bizarre postulates of the quantum world, the equations describing its mechanics are extremely reliable. Microchip-powered computing devices, like the laptop on which I am typing this text, work undeniably well, because of the accuracy of quantum mechanical predictions, even though most of us have very hard time accepting the picture painted by the underlying theory.

Obviously, this is not a text on quantum mechanics or paper folding trivia. However, these two examples point to an interesting assertion: The believability of analytically derived explanations should not always be the ultimate determinant of whether or not we accept—and more importantly, act upon—the findings. This is not to say that we should totally disregard our intuition, for that would mean depriving ourselves of lifetime worth of accumulated, though not always well catalogued knowledge. Quite to the contrary—I am arguing that true edge producing knowledge needs to combine the elements of truths that might be intuitively obvious to us with those that may not make sense to us, but have been shown to be empirically true. In other words – why not try to get the best of both worlds?

---

[2] Rosenblum, B. and F. Kuttner (2008), *Quantum Enigma, Physics Encounters Consciousness.*, Oxford University Press, New York, NY.

Data, Knowledge & Decisions

As ably detailed by Quinn and his colleagues[3], success of organizations depends more on their intellectual and systems capabilities than physical assets. To a large degree, Quinn's conclusion is somewhat intuitively obvious: Physical assets are, for the most part, generic, thus it is the application or deployment of those assets that determines the overall success of organizations. Stated differently, it is the uniqueness of organizational know-how, coupled with the ability to utilize that knowledge that are the greatest influencers of success. Hence it is of considerable importance to organizations to systematically develop competitively advantageous insights in a way that will aid their decision-making processes.

It is not an easy task. Unlike the objectively measurable physical assets, knowledge is highly abstract and difficult to measure, both in terms of quality as well as quantity. In the organizational context, it is often either confounded with individuals or buried deep inside various reservoirs holding it. An even more fundamental challenge is that of knowing what we know, especially given the pervasiveness of the use of terms such as 'data', 'information', 'facts', 'insights' or 'knowledge'. When is what we know an inconsequential, as far as the ability to enhance the quality of decisions, informational tidbit and when is a true, difference making insight? The next section hopes to provide some clarification.

---

[3] Quinn, J.B., P. Anderson, and S. Finkelstein (1996), 'Managing Professional Intellect: Making the Most of the Best', *Harvard Business Review*, March-April, 71-80.

Knowledge

Plato[4] defined *knowledge* as 'justified true belief'. Oxford English Dictionary lists several definitions of knowledge including 'expertise, and skills acquired by a person through experience or education', 'the theoretical or practical understanding of a subject', 'what is known in a particular field or in total', 'facts and information', and 'awareness or familiarity gained by experience of a fact or situation'. Wikipedia offers probably the simplest definition, by equating knowledge with 'what is known'.

Oddly (in view of its 2,500 years or so vintage), Plato's definition of knowledge comes the closest to what it means to business decision making. In business in general, and risk management in particular, decision making is necessitated by plurality of alternatives—if there are no alternatives, defined here as substitutable courses of action, there are no decisions to be made. In view of that, knowledge can be construed as the degree of understanding (of relative advantages and disadvantages) of the competing options, or in Plato's terms, beliefs that are justified and true, thus enabling one to select the most advantageous alternative[5]. Hence from the standpoint of risk management decisioning, knowledge represents justified and true beliefs regarding the relative efficacy of competing courses of action.

Taking this line of reasoning a step further, knowing more will give rise to *informational advantage*, which is the ability to make more effective decisions stemming from better understanding of the potential outcomes of competing courses of action. In other words, better risk management know-how will contribute to the organization's competitiveness—in fact, under some circumstances, it could be a source of competitive advantage (a more in-depth description of the notions of competition and competitive advantage is offered in the *Risk Profile Measurement* chapter). However, in order to have that type of a profound impact, organizational knowledge has to exhibit several broadly

---

[4] A Greek philosopher and mathematician, born around 428 B.C and a founder of the Academy of Athens, the first institution of higher learning in the western world.

[5] The processes governing making the said choices are subjects of an interdisciplinary field known as decision theory, which is concerned primarily with goal-directed behavior in the presence of options, under the assumption of non-random selection. In a very broad sense, decision theories fall under two general umbrellas: normative and descriptive. A *normative decision theory* is a theory about how decisions should be made, and a *descriptive theory* is a theory about how decisions are actually made. Obviously, the availability of decision-guiding knowledge is essential to each of the two sets of theories.

defined characteristics—most notably it needs to be codifiable, teachable and systemic.

Codifiability of knowledge is its ability to objectively encode facts and inferences into clear behavioral guides. In a practical sense, it is a degree to which a particular set of insights or know-how can exist independently of those creating it. Examples of codifiable knowledge include multivariate statistical models-generated behavioral expectancies or propensities, such as the probability of adverse development of recently filed liability claims or the likelihood of securities or employment practices class action. On the other hand, risk manager's or claims adjuster's experience or intuition are not easily, if at all, codifiable. As discussed in the next section, not all knowledge can be encoded and as a result, communicated.

Teachability of knowledge reflects the degree to which it can be absorbed by the organization. In general, the more understandable and parsimonious the knowledge, the simpler it is to teach. That said, we sometimes do not draw a sufficiently clear line of demarcation between knowledge creation and its application, which is particularly the case in business analytics, where many potentially valuable insights are lost in the web of methodological complexities. In most circumstances, there is a significant difference between teaching how to conduct analyses and how to use the results, which is an important distinction explored in more detail in subsequent chapters. For now, let it suffice to say that insights communicated in a user-friendly format and dispensed in manageable quantities tend to be easy to absorb by the organization, which means that over the long haul will have more impact on decisions.

Lastly, knowledge has to be *systemic*, which is to say that it needs to permeate the organization. This is important simply because organizations are effectively systems of diverse functions that need to act in harmony to meet its stated objectives. For example, in order for the knowledge of expected future claim development to contribute to systematically reducing the total cost of risk, it needs to be made accessible (and taught) to multiple organizational functions, such as claims management, financial planning, human resources and others.

Components of Knowledge

Creation of knowledge will continue to be a largely human endeavor for the foreseeable future. By making that statement I am not trying to deny that information technology will play a progressive bigger role in the development of organizational know-how – my intent is to draw attention to an important distinction between *knowledge* and *information*, which are often used interchangeably. Definitionally, information is best described as facts placed in a context, while knowledge is the sum of interpreted information—in other words, information constitutes input while knowledge is the final outcome. It means information is singular and for the most part non-evaluative (i.e., it contains no cause—effect delineation), while knowledge is cumulative and interpretive (i.e., observed outcomes are presented as results of specific actions). Hence, while information technology will certainly play an ever-increasing role in the generation and dissemination of information, the creation of decision-guiding, competitively advantageous knowledge is simply too complex, and to some degree too intangible to be automated, at least in the foreseeable future.

The cumulative character of knowledge gives rise to what is often called *explicit knowledge*, which is factual, objective and relatively easily codified and communicated. In essence, it is an analog to a database. The interpretive dimension, on the other hand, is evident in what is known as *tacit knowledge*. It is a subjective, hard to codify, teach and systematize though uniquely human aspect of knowing exemplified by skills, intuition and experience (hence the aforementioned intangibility of knowledge creation). In short, what we tend to regard as knowledge is essentially a product of the interplay between hard facts and 'fungible' interpretation, as shown below in Figure 2.1. Combining these two, quite different though equally important dimensions is the primary difficulty in automating the creation of knowledge processes, which is the reason for my earlier claim that the creation of knowledge will remain a largely human endeavor, at least in the foreseeable future.

Figure 2.1
Components of Knowledge

A somewhat different way of thinking about the building blocks of knowledge is to look at it from the standpoint of epistemology, which is a branch of philosophy concerned with the nature and scope of knowing. An epistemological definition points to four distinct types of knowledge: logical, semantic, systemic or empirical. Logical knowledge is the result of the understanding of how ideas relate to one another. Here, knowing manifests itself in applying accepted rules of logic, which stipulate additional truths. For example: All human beings are fallible. John is a human being, therefore, John is fallible. Semantic knowledge is the result of learning the meaning of words, which is simply the familiarity with definitions. The definition of epistemology mentioned earlier is an example of semantic knowledge. Systemic knowledge is the learning of a particular system, its symbols and their interpretations. For instance, one's mathematical skills are an example of systemic knowledge. Lastly, empirical knowledge is the learning resulting from our senses. Much of the scientific knowledge falls under that umbrella—in the fact the scientific method discussed later relies heavily on empirically-derived understanding.

A yet another way of categorizing knowledge is to think of it in terms of a broadly defined purpose it serves, which can be either descriptive (also called declarative) vs. procedural. The former captures the essence of our understanding of "what is", while the latter encompasses our understanding of "how to" accomplish something. For example, knowing the frequency of certain types of loss-generating events and/or the severity of those events constitutes descriptive knowledge; knowing how to reduce the said frequency and/or severity exemplifies procedural knowledge. In the area of risk analytics, much of what falls under the umbrella of descriptive knowledge constitutes relatively generic information—the truly competitively advantageous insights usually exemplify procedural knowledge.

Knowledge Creation

How is knowledge created? Although specific mechanisms are probably too diverse and numerous to summarize here, knowledge creation can be either a conscious, end objective-guided endeavor or it can be a result of an unintended accident. In other words, knowledge is created purposefully or incidentally. The former is quite familiar to most in the business world, as it is the primary mean of generating decision guiding insights in business. For instance, we notice a sudden upturn in the frequency of certain type of work related injuries, which then precipitates the question of why. The process of answering this question is essentially the process of creating purposeful knowledge. On the other hand, the insight that ultimately led to the invention of the now-ubiquitous microwave oven was an unintended byproduct of unrelated research into physical properties of very short wavelengths, i.e., microwaves[6]. The researchers were not seeking to gain an understanding of the heating or cooking properties (they were researching radar properties of microwaves; in fact, the first commercially sold microwave oven was called Radar Range), and it was a pure accident that one of the researchers put a candy bar in his shirt pocket which began to melt as a result of direct exposure to microwave radiation…

Stories like the accidental microwave invention certainly stir our imagination, but, at least in business research, it is the often painstaking, systematic, purposeful pursuit of knowledge that can contribute to the creation and sustainment of competitive advantage. Stated differently, to be effective, analyses of business data should be directed toward answering specific questions. Thus as approached in this book, knowledge creation is a teleological[7] process which needs to be directed at a specific purpose to yield worthwhile results.

It all seems straightforward, though it is not. Most organizations are far more adept at capturing data than they are at turning it into decision aiding insights; in fact, the sheer volume and diversity of the available data can get in the way of using its informational content productively. Strategies often get lost in a sea of interesting, albeit accidental findings generated and disseminated not because they support specific objectives, but simply because they are…well, interesting. More importantly, these often trivial informational pursuits tend to draw the same level of vigor (frankly, oftentimes even more as interesting tends to be more captivating than important) as does the pursuit of insights to guide the firm's stated strategic goals. Hence in some instances it is not the scarcity but the overabundance of data that impedes the creation of competitively advantageous knowledge, which when coupled with ineffective information filtering processes can significantly diminish the potential value of corporate data.

And thus the challenge: To create hard to imitate knowledge base to serve as a foundation of sustainable competitive advantage, by means of injecting unique insights into the organization's decision-making processes. As pointed out earlier, it means pulling together of the two, frankly quite different dimensions of knowledge: explicit and tacit.

Starting with the former, the creation of a robust *explicit knowledge* reservoir requires the translation of data-derived information into higher-level insights. This entails two somewhat different and temporally sequential steps.

---

[6] Microwaves are very short wavelength/frequency electromagnetic waves, much smaller than those used in radio broadcasting.

[7] Purposeful; derived from the Greek word *telos*, meaning *end* or *purpose*.

First is the informational reduction, which is a set of statistical procedures-based activities (discussed in more detail in subsequent chapters), designed to expressly differentiate between facts that are critical to reaching the stated strategic objectives and those that are not. The second step is that of *meta analyses,* which entail summarizing the critical, based on informational reduction results, but still too granular information into higher-order insights. The entire data—to explicit knowledge process is depicted in Figure 2.2.

Figure 2.2
Creating Explicit Knowledge

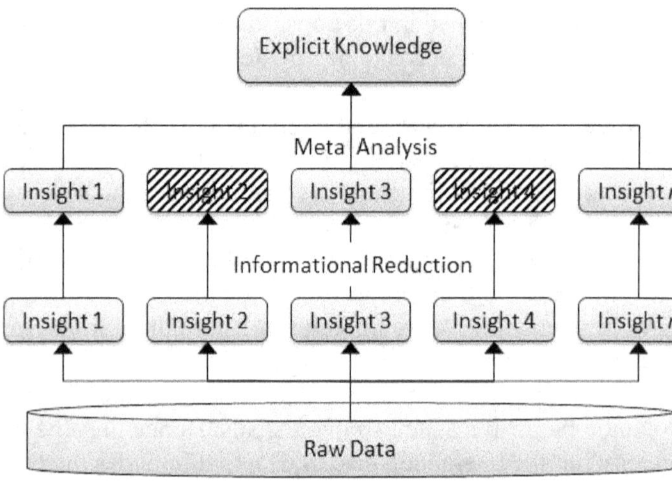

Explicit knowledge alone, however, rarely gives rise to competitive advantage because it is still devoid of experience based fact interpretation, thus it is usually not sufficiently indicative of the most advantageous courses of action. In other words, the absence of the experiential dimension, such as an experience in a particular industry to help contextualize company-specific loss experience, or hands-on claim management or loss prevention experience may both limit the potential applicability of the fact-only based explicit knowledge. This is particularly important considering that in many industries most of the competitors have access to a wide array of fundamentally the same information; hence, working from the same factual base, they are likely to arrive at similar insights, if their knowledge creation pursuits are limited to the explicit dimension of knowledge.

Adding the experiential or tacit component of knowledge into the knowledge creation mix helps to draw attention to what matters from a competitive standpoint. Thus to gain informational advantage over its competitors, an organization has to develop proprietary sources of factual information or find an effective method of personalizing its factual knowledge by combining it with the elements of *tacit knowledge*. There are numerous examples of successfully pursuing both alternatives. The world's largest retailer, Wal-Mart, in contrast to most of its competitors has consistently refused to sell its store movement data (i.e., sales data collected from the point-of-sale devices) to the outside syndicated information aggregators (most notably, AC Nielsen and Information Resources) to assure the uniqueness of its knowledge. The results are self-evident...On the other hand, Capital One Bank, working fundamentally with the same type of data as its competitors invested heavily in its own, proprietary data analytical processes (i.e., tacit knowledge) which enabled it to consistently deliver above average financial results. The competitive and other circumstances in which these two companies operate pushed them in somewhat different directions, but both organizations made the most of their circumstances, largely because they were purposeful and systematic.

Harnessing the value of tacit knowledge is in many regards more challenging as so much of it is subjective and difficult to codify. That said, a systematic process, framed in the larger context of risk analytics can serve as a conduit to extracting, normalizing and ultimately, incorporating the tacit dimension into the overall organizational knowledge base. The recommended process is depicted in Figure 2.3.

Figure 2.3

Analysis of Data as a Knowledge Creation Conduit

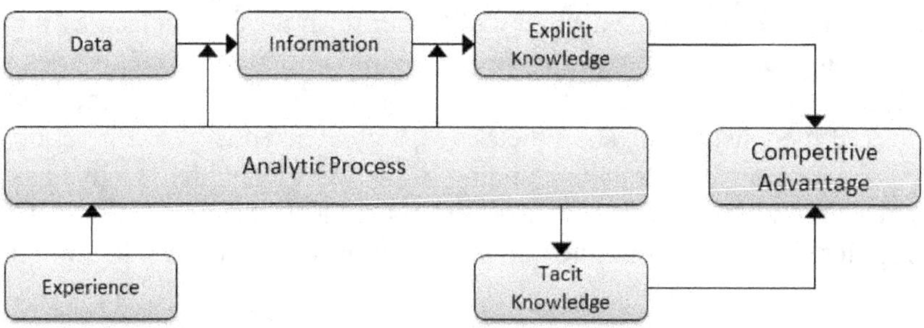

As suggested earlier and graphically shown in Figure 2.3, the broadly defined analytical process is a conduit to systematically transforming data into information and, ultimately, (explicit) knowledge. Furthermore, it is also as a source of the more experience-based tacit knowledge, which is important from the standpoint of maintaining the objectivity of the resultant insights. In other words, the data analytical skill set (*analytical process*), coupled with accumulated industry and related expertise (*experience*) support both the process of extracting explicit knowledge out of data (*data* → *information* → *explicit knowledge* progression) and the accumulation of tacit knowledge. The end goal of the knowledge creation efforts—which is sustainable *competitive advantage*—is the product of a unique combination of explicit and tacit knowledge at the organization level. In a conceptual sense, the entire process outlined above it is a reflection of the teleological nature of the business knowledge creation and accumulation: competitively useful knowledge creation is directed at a specific purpose, rather than 'fishing' for whatever can be found in the seemingly endless ocean of data.

Theory or Data Driven?

How do we know that we know? Ascertaining the validity and reliability of what is considered knowledge is probably one of the oldest controversies in science. At issues here is not only the availability of objective evidence—i.e., knowledge, but also its believability. In other words, how do we separate facts from fiction? Consider the so-called Galileo Affair[8] to appreciate the potential difficulty of distinguishing between objectively verifiable facts and subjective beliefs. The Galileo Affair is anchored in the idea of empirically testing the key postulates of the heliocentric system proposed by Copernicus. As the inventor of telescope, Galileo was the first to be able to gather closer celestial observations and more precise measurements empirically verifying the accuracy of Copernican thesis. Yet lacking an appreciable understanding of optics, many of Galileo's contemporaries were skeptical of his findings, suspecting the apparent celestial phenomenon to be tricks of the lenses. And so in their eyes, a great scientist was a heretic.

Obviously, our understanding of the world in which we live has increased immensely over the nearly four centuries that elapsed since Galileo's struggles. Yet as we continue to push the limits of our knowledge, we continue

[8] The trial and the resultant abjuration of Galileo before the Holy Congregation of the Catholic Church at the convent of Minerva on June 22, 1633.

to struggle with the same basic task of being able to differentiate between objectively verifiable knowledge and subjective beliefs.

From the standpoint of philosophy of science, the creation of objective knowledge can be either *theory* or *data laden*. The former is carried out by means of hypothesis testing, which is a method of empirically assessing specific theory-derived claims. It means that theory laden knowledge creation springs from the foundation provided by a particular conceptual and rational paradigm—and, it is limited to testing specific claims of predictions derived from that framework. It also means that results of empirical analyses are interpreted within the confines of the theory being tested. There is a certain amount of intuitive appeal associated with that stance, but more importantly, it is supported by neuroscience studies detailing the mechanics of the functioning of the brain. These studies suggest that cognitive processing of information requires that our brains hold some beliefs about reality, as absent those, we would be unable to learn from the available information[9]. In other words, the human knowledge creation process appears to be somewhat confirmatory, i.e., theory laden, in nature.

In the way of contrast, the *data laden* approach assumes no existence of an underlying theory and instead approaches the analysis of the available data as a purely exploratory endeavor. Hence the resultant knowledge is built from scratch, as it is cobbled together from individual insights found while exploring the available data. The data laden approach certainly has merit, but at the same time it is more likely (than the theory laden approach) to be blotted by data imperfections, which is a significant drawback, both in science and in business.

Business analysts need to carefully consider the strengths and weaknesses of these two competing knowledge creation frameworks. The theory laden method requires the availability of a somewhat mature—i.e., testable theoretical framework. It is important to keep in mind that a handful of loosely stated suppositions or insights generated by past analyses do not necessarily constitute a theory, at least not one that can offer an adequate explanation and/or prediction of the phenomenon of interest. On the other hand, often there can be multiple competing theoretical frameworks available, which can be confusing, to say the least. This brings us back to the earlier-made distinction between purposeful and incidental knowledge. Directing knowledge creation efforts toward clearly stated objectives, analysts can

---

[9] See Churchland, P. S. and T. J. Sejnowski (1992), *The Computational Brain*, MIT Press.

usually take advantage of conceptually robust and empirically validated conceptual frameworks emanating from a long list of business-related disciplines, such as psychology, economics and neuroscience. In fact, the risk analytical framework outlined in this book makes a heavy use of several such frameworks, most of all the persuasion theory, the theory of reasoned action (both adapted from psychology) and the equimarginal principle (as developed in economics).

The challenges faced by the data laden approach to knowledge creation are more formidable, which is a result of the combination of heightened dependence on the accuracy of data associated with this approach and the inherent imperfections of most databases. As it is intuitively obvious, greater dependence on open-ended exploration of data will create significantly more stringent data quality requirements. In purely exploratory (i.e., open-ended) data analyses, the absence of a supporting theoretical framework makes the task of differentiating between actual and spurious relationships particularly difficult, at times even impossible. Hence the question asked earlier – how do we know that we know? – becomes particularly difficult to answer.

Especially important to the assessment of the overall informational correctness of data are the notions of quality and representativeness. The *quality of data* manifests itself through data accuracy and completeness. The former represents the degree to which the coded values comprising a dataset are error-free, while the latter communicates the availability of actual (as opposed to missing) data values for all records contained in a file. *Representativeness of data*, on the other hand, is an outgrowth of the inherent incompleteness of virtually all business databases. Even the largest data reservoirs contain, in effect, only a subset of all events of a particular type (such as workplace accidents or insurance claims), which then raises the question: How representative is a particular sample of the overall universe? However, unlike the previously discussed data quality which tends to limit the reliability of overall findings, the representativeness of data plays a role in the generalizability of insights.

All of these considerations can be distilled to a few key takeaways. First and foremost, of the two competing knowledge creation approaches, data laden knowledge creation is significantly more demanding in terms of data quality and representativeness. Hence, relying on this approach to the creation of business knowledge will result in a higher likelihood of arriving at erroneous conclusions, when the available data is imperfect either in terms of quality or representativeness. This limitation is well illustrated by the drawbacks of automated data mining applications frequently used in conjunction with large event-tracking databases. It is one thing to flag statistically significant effects, it is yet another (and a significantly more difficult task) to reliably differentiate between persistent relationships and spurious ones.

Theory laden knowledge creation is certainly not immune to the dangers presented by poor data quality, but it is significantly less impacted by it, for a number of reasons. First, virtually no theory is ever validated or refuted on the basis of a single test, or even a handful of tests, which obviously reduces the danger associated with a single, low quality dataset. Second, a single study typically tests multiple hypotheses derived from the theory of interest and under most circumstances, not all of those hypotheses would be impacted in the same fashion by data imperfections. Perhaps most importantly, theory laden approach takes fuller advantage of the cumulative nature of knowledge creation, by offering a way of leveraging previously uncovered insights and building on that base with the help of additional analyses.

Knowledge as a Strategic Asset

An organization that knows how to produce something at a lower cost than other producers will enjoy cost advantage over its competitors. If its goal is to grow market share, the cost advantage will give it the ability to do so without sacrificing profitability, or it can simply enjoy higher margins and use the resultant profits elsewhere. Either way, being able to make the same product for less is clearly advantageous—does the same reasoning hold true for an organization that knows how to reduce its total cost of risk? I believe so.

From an accounting standpoint, the cost of risk represents an expense. Insurance premiums, which are a common component of the overall cost of risk, have no appreciable residual value[10] past their effective time horizon, nor do most other risk financing mechanisms. The same generally holds true for captive insurance[11], though it is possible, at least in principle, to structure a captive to be a profit-seeking entity. Of course, contractual risk transfer costs are not the only risk-related expenses; in fact, for some companies that particular aspect of the total cost of risk represents a relatively minor portion of the total. Organizations in heavy manufacturing, retail and hospitality industries, to name a few, employ large numbers of workers engaged in activities which are conducive to physical injuries—many of the larger firms in those industries spend tens of millions of dollars annually on work-related accidents. These costs are as much a part of the total cost of risk as commercial insurance premiums. And furthermore, these costs usually have a direct, and obviously adverse impact on earnings. Hence it follows that knowing how to systematically and sustainably reduce the total cost of risk will enhance the organization's competitiveness.

Much of the decision-aiding knowledge comes from insights derived from event-tracking data, which encompasses a wide range of business-to-consumers and business-to-business interactions[12]. Thanks in a large part to the brisk growth of electronic transaction processing (ETP) systems, event-tracking data became ubiquitous over the past couple of decades. Starting with the

---

[10] Even while a given insurance policy is in effect, the contingent capital it provides is typically not recognized as an asset on the organization's balance sheet.

[11] An insurance company established with the objective of underwriting only the risks emanating from its parent company; it is discussed in more detail in the next chapter.

[12] Perhaps the most familiar to most of us example of event-tracking data is the *point-of-sale*, or POS, transaction recording taking place in a retail setting. A customer paying for his/her purchases creates multiple event-tracking records, with each item comprising the shopping basket creating a separate electronic record.

introduction and subsequent proliferation of bar code-reading electronic scanners (first used in an Ohio supermarket in 1974), followed by digitization of inter- and intra-company record-creating events and further fueled by rapid advances in computing and data storage technologies, the ETP systems now generate enormous amounts of relatively accurate and detailed data describing just about every aspect of business, risk management included.

ETP was taken to a new level by the explosive growth of internet-based connectivity, which contributed not seen before volumes of event-tracking information. In addition, it also created a natural venue for broader data cross-pollination, by enabling organizations to more readily gain access to broader swaths of data from the outside.

Another important aspect of the wide spread adoption of ETP as the primary mode of processing business transactions has been the commoditization of the resultant data. Stated differently, most organizations competing in a given industry have comparable data assets, hence it follows that any cross-organization data-related knowledge differences are most likely a function of data analytical advantages. Just about every organization has lots of data, but some are simply better at squeezing competitively advantageous insights out of it.

It seems fair to say that, at an organization level, data crunching capabilities evolve primarily in response to organizational priorities and the growth in the availability of data. It follows that as more data becomes available, data crunching capabilities of organizations will also steadily expand. However, since the expansion of data analytic capabilities is also contingent on organizational priorities, not all companies will develop at the same pace. In the end, a common pool of data brought about by the proliferation of electronic transaction processing systems (such as computerized casualty claim processing systems) will bring about some common-to-all, generic data analytical capabilities, while at the same time creating competitive disparity in terms of more advanced data analytical competencies.

This trend is particularly evident in the area of marketing promotion evaluation. The vast majority of organizations that have access to the requisite data will typically also have basic data analytical capabilities, usually built around data summarization and reporting. Chances are that risk managers at firms competing in the same industry are looking at very similar claims reports. Much of that basic informational parity can be attributed to the proliferation of third-party developed reporting applications, such as the widely-used business intelligence tools offered by a number of different vendors, such as Business Objects, Cognos or MicroStrategy.

By all accounts, the convergence of widespread data availability and reporting capabilities should have produced a leveled informational playing field—in other words; most firms competing in a particular area ought to have comparable informational competencies. Yet, that is not the case. In virtually all industries only a handful of firms are able to consistently use data—readily available to most—to their advantage. To paraphrase an old cliché: Most companies are data-rich, but (still) information-poor. So even though data is accessible to the vast majority of organizations, it tends to widen the competitive divide rather than narrowing it. As discussed in a growing number of popular business texts, such as Davenport and Harris' *Competing on Analytics,* Levitt and Dubner's *Freakonomics,* Ayres' *Super Crunchers*, or Baker's *The Numerati,* advanced analytical know-how has become one of the key determinants of firms' marketplace competitiveness.

As noted earlier, in the knowledge-intensive environment, informationally competent firms are able to consistently outperform their competitors, primarily because they are able to make better use of organizational resources. Whether it is better understanding of consumers' needs and preferences, a more accurate assessment of the impact of competitive actions or more reliable estimation of likelihood and severity of major risk exposures, better information typically leads to better decisions. Knowing less, on the other hand, tends to introduce an element of randomness into the organization's decision making process (as the shortage of robust information necessitates guessing), which over the long run translates into a more uneven performance, often reflected in more volatile stock. And finally yet importantly, informational competency enables organizations to take a more proactive decision making stance, which is generally viewed as a prerequisite to both winning and maintaining market leadership. The lack of reliable decision insights tends to impose a more reactive decision making mode, which tends to force organizations into playing catch-up with their better-informed rivals.

It is important to note that persistent informational deficiency does not just negatively affect the organization's performance—it may actually pose a threat to its very survival. The steadily accelerating pace of globalization coupled with the broadening trend of de-regulation continues to stiffen the competitiveness of markets, which in effect is raising the cost of poor decisions. Under most circumstance, there is simply too little time and too much competition to practice trial and error decision making.

As demonstrated by the likes of Microsoft, Proctor & Gamble or Marriott, timely, accurate and unique business insights are among the key pathways to sustainable competitive advantage. IBM takes those ideas even further, by building mathematical models of its employees, with the goal of improving productivity and automating management. The degree to which market leaders are able to consistently outperform their competitors is now inextricably tied to their proficiency in translating large volumes of data into decision-guiding insights. The speed and precision with which an organization can translate raw data into decision-guiding insights determines whether it will be able to pinpoint competitive weaknesses and to identify the most advantageous courses of action, or be among the first to spot and take advantage of emerging trends and opportunities. And as the marketplace competition continues to heat up, fueled by growing privatization, accelerating product innovations and the widening trend of deregulation, it is not just the success, but even the very survival of organizations that is becoming increasingly more dependent on their ability to make sound and effective decisions. In a sense, all organizations are now in the information business but their competencies in that area are highly uneven.

In view of the enormous scope and the depth of what can be included under the broad label of 'business analytics', this book does not pretend to offer a "one size fits all" solution that could be applied to all data analysis-related business problems. My focus is on one particular aspect of business informatics: risk analytics. More specifically, it is on delineating a clear, operationalizable process of using the readily available data for the purpose of developing cost-effective methods of protecting earnings of non-financial organizations. A lot has been written in the area of quantitative credit and market risk, but disproportionately little effort has been put into the development of similarly robust analytical frameworks in the area of strategic and operational risk. The goal of this book is to contribute toward filling that gap.

An old Taoist proverb teaches that 'a journey of a thousand miles begins with a single step'; here, the journey toward the development of a robust analytical framework starts with an explicit recognition of the tacit differences separating raw data, information and finally, decision-aiding knowledge.

From Data to Information to Knowledge

Although often used interchangeably, the notions of *data, information* and *knowledge* all convey fundamentally different meaning. From the standpoint of decision making utility, data is potential information—information is potential knowledge—and knowledge is potential competitive advantage. Implicit in these differences is a tacit value creation progression, where the initially low value *raw* data is being transformed into higher value information, and ultimately into the finished product, which usually takes the form competitively advantageous knowledge. Hence the notions of data, information and knowledge are all linked together by the value-adding transformation of the low impact, generic commodity (data) into high value, decision-aiding corporate asset (knowledge). The earlier mentioned cross-firm invariance in informational proficiency is in itself a manifestation of differences in firms' analytic capabilities. An analytically proficient organization has the requisite skills and processes allowing it to reliably and consistently turn the competitively generic data into competitively unique and advantageous knowledge, while an analytically deficient organization lacks either the necessary skills or processes. Hence the attainment of informational proficiency is rooted in the development of a *knowledge creation process* as the primary conduit to the establishment of a fact-based decision making framework.

Within the confines of business—and specifically, the management of risk, the knowledge creation process is defined as a set of operationally-clear data analytical activities aimed at extracting unique, competitively advantageous insights out of the otherwise generic raw data. The operationally-clear data analytical activities are further defined as *specific* statistical techniques or computational algorithms[13] offering the most effective and efficient means of transforming specific types of data into well-defined decision inputs. As implied in the above definitions, the data analytical process

[13] In principle, the term 'algorithm' is sufficiently broad to include virtually all statistical techniques. However, as used here, *statistical techniques* refer to general problem solving methods readily available to anyone, while *computational algorithms* denote custom-built computational methods. For example, cluster analysis is a statistical technique widely used for grouping customers into segments; it is typically included in many of the popular statistical analysis software packages (e.g., SAS or SPSS) and as such readily available for anyone to use. A proprietary approach to customer value quantification, developed in-house and not readily available to others is an example of a computational algorithm.

makes an extensive use of a variety of quantitative techniques, with the goal of bringing about edge-producing insights, not readily available to others in the marketplace. Culled together into a single reservoir, the collection of these insights comprises the organizational knowledge base, which is an increasingly important component of organizational equity. As it is intuitively obvious, the quality of the organizational knowledge base is highly dependent on the robustness of the process producing it, which as discussed later, is one of the primary drivers of cross-firm informational inequalities. Perhaps less intuitively obvious is that the ultimate measure of its efficacy is the degree to which the results attributed to that knowledge contribute to the establishment or maintenance of sustainable competitive advantage.

Some of the most revolutionary and admired companies, including General Electric, Wal-Mart, Microsoft, Google or Amazon can attribute much of their success to informational proficiency and the impact it has had on their decision making. Although operating in vastly different industries and governed by considerably dissimilar operating models, these organizations nonetheless have one thing in common: They excel at extracting knowledge out of data and using it to their advantage. In fact, in most industries, knowledge leaders are also performance leaders, because knowing more means making better decisions in anything from resource allocation to opportunity identification. It is important, however, to consider their informational proficiency in the confines of their respective industries to account for cross-industry data inequalities. Some sectors of the economy, such as retailing, financial services or hotel and hospitality are event tracking data-richer than some other ones, such as energy or materials. (This difference is primarily due to the dominant transaction type distinctiveness—e.g., retail entails business-to-consumer sales of specific items, while the materials industry is most often characterized by bulk business-to-business sales.)

In addition to data availability inequalities, the individual segments of the economy are also characterized by dissimilar levels of competitive intensity. Retail, hospitality, consumer package goods, financial services or gaming and entertainment sectors tend to be among the most competitive, in terms of the sheer number of firms offering directly substitutable products. Operating in more competitively intense environments results in firms having a greater incentive to invest early and invest more in data-supported decision-aiding infrastructure. Not surprisingly, the best known and probably the most compelling and talked about examples of unique knowledge-driven competitive advantage come from those industries. Household names, including Wal-Mart, Capital One, Proctor & Gamble or Marriott became recognized performance leaders in their respective industries as a direct consequence of first becoming data-based knowledge leaders. These companies had the foresight to invest in the development of superior business intelligence systems and also had the discipline to make objective information the bedrock of their decision-making. They have been able to consistently outperform their competitors because they are in a position to better read the marketplace and make more effective use of their resources. To them, as well as a host of other, analytically advanced data users, informational proficiency simply diminishes the amount of guesswork in such critical areas as pricing, merchandising, promotional allocation or new product design, which offers ample competitive cushion to knowledge-enabled firms.

It is remarkable that in spite of the compelling evidence pointing to significant competitive benefits associated with superior, fact-based knowledge, so many organizations continue to bet their future on intuition of individual decision makers. Obviously, there is value in the accumulated experience, but its impact can be considerably more pronounced when coupled with broader learnings stemming from objective data. The goal of building a robust organizational knowledge base is not to replace the decision maker, but rather to enhance his/her efficacy by systematically reducing the level of uncertainty inherent in virtually all decisions. Knowing more enables one to spot and take quicker and fuller advantage of emerging marketplace opportunities and it is well-known that the first-mover advantage often translates into higher profits (which is an obvious consequence of no or very few competitors). And last, but certainly not least: Superior knowledge is also more difficult to replicate by the competition than other sources of competitive advantage. Successful products can be copied relatively quickly, just as eye-catching promotional campaigns can be mimicked and winning strategies imitated, but because superior information is the invisible force behind better products or more effective campaigns, it is extremely difficult for others to replicate. Not surprisingly, firms that mastered turning data into better decisions continue to outpace their peers.

Sources of Proficiency

Informational competency is rarely, if ever, a product of an accident. Its genesis can be usually traced to careful planning of data capture/acquisition, strong execution of data analytical strategies and disciplined, system-wide embrace of fact based decision-making. It all translates into a well-defined set of 'hard' and 'soft' assets. In terms of the former, superior knowledge requires robust computer hardware and software, both of which are needed to support data capture or acquisition, compilation and the initial processing of the accumulated data as well as the subsequent in-depth analyses. The latter entails the availability of an appropriate data analytical skill set, without which, even the best of breed hardware and software will not catapult the organization to informational competency. In other words, it is entirely possible that an organization could make substantial investments in information technology and still only keep up with the competition. That is because getting ahead of the competition in terms of decision-aiding knowledge—i.e., gaining and sustaining informational, and ultimately, competitive advantage—demands looking beyond the common-to-many data analytic mindset in search of unique, advantage creating insights. It means pursuing a more ambitious, forward-looking informational vision.

But what does 'forward-looking informational vision' mean? In broad, conceptual terms it amounts to looking at a right problem in a right way. In more precise analytical terms, it is simply the creativity surrounding the analysis of the available data.

Knowledge leaders work at being at the forefront of informational proficiency by molding data to questions posed by critical business challenges, rather allowing computational convenience to dictate what type of information is extracted from the data on hand. They seek specific, decision-aiding insights into such key competitive edge producing problems as quantification of incremental sales or revenue impact of competing price and promotion strategies. They understand that in many regards, the pursuit of business knowledge is the antithesis of mass-producing generic reports that capture every imaginable nuance and detail contained in the raw data, while answering few if any of the outcome-deciding questions. That is why organizations that ultimately become performance leaders have the drive, conviction and skills to enable them to leave the comfort of the tried and true traditional—i.e., generic—data reporting and analyses to look for answers not yet found by their competitors. They are not satisfied with knowing as much as their competitors—instead, they search for unique, competitive edge producing insights. That, in a nutshell, is the essence of forward-looking informational vision.

Similar to other mold-breaking behaviors, analytic innovation has its own share of impediments that need to be overcome. Probably the most significant, at least from the behavior-changing standpoint is the organization's ability to sharpen its informational focus. In short, there is a fundamental difference between the *availability* and *applicability* of information. This distinction is important when thinking about data analysis—i.e., information creation—vs. data usage—i.e., information deployment. In principle, edge-producing analytics entail the inclusion of all available data, but the effective use of the resultant insights is contingent on focusing on only the sub-set of all available knowledge that is directly related to the decision at hand. Quite often, to know more at the decision time demands setting aside the bulk of the available information. Frankly, this is among the reasons the previously discussed broad base reporting tends to be an ineffective decision aid. Organizations that become knowledge leaders cultivate not only robust knowledge creation, but also rational and disciplined information usage guidelines. In a nutshell, making better decisions calls for specific, decision-related set of insights—everything else, interesting or not, is superfluous to that process.

It is a lot easier said than done, though. Many organizations' MIS/IT functions are permeated by the volume production mentality, which usually manifests itself in a string of detailed reports that overwhelm most, while informing only a few. It is the unspoken, though enduring belief that generating large volumes of information represents a return on the often-hefty data infrastructure expenditures. In one form or another, the emphasis on volume is quite common, which is in a large part due to the often-significant divide separating those who create information from those ultimately using it. This analyst—user divide is one of the reasons that the often-significant investments in database and reporting technologies rarely translate into noticeable marketplace benefits. Stated differently, technologically advanced database management systems (DBMS) can be a source of informational parity, but not of competitively advantageous knowledge. This is a critical distinction and one of the key reasons behind the development of the analytical process outlined in this book.

In a strange sort of a way, the trend toward DBMS application standardization is to some degree responsible for the low business impact of many of these often-pricey data management systems. The ever more robust capabilities of the off-the-shelf applications along with their progressively greater ease of usage, vis-à-vis the mounting technological challenges of the custom-built data processing solutions[14] have led to the virtual disappearance of the latter. Though otherwise a very positive development, the widespread adoption of generic decision support systems also carries with it some not-so-

[14] Most notably, the difficulty of integrating these typically special application oriented systems with the growing number of other applications.

positive consequences, such as the informational conversion. Simply put, similar (at times, identical) data combined with generic data management and analysis systems often lead to very similar informational bases, quite unintentionally shared by organizations competing in a given industry. In the end, multiple firms competing for more-or-less the same customers and offering functionally very similar products often end up trying to outwit each other with the help of fundamentally the same information.

Still, as mentioned earlier, a relatively small but highly successful segment of companies have found a way to consistently extract competitively unique insight out of the otherwise generic data. Their data and data management systems are usually quite similar to their competitors', but their knowledge creation is typically far ahead of the rest. The key to those organizations' success lies in how they approach the task of mining data. Unlike their less able peers, the analytically-proficient firms tend to look beyond the *retrospective* (i.e., a detailing of past results), metric-centric report generation, instead focusing on *prospective* (projections supporting future decisions), business issue-centric and decision-directing insights. Reflecting fundamentally different informational paradigms, the retrospective and prospective data analytical postures differ on a number of key dimensions, with the two most important being the degree of informational specificity, or the volume of the resultant information.

It is axiomatic that the more tailored the information is to the business problem at hand and the specifics of the organization, the more it will benefit the organization's decision making. Particularly, in order for data analyses to make positive contributions to the firm's success, its outcomes have to be objectively evaluative of competing courses of action. This means that the resultant knowledge should be sufficient to point the decision maker in the direction of the greatest anticipated benefit. Although it seems like a simple enough task, making this conceptual goal an operational reality can be complex. The reasons behind the complexity are rather apparent: Many of the traditional data analytic techniques are ill suited to the realities of modern event-tracking databases and the informational demands the fact-based decision-making. As shown throughout this book, some of the more basic techniques, such as statistical significance testing or impact (i.e., lift) quantification, are at odds with the intended use of the resultant insights—in other words, usage limitations imposed by computational processes conflict with the intended or desired business applications. Some other techniques, such as experimentation, are not per se at odds with business applications, but their usability limits are often outstretched by informational demands placed on them.

The area demanding perhaps the most fundamental re-evaluation is the broadly defined results or outcomes reporting. Virtually all organizations rely on tabulating and trending their period-by-period revenues and expenses, which are often 'sliced and diced' in a myriad of ways. Although it is certainly important to keep abreast of historical performance metrics, this information is of little help in forward-looking decision-making. Choosing among competing courses of action, such as competing risk financing alternatives, requires the decision maker to be able to quantify option-specific expected impact. It ought to be done in a way that will enable the decision maker to estimate the net benefit associated with each option. Stated differently, making better choices demands objective estimates of *cause-attributable effects*, which is the ultimate measure of the *worthiness* of individual, competing alternatives. This is fundamentally different then topline cost or aggregate outcome based comparison, hence a closer look seems warranted.

Cause-Attributable Effect

Basic reporting is best exemplified by what has come to be known as *management dashboards*, which are reader-friendly, graphics-intensive[15] summarizations of key performance indicators. These reports are typically built around outcome tabulations, such as frequency and severity of certain types of losses aided by side-by-side comparisons, with metrics of interest typically broken down by type or geography. Management dashboards are clearly beneficial to decision makers insofar as they can—if well designed—present a relatively comprehensive snapshot of specific aspects of business, in a highly parsimonious format. The vast majority of dashboards, however, tend to be inconclusive. They focus on easy to measure outcomes, such frequency of the total cost, while failing to address the underlying *causes* – this is a considerable limitation. Most losses can have numerous causal explanations, which means that knowing which—if any—of those factors had a measurable impact on the outcome of interest is quite important to future risk mitigation and cost containment efforts.

---

[15] In fact, a typical report layout is somewhat reminiscent of a car dashboard (hence the name), given the heavy reliance on dials and gauges as means of communicating the information. See the *Knowledge Dissemination* chapter for an example of a management dashboard report.

To be of more benefit to their users, management dashboards should be built around *effect attribution*. In terms of the previously mentioned knowledge creation continuum, knowing the magnitude of the impact associated with specific causes will arm the decision makers with future action guiding knowledge by linking specific outcomes with the most important causes. It is, however, considerably more complex methodologically. It also represents a shift in information generation philosophy: The traditional observable outcome oriented reporting is focused on churning out reports encompassing all that *can be known*, while the cause-attributable effect quantification focused reporting advocated here is focused on specific insights into *critical to know* areas.

In practice, the difference between these two methodologically and substantively distinct result measurement approaches translates into two fundamentally dissimilar sets of activities: The former are typically built around simple metric-by-metric tabulation and summarization of aggregate results, while the latter emphasize translating of large volumes of either inconclusive or incomplete pieces of data into probabilistic cause—effect estimates. From the analytical standpoint, the observable outcome based reporting is computationally straightforward and nowadays the task is almost always handled by highly automated, functionally elegant data reporting software packages. The opposite is true for effect attribution based reporting, which demands highly involved, often complex and manual statistical modeling preceded by a considerable amount of data preparation. Although some parts of the requisite process are prone to standardization (hence this book), cause—effect estimation is considerably more effort and expertise intensive. The payback however, as illustrated later in this book, can be substantial.

Volume

The volume of information also matters. Interestingly, more often than not there tends to be an inverse relationship between the sheer amount of information and its business utility. This may sound counterintuitive, particularly considering our enduring belief that it is better to know more rather than less. The pitfall in this line of thinking, however, is the implicit assumption that more information translates into deeper knowledge. That is simply not true, mainly because a considerable amount of the available information often has very little to do with a particular business decision (or any decision, for that matter). For instance, the decision as to which of several competing risk financing alternatives should be selected requires an objective assessment of the net present value of each option. Other information, such as the last year's claims trends or cross risk type cost distribution comparisons might be deemed interesting, but ultimately will offer little-to-no help in identifying the most economically appropriate option. In short, one can have lots of information but little-to-no knowledge. It follows that to yield the maximum benefit, information creation needs to be rooted in the give-and-take considerations of quality over quantity and need-directed problem solving over propagating spurious informational details. Frankly, it is counterproductive to disseminate interesting but not decision aiding informational tidbits, simply because processing it takes time and attention away from the task at hand, while making no substantive contributions to decisions at hand.

From the viewpoint of science, there is nothing new about the notion of less being more. As one of the key tenets of scientific inquiry, this idea traces its philosophical roots to Ockham's razor[16], which is a centuries-old axiom guiding the process of scientific theory building. Better known as the *principle of parsimony*, this basic 'keep it simple' prescription tells us that the best explanations are those that involve the fewest number of concepts or informational details. A business decision maker will benefit much more from a relatively few, but highly action-directing insights than from a large number of mostly inconclusive and often unrelated details.

This is not to say that whatever information is not applicable to an issue at hand should be discarded—quite to the contrary, more effort should be put into cataloging and meta analysis as the means of making effective use of all informational assets (more on those in later chapters). Of the two, the latter can be particularly beneficial, though it is rarely used in applied business research. Operationally, *meta analysis* is data about data, which in essence is the exploration of results of data analysis in search of underlying patterns and other communalities. It can be particularly beneficial to database analyses because it offers a robust and an objective method of summarizing the often quite voluminous basic insights. It can serve both as the means of uncovering of new insights as well as succinctly communicating of the otherwise excessively detail findings.

Clearly, informational excellence can be quite beneficial to firms' economic well-being which brings us to an obvious question: What is required of an organization for it to develop a high level of informational proficiency?

---

[16] *Entia non sunt multiplicanda praetem necessitatem,* Latin for 'entities should not be multiplied unnecessarily'; it is often paraphrased as 'All things being equal, the simplest solution is the best'. William of Ockham was a 14th Century Franciscan friar and logician.

Or, stated differently: What separates informationally advanced organizations from the rest of the pack?

Impact of Analytics

Informational competency is rarely, if ever, a result of data access inequalities. As previously discussed, most of the same-industry organizations today have access to more-or-less that same type of raw data, largely due to the fact that the vast majority of it comes from functionally generic sources[17]. For instance, the bulk of Wal-Mart's data comes from its point-of-sale systems which are functionally quite the same—i.e., capture the same type of basic data—as are those used by K-Mart or other major discounters (after all, these are standard applications sold and developed by outside vendors). In that sense, Wal-Mart's informational superiority should not be attributed to (raw) data inequalities. The previously noted standardization of electronic transaction processing systems just about guarantees that most competitors in an industry will have access to the same types of event-tracking data.

That is not to say that there are no instances of firms enjoying access to unique sources of data. A handful of organizations (the names of which I am, unfortunately, not at liberty to disclose) supplement their worker compensation claims data files with not only the basic employee demographics, which is relatively common, but with in-depth behavioral and attitudinal profiles collected with the help of detailed employee surveys. Hence, not only do these organizations have at their disposal the standard event-tracking claim details passively collected by claims management systems, but they are able to augment it with behavioral and attitudinal data. Of course, taking that extra step is often contingent on highly specialized skill set, which means that organizations pursuing the collection of such data are typically already far more informationally proficient than their competitors. In other words, the capture of the special purpose data is more a result of informational competency than its precursor.

Another possible source of informational proficiency could be the broadly defined data infrastructure, which is comprised of data storage as well as data processing hardware and software. Probably even more than data

---

[17] These include standard POS (point-of-sale) transaction recording systems; third-party data vendors, such as AC Nielsen in consumer packaged goods or RL Polk in automotive industries; or Standard & Poor's Compustat (quarterly, annual and ad hoc SEC filings submitted by all publicly-traded firms) tracking financial metrics across all industries; etc.

access, the data processing infrastructure is extremely unlikely to be the source of informational advantage for two basic reasons: Firstly, over the last several years the widespread standardization of warehousing and reporting applications has led to a certain degree of functional conversion, which means that differently branded applications are nonetheless quite similar in terms of their capabilities. Secondly, even the largest organizations more-or-less abandoned the earlier trend of developing from scratch their uniquely own (and thus different) decision support systems in favor of standardized, outside vendor-supplied solutions. In other words, there is little-to-no cross-user infrastructure differentiation.

In the end, neither the mere access to raw data, nor the availability of a state-of-the-art data processing infrastructure are likely to be a source of a sustainable informational advantage. This leaves only two other plausible explanations: 1. organizational culture, and 2. the data analytical *know-how.*

Culture, defined here as the institutionalization of fact-based decision making, holds quite a bit of intuitive appeal as the source of the cross-firm knowledge disparity. After all, if an organization does not value information, in the sense of embracing data-driven decision-making, it could not possibly develop a superior data-based knowledge foundation. However, one could also argue the flip side of this reasoning, namely, that it is unrealistic to expect a rational firm to value anything prior to the existence of convincing evidence. Since both sides of this argument have merit, this has the characteristics of the proverbial 'chicken and egg' circular argument, with no clear way of settling which came first. However, looking to organizational culture as the source of informational proficiency implicitly assumes that the organization has the skills required to extract uncommon insights out of the otherwise common data. And this indeed could be the crux of the problem—many firms do not.

To put it simply, the biggest single source of informational advantage is the superior knowledge creation know-how. Overall, the most significant factor that consistently explains why some data-rich organizations are also knowledge-rich while other, equally data-rich and technologically enabled firms are comparatively knowledge-poorer is the advanced data analytical skill set of the former. At the time when data is ubiquitous and the basic data processing increasingly informationally generic, it is the ability to go beyond the basic data crunching functionality that is the key determinant of the value of the resultant information.

Though manifestly important, the knowledge creation know-how is arguably the least developed and certainly the least formalized aspect of the new, digital world. Many will balk at this statement, as after all, quantitative data analysis itself is a well-established, long-standing field of study. And indeed it is, in the academic sense. However, as shown throughout this book, it is not in the practical, particularly business sense. Similarly to a number of other fields of study, quantitative methods tend to be inwardly oriented and primarily focused on methods, rather than outcomes. Those trained in it tend to acquire substantial amounts of domain-specific knowledge, but very little understanding of the contextualizing influences of different data types or business objectives. Analysts' understanding of even the most rudimentary characteristics of modern business databases tends to lag far behind their comprehension of the specific inner-workings of the individual quantitative analysis methods, which is to some degree a reflection of many academics' limited exposure to the more complex business data sources. Frankly, that poses a problem, as extracting unique and competitively advantageous insights is as dependent on the in-depth knowledge of statistical techniques as it is on the comparable knowledge of data.

The Pursuit of Knowledge

In his 1969 book, *The Age of Discontinuity; Guidelines to Our Changing Society*, Peter Drucker wrote about knowledge-based economy, which is the use of knowledge technologies (e.g., data management and reporting; predictive analytics) to produce economic benefits. The essence of Drucker's argument was that industrial society was being gradually replaced by information society, where the creation, diffusion and integration of information became the thrust of political, cultural and business activities. His conception of knowledge economy, as the economic equivalent of information society, was one where wealth was created through the exploitation of understanding, rather than the traditional means of land, labor and capital. Some of the most admired companies today, such as Google, Microsoft, Apple or eBay are a testament to the astuteness of Drucker's observations.

One of the most persistent indicators of the informational maturity of organizations is their outlook on data. Though virtually all firms recognize the importance of raw data as a source of information, not all take a full advantage of its informational content. To the vast majority, event-tracking data needs to be *reduced* to be of value, which means tabulated, summarized, described and distributed via a wide range of reports, such as those showing total number of losses, losses per geography, time period, etc. On the other hand, a relatively smaller set of organizations take a far more expansive and exploratory approach to data. Their more inquisitive stance stems from the desire to understand the causes of the observed outcomes, rather than merely tabulating unexplained results. Not surprisingly, their data mining capabilities are, almost always, far more developed, particularly in the sense of a wide-scale (i.e., organization-wide) use of multivariate statistical analyses and experimental design. These are the knowledge leaders discussed earlier—the organizations whose data crunching capabilities evolved beyond the often pointless report propagation in search of unique, competitive edge producing knowledge.

Interestingly, both types of organizations, the 'causal knowledge seekers' and the 'result summarizers' tend to speak of data as a corporate asset. In case of the former, exemplified by firms such as Capital One, Marriott, Proctor & Gamble or Wal-Mart, data is clearly a corporate asset—after all, those firms were able to gain and maintain competitive advantage through an innovative and an effective use of it. Looking at data's asset-worthiness through that prism, it is hard to see how the latter category of companies, the result summarizers, can make the same claim. If the firm's competitive position has not been enhanced by data, is that data really an asset to the organization? Probably not.

The reason for that is simple: Data, as a digital representation of certain outcomes (e.g., losses or claims) or states (e.g., demographics) is merely a raw material with a *potential* to inform the firm's decision-making. Absent the know-how necessary to extract competitive edge-producing insights out of it, raw data offers little-to-no utility to an organization, in addition to which, its informational (and any monetary) value diminishes over time[18]. For instance, 10 years old workers' compensation claim details offer little in a way of insight into present-day likelihood of adverse claim development. In other words, virtually all business data have a certain period of applicability, beyond which its informational contents become simply too dated and in effect, obsolete. At the same time, just having data (i.e., its capture, storage and ongoing maintenance) can be quite costly, often requiring millions of dollars of capital expenditures on computer hardware and software, not to mention dedicated stuff (database administrators, programmers, etc.). These considerations point to the question of business value: If the data residing in our IT systems does not make clear and consistent contributions to revenue-generation or cost savings, why should it be considered an asset? After all, basic business logic suggests that an asset should not consume more than it either currently or potentially can contribute. Let us take a closer look.

Is Data an Asset?

An *asset* is defined as something of economic value that the organization owns and controls and that is expected to provide future benefits. In an investment sense, an asset increases the value of a firm or benefits the firm's operations. Although data can be viewed as having intrinsic economic value, since in many instances it could be sold in the marketplace, that argument is only applicable to a certain sub-set of firms (e.g., retailers often sell their event-tracking data to outside vendors, such as AC Nielsen or IRI, who then re-sell it, typically as packaged solutions to manufacturers) and data types. In a broader context, it is fair to say that few if any organizations would be willing to sell their claims, loss history or product sales data, as any

[18] This is particularly the case with event-tracking data, where the *recency* of behavioral outcomes is one of the key factors in deriving robust explanatory/predictive insights. It is a manifestation of the intuitively obvious notion that behaviors are most influenced by factors and events closest to them in time.

potential monetary gains would be far outweighed by the potential competitive self-hindrance. Furthermore, there are a number of regulations governing sharing of certain types of data, such as the recently enacted Shelby Act which places severe limitations on the use of vehicle registration data, or the Health Insurance Portability and Accountability Act of 1996 which sets limits around accessing and sharing individuals' health information. All considered, outside of the data service provider industry, few companies decide to invest in data capture and its ongoing maintenance capabilities because of the expectation of deriving an income stream from future sales of that data.

Under most circumstances, the real asset-worthiness of data stems from its potential to improve the firm's operations through the generation of unique knowledge, which in turn can give rise to competitively advantageous decisions. This leads to an obvious conclusion that data that do not contribute, meaningfully, to the development of competitive advantage should not be considered an asset. In fact, keeping in mind the often high cost of its capture and maintenance, poorly utilized data could even be viewed as an expense from a strictly cashflow point of view. There simply is no getting around the obvious conclusion that unless properly used, data investments can lead to an economic loss when evaluated in the confines of basic cost—benefit analysis.

All considered it is then more realistic to think of data as a *potential* asset; as such a categorization highlights the importance of the analysis of the available data. This more tenuous expression of data's asset-worthiness underscores the obvious fact that without a significant amount of effort put into analytics; even the 'best' data will not contribute enough to the organization's well-being to warrant an unconditional asset designation. Also, thinking of data as a potential, rather than an actual asset also draws attention to the importance of taking steps to extract economic benefits out of data that are at least equal to data's cost of ownership.

Thinking of data as a potential asset also has a secondary benefit of redirecting the emphasis away from storage and maintenance infrastructure and toward the usage. Since the 1980's, organizations across industries have been investing heavily into data capture and maintenance related infrastructure, while dedicating disproportionately little effort and resources to data exploration. It has been estimated that approximately 85%-90% of total data related expenditures were directed at the hardware and software infrastructure, with only the remainder going toward extracting insights out of data. In other words, only about 10¢ out of every $1 of data related spending went toward actually making data into a true organizational asset. As a result, the well-known expression of a firm being data-rich, but information-poor is often quite on point...

But even the 10% or so of the total information technology expenditures that in one way or another was dedicated to data exploration has not always been utilized as much as possible. Oftentimes, a good part of that spending went toward the production of generic information (e.g., the standard, measurable outcome focused management dashboard reports discussed earlier) that could bring the organization up to the level of competitive parity, though not sustainable competitive advantage. Some of that is due to the previously discussed convergence of technological data capture and storage platforms combined with a generic approach to data analysis, together leading to further informational convergence. Further fueling the informational convergence is the recent proliferation of third-party analytics, or data analysis vendors offering fundamentally the same type of information to multiple competitors in an industry. Unlike the technological standardization, however, the degree of analytical convergence varies across industries, as it tends to reflect of the availability of data to vendors. Nonetheless, there is a distinct trend of relatively few, large data providers and aggregators providing informationally non-distinct analytical products and services to a wide cross-section of the marketplace.

The slow but persistent process of technological and informational convergence underscores the importance of the earlier discussed forward-looking informational vision built around analytically innovative approaches to data analysis. Raw data has the potential of becoming an asset, but its asset-worthiness hinges on the organization's analytical skills. Data is an asset to organizations that are able to systematically extract competitive edge producing insights out of it. To others, specifically those whose data crunching capabilities are limited to standard, off-the-shelf tools and whose informational vision does not extend beyond basic outcome reporting, data is yet another component of the cost of doing business.

Data as a Source of Competitive Advantage

The last couple of decades have been particularly eventful from the standpoint of business information. Some of the more noteworthy trends, from the standpoint of knowledge creation, include the following:

- A combination of rapid gains in data processing capabilities, decreases in storage and processing costs and the proliferation of

powerful software applications resulting in database technology become affordable to an ever-growing number of organizations.
Result: Leveraging the organization's own and competitive data became a key ingredient of firms' business strategies.

- The growing digitalization of business processes, including event and transaction processing, spawns an overabundance of event-tracking data often leading to potential users 'drowning' in data but lacking information.
  Result: Organizations spent large sums on customer data warehouses, yet to-date only a handful truly leverage their data assets.

- The forces of deregulations coupled with growing business globalization lead to the heightening of competition, ultimately amplifying the importance of timely, accurate and topical insights.
  Result: Increasing competition accentuated the need for speedy extraction of actionable business insights from databases.

- Information availability and immersion become a part of everyday business culture and data analysis techniques, slowly making their way into the common business lexicon.
  Result: As database analytics is no longer a domain of a few, large organizations, the demand of skilled analysts exploded.

Taken as a group, these developments are to a large degree responsible for the growing importance of unique (to the organization), fact-based knowledge in building and sustaining competitive advantage. In a sense, all organizations are now in the information business, to the degree to which their competitive well-being has increasingly grown dependent on the access to timely and accurate decision guiding insights. Stated differently, knowledge surrounding the key decisions, such as product design (i.e., what is the most desirable bundling of product attributes?), promotional mix allocation (i.e., how should the finite promotional dollars be allocated across the available promotional alternatives to deliver the highest incremental benefit?) or the total cost of risk management (i.e., how to provide sound protection against loss-causing events at the lowest possible total cost?) is now among the most pronounced determinant of firms' success.

In a recent, insightful look at the impact that the persistent and well thought out data analysis—defined as reliable conversion of raw data into competitively advantageous knowledge—can have on organizations' long-term success, Davenport delineated a number of key factors characterizing information-driven organizations[19]. These included the widespread use of modeling and optimization, enterprise-wide deployment of data-derived insights and solid support from the top echelons of management. Of those, the *widespread use of modeling and optimization* comprises the general set of skills needed to translate the mounds of often-dissimilar raw data into useful information. As detailed by Davenport, the quality of the resultant analyses requires the coming together of three key components: the right focus, the right people and the right technology. Implicit in the interplay of those three information-quality-shaping forces is the analytic know-how, which is that somewhat intangible quality that, on the one hand, calls for strong quantitative methodological skills, while at the same time contributing a healthy amount of problem solving creativity. A disciplined and rational left brain meets the spontaneous and untamed right brain…not impossible, but at the same time, not an everyday occurrence either.

As previously outlined, organizations that excel at extracting competitively advantageous knowledge out of the otherwise generic data are able to do so because of their data analytical prowess and the organization-wide fact-based decision making discipline. Processes ranging from high level strategic planning to tactical decisions surrounding product mix, logistics, inventory and distribution or promotional mix spending allocation are all making increasingly better use of the available data. To that end, one of the key drivers that fueled Wal-Mart's growth and its eventual ascendance to the world's largest retailer (and the #1 ranking on the Fortune Magazine listing of the largest U.S companies, based on gross revenue[20]) was its early embrace of the information-driven decision model. While its competitors continued their march forward, or so they believed, guided mostly by their intuition, anecdotal evidence and rarely empirically validated generalizations, Wal-Mart looked to objective and representative data insights for decision cues. As a result, its merchandising mix consistently outperformed its peers, while its simulation and optimization based supply chain management mercilessly squeezed unnecessary inventory and stock-out costs, enabling it to offer competitive prices while still generating attractive returns for its shareholders. It is no

---

[19] See Davenport, T. H. (2006), 'Competing on Analytics', *Harvard Business Review*, January, 98-107.
[20] $469.2 billion in 2013.

surprise that the now industry-leading organizations such as Dell and Amazon emulated Wal-Mart's supply chain philosophy as one of the engines catapulting them to the position of prominence.

But Wal-Mart's way is not the only way—frankly, blindly copying methods of successful companies' practices can be a slippery slope, as it cannot be assumed that just because a particular practice or a method works well in one instance, it will work equally well for others. Inherent in the development of effective data analytical capabilities is a certain element of organizational self-discovery, which entails the identification of the most adaptable (to the specific of the organization) ways the organization can use data to gain and sustain competitive advantage. After all, the retail industry's dynamics are quite different from the pharmaceutical, financial or other sectors of the economy, as is the available data. Neither are any two firms in a given industry exactly the same, particularly in the cultural sense (for instance, some firms are highly centralized while others are de-centralized in terms of their decision making models; some are overt risk takers in terms of heavy emphasis on new, trend-setting products, while others are risk avoiders, preferring instead to focus on the tried and true ideas or technologies). Therefore, the specifics of what data and how it can be used effectively are shaped by both industry-wide forces (e.g., what type of data and data insights can offer the greatest potential competitive levers?), as well as by company-specific competencies and goals (e.g., company's intrinsic capabilities and its organizational culture).

Capital One, as one of the leading credit card issuers in the U.S and one of the leading credit card industry innovators has consistently delivered above average results by an almost religious dedication to objective data analysis, especially customer mix optimization. Harrah's, a major casino entertainment organization and a relative risk-taker in its industry, systematically improved its profitability by using data analysis to attract and retain customers with the greatest profit potential. A resource-constrained baseball club, the Oakland A's consistently posted one of the league's best regular season records by identifying the otherwise undervalued players that could perform the desired assortment of tasks, something Oakland was able to do in spite of working with a far below average budget. Honda developed a second-to-none brand loyalty by using data for early detection of potential problems, thus greatly increasing the reliability of their automobiles. A leading hotel chain, Marriott, uses advanced analytics to optimize the price-profitability relationship, while Novartis, the giant pharmaceutical firm leverages data analysis to improve the quality and the efficacy of its R&D efforts. Last but not least, Procter and Gamble, a leading consumer packaged goods manufacturer continues to prosper in a very competitive, mature industry segment in a large part due to organization-wide embrace of data-driven new product development, as well as promotional mix allocations and evaluation practices. Progressive's market capitalization grew more than four-fold as a result of the insurer's deployment of statistical models-based automotive policy underwriting technology.

Yet overall, the use of advanced statistical modeling techniques has been comparatively slow in a broadly defined area of risk management. While many organizations, as exemplified above, readily recognize the value of using data as one of the basis of consistent revenue growth, considerably fewer see statistical data analyses as an effective mean of cost containment. This is beginning to change, however. In his recent book, *The Numerati*, Stephen Baker discusses IBM's efforts to use behavioral modeling techniques to improve the productivity of its vast legion of business process consultants and technologist, as well as to automate project management.

There are numerous other areas where behavioral modeling can be a vehicle of systematic cost reduction. The bulk of larger retailers and manufacturers, among others, spend tens of millions of dollars on workers' compensation and/or general liability claims. As detailed later in this book, considerable savings can be realized by deploying organization-tailored predictive modeling technologies to automate claim processing, flag individual claims deemed to be most at risk of adverse development and delineate specific causal factors leading to higher costs. By taking these steps, an organization will be able to effectively process larger volumes of claims more expeditiously and with fewer resources, take proactive steps (e.g., more aggressive claim management and monitoring) against specific, potentially explosive claims and develop more effective cost containment and safety protocols.

In a similar vein, organizations routinely allocate $millions to insurance coverage procurement without sound informational foundation relating the actual cost to anticipated benefits. In many instances insurance coverage is clearly needed, but in all instances it is an expense with little-to-no residual value. Stated differently, the amount of coverage purchased should reflect both the company specific likelihood and severity—it should also contemplate the threshold impact of loss on earnings. Furthermore, what if, through diligent analysis of the available data (which, by the way, is readily available for risk analysis, and it is quite rich) it could be discerned that an organization would be better off to pursue altogether different means of risk protection?

3

The Art of Communication

One of the unintended and unforeseen consequences of the rise of the 'age and the science of data' has been a relative abandonment of the art of communication. While social networking did indeed bring a lot more of us a lot closer together, it also brought with it an onslaught of bad communication habits and practices: texting often takes the place of a verbal call, informational tidbits more and more replace full-sentence expressions, emoticons are here to convey complex feelings…Announcements that once were reserved for key turning-point-type events are now promulgated for most inconsequential of events…More and more, the information age society funnels excessive time, effort and resources toward largely immaterial communications, while allowing the quality of communication to wither…

It is easy to argue that it is not quite as bad in professional settings, where more formal norms and standards are still in place and indeed, there is probably merit to that point of view. At the same time, given that organizations are ultimately just groups of individuals joined together in pursuit of some shared goals, when the quality of communication begins to diminish on a personal level, at least some of that will likely trickle into the professional domain. As noted earlier, effective communication is one of the three pillars of the Threat Exposure Management, or TEM for short, framework discussed in this book (the other two being *knowledge* and *agility*), hence its quality and effectiveness play a fundamental role in the efficacy of the threat abatement approach discussed here.

Communication Defined

Wikipedia defines *communication* as '…the purposeful activity of information exchange between two or more participants in order to convey or receive the intended meanings through shared system of signs and semiotic rules'. It can take place in three general contexts: human, living organisms in general and communication-enabled devices, such as computerized control systems. Furthermore, all communications are usually categorized as verbal, or spoken, and nonverbal, or taking the form of non-word messages. That distinction, however, is somewhat unrealistic insofar as it attempts to draw a line of demarcation where such distinction may not be warranted. For example, facial expression, eye contact, voice intonation or emphasis are all considered to be a part of nonverbal communication, yet all those elements are inseparable parts of verbal communication, which effectively renders the verbal vs. nonverbal distinction somewhat meaningless.

The first formal model of communication was introduced in 1949 by two Bell Labs researchers, Claude Shannon and Warren Weaver[1]. Mirroring the telephone and radio technologies, the initial model conceptualized human communication as being comprised of three distinct elements: sender, channel and receiver, while also allowing for noise, which could be any factor adversely affecting the communication process. Among the criticisms levied against Shannon and Weaver's transmission model was that it made no allowances for content, context, situational or interpretive factors. In effect, the model imposed monotonicity when there was often a need to account for both the substantive (which the model recognized) and affective or emotional (which the model did not recognize) communication components. Expanding on Shannon and Weaver's original work, David Berlo introduced the Source-Message-Channel-Receiver, or SMRC model in 1960[2], which is still widely used as a standard communication tool today.

---

[1] Shannon, C. E. and W. Weaver (1949), *The Mathematical Theory of Communication,* University of Illinois Press, Urbana, IL.
[2] Berlo, D. K. (1960), *The Process of Communication,* Holt, Rinehart & Winston, New York, NY.

Communication as a Management Tool

Although the SMRC model offers worthwhile insights into a general communication process, it is nonetheless too coarse a tool for more detail-demanding business communication analyses. Hence rather than focusing generic communication transmission considerations, it is more pertinent, at least from the standpoint of organizational management, to draw a distinction between the *mode* and the *content* of communication. Regarding the former, the three general modes of communication are:

1. *Interpersonal* – exemplified by individuals engaging in conversation, exchanging opinions, feeling and emotions.
2. *Interpretive* – exemplified by individuals making sense of written and spoken descriptions.
3. *Presentational* – exemplified by individuals presenting concepts and ideas to an audience of listeners or readers.

Each of the above three modes entails somewhat different challenges, which in turn bring about varying chances of success. The interpersonal mode is characterized by active negotiation of meaning among individuals, which allows each individual the ability to monitor how his/her meaning and intentions are being received, which in turn allows for timely adjustments and clarifications. As such, the interpersonal mode yields the highest overall chance of achieving successful communication, thus it should be the preferred communication mode for conveying any critical information.

In contrast to the 'two-way' character of the interpersonal mode, the 'one-way' oriented interpretive and presentational modes do not offer active negotiation of meaning, which raises an important distinction between the notions of comprehension, which refers to understanding of words or other symbols, and interpretation, which implies the ability to 'read (or listen) between the lines'. Not surprisingly, the likelihood of successful conveyance of intended meaning is generally lower for the two 'one-way' communication modes; thus it follows that those modes are suboptimal choices when the message being communicated is critical and/or complex.

The second of the two core communication characteristics, the content, is more difficult to capture in a simple typology, largely because it is extremely varied and situation-dependent. That said, one possible way of deriving some meaningful and generalizable content types, at least insofar as business management is concerned, is to consider the three broad purposes of business communication. Naturally, there are numerous possible ways of grouping business communications – some are based on the means of communication, e.g., verbal, written and electronic, while others emphasize the target, e.g., internal (which can be further subdivided into upward, downward and horizontal flows) and external. Although instructive in their own right, those typologies make no allowances for what can be termed 'innate cross-message importance'. For example, communications detailing regulatory compliance requirements or emergency evacuation procedures would generally be deemed more critical than those conveying new corporate branding philosophy.

Approaching communication types from that perspective is suggestive of an alternative, purpose-minded communication content typology grouping all information into the following three categories:

1. *Compliance* – focused on conformance to externally mandated rules, compliance oriented communication encompasses the conveyance of requirements, processes, timelines and other details.
2. *Governance* – pertains to the mechanisms used by organizations to ensure that their constituents follow internally mandated, established processes and policies.
3. *Leadership* – encompasses any internally- and externally-focused information geared at displaying the ability of an organization's management to make sound decisions and inspire their constituents.

Contrasting the three distinct content types with the earlier delineated modes of communication (interpersonal, interpretive and presentational) suggests the following possibilities:

Table 3.1
Communication Mode vs. Content

Communication Content	**Communication Mode**		
	Interpersonal	Interpretive	Presentational
Compliance	*very good*	*poor*	*good*
Governance	*very good*	*poor*	*good*
Leadership	*very good*	*good*	*very good*

The conclusions summarized in Table 3.1 are very general and non-context specific, which is to say they are meant to offer general guidance only. It is important to keep in mind that the focus of the contrasts summarized above is limited to the context of risk only, which is why the interpretive communication mode is deemed to be comparatively ineffective for all three different communication contents. There are numerous other contexts, such as creative problem solving, in which interpretive communications would likely yield superior results; however, when the scope of information conveyance is limited to only matters relating to diminishing the chances of noncompliance, misgovernance and misunderstanding of an organization's strategic vision, subjective interpretation of meaning might undermine the sought after conveyance of exact meaning.

Overall, the 'two-way' interpersonal communication mode offers the most effective means of conveying risk related information primarily because it is built upon the foundation of negotiation of meaning, which makes it very easy for the receiver of information to resolve any ambiguities. The second best option is the 'one-way' presentational mode: It is not as effective as the interpersonal mode because it does not have a built-in meaning negotiation provision, while at the same time it is more effective than the interpretive mode because it aims to bring about uniformity of message, something that as noted earlier the interpretive mode lacks.

Communicating Risk

The management of risk is a subdomain of broader organizational management thus it can be viewed from the standpoint of the same mode vs. content duality discussed in the previous section. Although the Threat Exposure Management (TEM) framework, which encompasses the historically standalone disciplines of *risk, business continuity, emergency* and *change management,* itself has a broad scope, relative to the traditional view of risk, it is nonetheless still concerned primarily with identification of threats, assessment of their impact and selection of the most appropriate responses, hence its communication scope can be expected to be narrower (than the general business communication) in scope and more specific. More specifically, risk communication can also be expected to be anticipatory or proactive, in a sense of conveying warnings, as well as instructive or reactive, in a sense of conveying directions or instructions. Cast in the context of the individual disciplines comprising the TEM framework, *anticipatory communications* are intended to communicate risk assessment, business continuity plans and organizational change related considerations, while *reactive communications* are intended to convey emergency or crisis related details. In a more general sense, the former is primarily concerned with what might happen at some point in the future, while the latter is focused on responding to events that are currently underway.

Anticipatory Communications

Anticipatory communications are not limited to disseminating risk assessment-stemming warnings to organizational stakeholders – there are numerous legislative acts that mandate certain disclosures and preemptive notifications. For example, the US Comprehensive Environmental Response, Compensation and Liability Act includes 'community relations' provision which calls for developing working relationships with the public to determine acceptable clean up ways; the US Emergency Planning and Community Right-to-Know Act requires public disclosures about hazardous chemicals in the community; the US Occupational Safety and Health Act mandates that employers clearly communicate any workplace hazards to employees; the US Food & Drug Administration's Regulations on Prescription Drug Communication require truthful, balanced and accurate disclosures of all known drug effects. Failure to comply with the established regulatory requirements can result in severe civil and criminal penalties and fines, as well as the imposition of remedial solutions and direct oversight by government regulators, which is why all-too-often the compliance function can become the organization of 'No', leading to business managers coming to view the onus of compliance obligations as more of an exasperation than a responsibility. If the compliance function becomes marginalized, or worse, ostracized, in the organization's business operations, the company is at risk of a systemic breakdown of compliance, leading to substantial enforcement activities, which can become what it sounds like: a vicious cycle...This often happens when an organization embraces what is known as 'rules-based compliance.'

In the *rules-based compliance* program, the focus is on compliance with existing laws or regulations; most business organization start with that approach to compliance, because of its emphasis on employees knowing and following applicable rules. Employees focus on what they need to comprehend in order to conduct their business, while keeping themselves and the company from violating the letter of the law. In a large, complex organization, especially a diversified conglomerate that operates in multiple, often-unrelated industry verticals, rules-based compliance philosophy can spawn a mammoth corporate rulebook, consistently in need of revision but still failing to address every potential situation. Furthermore, the rules-based approach can drive minimalist behavior among the employee base, where individuals focus on meeting the minimum regulatory requirements of the standards, policies, laws, or regulations.

High-performing companies view compliance as a catalyst for substantial value creation within an organization, not only as good risk mitigation. Those companies tend to integrate and embed compliance into the business processes of their organization, which results in an interconnected approach to compliance, one that properly integrates the program with the business culture and processes, can significantly enhance reputational value, employee retention, and even revenue. This is known as the 'values-based compliance'.

A *values-based compliance* program will usually emphasize establishing of an organizational culture of compliance, one that is built upon a foundation of ethical principles such as integrity, dignity, and professionalism. Guided by a commitment to ethical values, employees are then expected to comply with the letter and the spirit of all laws, regulations, and obligations to which the corporation is subject. In the values-based culture, the employee knows not only what the rules and policies allow, but also begins to have a comprehension and appreciation of the purpose behind the rules. This understanding goes beyond simply following the rules because it is required; it also evidences a strong commitment to conducting business in a manner that upholds the highest standards of ethics and integrity.

Reactive Communications

As suggested by the name, *reactive* communications are highly situation-dependent and, in many regards, tend to be a lot more spontaneous than *anticipatory* communications. In the majority of instances, emergencies and crises come with little-to-no warning necessitating impromptu communications between the effected organization and its various stakeholders. However, as much as the actual occurrence, timing-wise, of a crisis may be unforeseen, the very idea of that crisis should not necessarily be a surprise. Whether it is a man-made crisis, such as an accounting scandal or a major labor dispute, or a natural emergency, such as catastrophic flood or an earthquake, chances are it happened elsewhere at another point in time, hence proper communication protocols, and even some general content can be prepared and fine-tuned ahead of time. The essence of Threat Exposure Management is to anticipate any and all known and knowable organizational threats and then carefully mapping out sound responses, which includes communication-related preparations.

Thorough and sound identification of any threat response related communication needs is an important first step in developing an effective risk-related communication strategy. Once the potential communication focal points have been identified, event- or situation-specific communication plans should be developed, which necessitates addressing some key communication challenges.

Risk Communication Challenges

The essence of managing threats confronting business organizations is to act knowledgeably and proactively. It begins by taking steps to identify and estimate known and knowable risks, which then ought to be followed by sharing appropriate information with appropriate organizational stakeholders. It may sound simple, but it is not. As pointed out by Rowan[3], there are three distinct challenges to effective risk communication: 1. knowledge challenge, which stems from the need to make sense of technical risk assessment

---

[3] Rowan, F. (1996), 'The High Stakes of Risk Communication', *Preventive Medicine,* vol. 25(1), 26-29.

information, 2. process challenge, summarized earlier in Table 3.1 and highlighting communication mode-specific situational effectiveness differences, and 3. communication skill challenge, which is a consequence of the inherent difficulty of conveying messages that combine factual risk assessment details and affective or emotion reactions. Further compounding the communication difficulties are *mental noise* and *social amplification* – the former manifests itself in diminished capacity of audiences to hear and process information resulting the feeling of danger, while the latter is a consequence of social media-fueled speculation.

Further compounding the difficulty of effective anticipatory risk communication are various organizational constraints, which often include one or more of the following:

- Inadequate resources. Simply put, an organization's communication 'apparatus' may be understaffed and lacking in financial and other needed resources, such as proper training in what might be somewhat esoteric language of risk;
- Management inaction or apathy. As suggested by the notion of 'threat rigidity response', when confronted with a possible threat, managers' may become more rigid and controlling by tightening control over staff, flow of information and decision-making processes;
- Cumbersome communication review and approval process. There is clearly a need to control the content and the quality of organizational risk-related communications, but care must be taken to make sure the review process does not impeded the primary objective;
- Conflicting organizational requirements. Nowadays, the organizational 'know-how' is often viewed as a key part of the organization's competitive advantage – at times, the desire to not disclose internal operational details may run counter to the need to clearly communicate risk assessment related information;
- Insufficient or not timely information. The communication staff may itself not be well-informed;
- Belief that 'others' will not understand technical risk assessment details;
- Panic and/or denial. The organizational decision makers might simply not find the risk assessment information credible, or they may panic when presented with very unaccepted information;

Unfortunately, the potential communication challenges do not end with the above considerations – the efficacy of human communication, whether it is spoken or written, formal or informal ultimately hinges on the selection of 'right' words to communicate the desired meaning. It is important to recognize that even highly literate individuals can misunderstand the words themselves or the implied meaning, which typically happens as a result of one or more of the following:

- Ambiguity, which typically arises when words have multiple meanings (e.g., words 'break', 'cut' or 'charge' all can assume numerous and very different meanings);
- Vagueness or under-specificity, which is when a given word may invoke different feelings or ideas in different people (e.g., the term 'significant');
- Context dependence, which arises when the meaning of words changes when placed near other words.

Principles of Risk Communication

ISO, the International Organization for Standardization, an independent, non-governmental international organization with a membership of 162 national standards bodies[4], developed a generic risk communication standard as a part of its broad ISO 14000, Environmental Management, family of standards. More tailored to the North American political and regulatory regimes are a number of more context-specific standards that have been developed by the North American Standards Institute, the American Society for Testing and Material, and the National Fire Protection Association. The risk communication standards falling under those general umbrellas are generally meant to address both the anticipatory and reactive communications discussed earlier.

More focused on crisis communication are *situational crisis communication theory*[5], which suggests that communication managers should match responses to the level of responsibility and reputational threat posed by a crisis, *image restoration theory*[6], which outlines strategies to mitigate image when confronted with reputational damage, and *social-mediated crisis communication model*[7], which describes interactions between an organization in crisis and the three types of publics who produce and consume information before, during and after crises: 'influential social media creators', 'social media followers' and 'social media inactives'. All of these conceptualizations offer worthwhile general guidance, though leave numerous, practically important matters open. For instance, none offer specific communication process (e.g., how frequently to communicate) or presentation (e.g., offer more or less detail); the next section offers a more specific set of recommendations.

---

[4] The commonly used 'ISO' name is not an acronym, rather it is a universally-constant short form of the organization's name; the term itself is derived from the Greek 'isos', meaning 'equal'.

[5] Coombs, T. W. (2007), 'Protecting Organization Reputations During a Crisis: The Development and Application of Situational Crisis Communication Theory' *Corporate Reputation Review*, vol.10(3), 163-176.

[6] Benoit, W. L. (2004), 'Image Restoration Discourse and Crisis Communication', in D. P. Millar and R. L. Heath (eds.), *Responding to Crisis: A Rhetorical Approach to Crisis Communication,* 263-280, Lawrence Erlbaum, Mahwah, NJ.

[7] Liu, B. F., Austin, L., Jin, Y. (2011), 'How Publics Respond to Crisis Communication Strategies: The Interplay of Information Form and Source', *Public Relations Review*, vol. 37(4), 345-353.

Process & Presentation Principles

In general, when communicating any (i.e., anticipatory or reactive) risk related message, there are some specific practice-tested 'principles' that when followed will greatly enhance the efficacy of risk communications. (From the standpoint of epistemology, or the study of knowledge, the following do not rise to the level of true principles; however, the use of that term is believed to be warranted given the wide acceptance of the following among expert practitioners.) Outlined separately are the principles of process and the principles of presentation.

Principles of Process:

- Know the limits and purpose of your communications, especially in regard to the following constituents:
    - Organizational requirements: What exactly should be conveyed?
    - Regulatory obligations: Are there specific demands that apply?
    - Audience expectations: How (channel, form) should individual audiences be reached?
- Whenever possible, pretest your message;
- Communicate early, often and fully;
- Remember that perception is reality;

Principles of Presentation:

- Know your audience;
- Do not limit yourself to one form or method;
- Simplify language and presentation, not content;
- Be objective and honest;
- Listen to and respond to concerns;
- Deal with uncertainty – for instance, acknowledge that the initial conclusions are based on estimates, thus are subject to change.

***

The remainder of this book offers an in-depth overview of the Threat Exposure Management (TEM) framework. Each of the three broad components of TEM (see Figure 1.4 in Chapter 1) – risk management, organizational resilience and change management – is detailed separately, starting with risk management.

Risk Management

Risk Management as Practice

The contemporary practice of risk management, as detailed in the ensuing chapters, can be seen as a product of centuries-long efforts to understand, assess and manage natural and man-made threats. However, given the very broad scope of the deceptively simple sounding term 'risk', the discipline of 'risk management' can be described as an archipelago of framework-, industry- or scope-dependent approaches, each offering sound ideas but none complete or comprehensive enough to serve as a core around which the entire discipline could coalesce. This state of being is clearly captured by the number and diversity of professional, risk management focused organizations jostling for the position of preeminence, but ultimately serving some sectors of the risk management industry better than others. With that in mind, it is worthwhile to take a quick survey of some of the better-known professional risk management organizations, with the goal of developing a better intuitive understanding of the scope and the depth of contemporary risk management practices.

Overall, the professional organizations serving the risk management community, which encompasses university-based researchers and industry practitioners, can be grouped into three clusters: general, industry-specific and topical associations. Listed below are some of the better-known organizations falling into each of the three clusters.

General Associations:

Risk and Insurance Management Society (RIMS): Founded in 1950, RIMS is now dedicated to all aspects of risk management, although historically has been particularly focused on insurance topics; the organization counts as its members more than 3.500 industrial, service, nonprofit and government entities throughout the world, including more than 11,000 risk management professionals in more than 60 countries.

Professional Risk Managers' International Association (PRMIA): Dating back to only 2002, PRMIA is a non-profit professional association focused on defining and implementing the best risk management practices and providing an open forum for the development and promotion of the risk profession.

Global Association of Risk Professionals (GARP): Established in 1996, GARP aims to help create a culture of risk awareness within organizations, from entry to board levels; the organization has more than 150,000 members in 195 countries and territories.

Institute of Risk Management (IRM): Founded in 1986, the Institute is a risk management professional education and training body with about 4,000 members in roughly 100 countries; it is currently one of only few organizations offering vocational post-graduate level qualifications entirely focused on enterprise risk management (ERM).

Industry-Specific Associations:

The Risk Management Association (RMA): The core purpose of RMA, one of the oldest risk management associations founded in 1914, is to advance sound risk management principles in the financial services industry to improve institutional performance and financial stability, as well as to enhance the risk management competency of individuals.

American Society for Healthcare Risk Management (ASHRM): Established in 1980, it is a personal membership group of the American Hospital Association with nearly 6,000 members; it is dedicated to promoting safe and effective patient care practices, preservation of financial resources and maintenance of safe working environments.

University Risk Management and Insurance Association (URMIA): Founded in 1969, it is focused on protecting the reputation as well as human and financial resources of institutions of higher education through the incorporation of sound risk management practices.

Public Risk Management Association (PRIMA): Made up of more than 2,000 entities in over 1,800 jurisdictions, the Association is dedicated solely to the practice of risk management in the public sector.

Private Risk Management Association (PRMA): It is focused on the high net worth private risk and insurance management niche; it offers its members specialized education and information and fosters the establishment of standards and credentials.

Topical Associations:

Society for Risk Analysis (SRA): Founded in 1980, it is a learned society dedicated to disseminating risk analysis related research; it offers its members a forum to discuss idea and methodologies for analyzing risk and solving related problems.

Society of Risk Management Consultants (SRMC): Founded in 1984 through a merger of The Institute of Risk Management Consultants and the Insurance Consultants Society, SRMC is dedicated to the promotion of professional and ethical guidelines and education and exchange of information through conferences and networking.

Society of Actuaries (SOA): Founded in 1949 as the merger of two major actuarial US organizations (the Actuarial Society of America and the American Institute of Actuaries), it is focused providing primary and continuing education for the modeling and management of financial risk and contingent events.

The above are just some of the better known associations devoted to promoting and furthering risk management related theory and practice; while all of the risk management associations listed above (as well as those not) offer their members informal training and education, some also established formal credentialing programs. Some of the better-known risk management related professional designations include Associate of Risk Management (ARM), Chartered Property and Casualty Underwriter (CPCU), Certified Risk Manager (CRM), Financial Risk Manager (FRM), Certified Risk Analyst (CRA), Chartered Enterprise Risk Analyst (CERM) and Fellow of the Casualty Actuarial Society (FCAS).

***

The ensuing three chapters offer a broad overview of the core elements of risk management practice: An in-depth analysis of the meaning and the scope of the notion of 'risk' (Chapter 4: Understanding Risk), the fundamental risk measurement concepts (Chapter 5: Measuring Risk), and a method for constructing multi-attribute risk profiles of organizations (Chapter 6: Risk Profiling).

4

Understanding Risk

Merriam-Webster dictionary defines *risk* as a '...possibility of loss or injury', positing that the term dates back to the latter part of the 17th century. The dictionary also suggests that the notion of risk stems from an older term (dating back to the 13th century) peril, which it defines as '...exposure to the risk of being injured, destroyed, or lost'. The notion of peril is itself related to the chronologically contemporary (also dating back to the 13th century) concept of danger, defined as '...exposure or liability to injury, pain, harm, or loss'.

It seems odd that something that clearly has been an inseparable part of humanity since the dawn of our civilization has not gotten a formal recognition until just a few centuries ago. Common sense tells us that *risk* did not enter the realm of human experience at some arbitrary point, such as the aforementioned 13th or 17th centuries—it has shadowed us throughout our history. It was the conception of risk it took quite a while longer to develop in our cognitive awareness. In a sense, the evolution of what we now describe as risk ran parallel to the maturation of our social and economic structures, both in terms of the types of risk as well as the acuity of our perception of it. As these structures grew in complexity, so did our awareness and fear of adverse outcomes.

Building on the Merriam-Webster definitions cited earlier, I start by defining risk as the possibility of adverse events occurring at some point in the future. It is a very broad definition, both conceptually and operationally. It is a combination of old and new, natural and man-made as well as tangible and abstract. There are many forms of risk that existed throughout the history and have been recognized as such, others that existed in principle, but did not become recognized as threats until relatively recently, and still others that are a direct byproduct of the socio-political-legal fiber of our society. For instance, the various forms of natural catastrophes, such as wind, floods or earthquakes have been our constant companion since the dawn of our civilization. At the same time, the possibility of a person getting injured while on someone else's premises certainly existed for many centuries, but it did not become a recognizable risk until relatively recent (in the sense of historical chronology) tort law developments. Similarly, corporations, as independent, legal business entities with outside shareholders and independent management have also been in existence for centuries[1], yet securities class action litigation (civil suits filed by shareholders alleging dishonest and/or deceptive practices on the part of management) did not become a threat until 1980's. Similarly, intellectual property or technological risks did not exist (as a concept and a form of threat) before the advent of the industrial age.

It is important to note that, in the strict sense of the word, we do not create or eliminate risk—rather, risk is a consequence of our actions. The action of erecting a building carries with it the possibility of property damage, by wind, fire or other means—in other words, the risk of man-made property damage[2] is a result of the decision to put up or otherwise assemble a property. In a more general sense, the risk of damage represents a liability associated with all damageable assets. This is also true in less tangible situations. For instance, if we enter into a service agreement with another party, that action gives rise to the potentiality of non-performance or non-payment. In this instance, risk is a consequence of the decision to enter into a service agreement with another party. The examples are virtually endless, all pointing to the same conclusion: The development of thorough understanding of risk starts with a careful delineation and study of specific risk-spawning actions.

This is particularly true of economic risk. Business interactions are ultimately about exchanging elements of value. Looking back in time, what is known as business transactions today started as barter trades, which are exchanges of goods or services not involving the use of money. There is no way of knowing when the first barter exchange took place (nor is it particularly important to be able to pinpoint the exact instance), though it is safe to say that

[1] Business entities which carried on business and were subject to legal right existed as far back as ancient Rome; the oldest, as it is believed, business corporation in the word is the Stora Kopparberg mining company in Sweden, dating its origins back to 1347.

[2] I am differentiating between man-made property, such as buildings, and natural property, such as land, because the latter is obviously not damageable.

it goes all the way back to the dawn of our civilization. What is important to note is that from the very first barter exchange, both parties assumed the risks associated with giving up what they had (the benefits of which were quite well-known to the owner) for something else (the benefits of which were less know to the prospective owner). It was that uncertainty gap that gave rise to the *exchange risk*. Conceptually, the action of economic exchange is rooted in properly valuing the anticipated benefits associated with what is being acquired, which means that the most rudimentary aspect of risk is that of over-valuing of the acquisition. Hence in the sense of risk analysis, a barter transaction can be described in the context of expected vs. realized utility, as shown below:

Exchange Risk = (Expected Utility - Realized Utility)

As time passed, barter trade gave way to monetary exchanges, i.e., buying and selling, and a good portion of individual traders began to group together to form business organizations. And as the economic plenty of an evolving society continued to expand, along with the socio-economic-political infrastructure, so did the varieties of economic threats. Stated differently, our conception of risk grew beyond its initial nucleus of (barter) exchange risk to become a function of assets, both tangible, such as factories, inventories or real estate, and intangible, such as rights or intellectual property and the environment affecting those assets, such as socio-political, regulatory or physical.

So, is risk simply the uncertainty regarding the future events and outcomes? As it tends to be the case with numerous other abstract notions, this too gave rise to a healthy debate. The analysis of some of the key points and conclusions follows.

Risk vs. Uncertainty

Intuitively, risk and uncertainty are noticeably different. The former implies more specificity in terms of what might happen, while the latter is a reflection of a general state of ambiguity regarding the future. In more concrete terms, the key risk consideration is whether or not the (known) event will occur, while uncertainty connotes a non-specific insecurity or ambiguity regarding the future in general. Not surprisingly, risk theorists tend to conclude that it is extremely important to draw a clear line of demarcation between risk and uncertainty. Perhaps the best set of original ideas trying to differentiate between these two concepts can be traced back to the work of Frank Knight, dating back to the early 1900's. In his seminal book, *Risk, Uncertainty & Profit*, published in 1921, Knight comes to following conclusions: '...Uncertainty must be taken in a sense radically distinct from the familiar notion of Risk, from which it has never been properly separated. The term 'risk', as loosely used in everyday speech and in economic discussion, really covers two things which, functionally at least, in their causal relations to the phenomena of economic organization, are categorically different. ... The essential fact is that 'risk' means in some cases a quantity susceptible of measurement, while at other times it is something distinctly not of this character; and there are far-reaching and crucial differences in the bearings of the phenomenon depending on which of the two is really present and operating. ... It will appear that a measurable uncertainty, or 'risk' proper, as we shall use the term, is so far different from an unmeasurable one that it is not in effect an uncertainty at all. We ... accordingly restrict the term 'uncertainty' to cases of the non-quantitative type'.

Building upon Knight's work, Hubbard offered a more operationally clear differentiation between risk and uncertainty[3]. According to him, risk always implies uncertainty, but not the other way around—uncertainty does not necessarily imply risk, which is in keeping with the definition of risk offered in the opening paragraph of this chapter. More specifically, Hubbard offers the following risk vs. uncertainty tests: An event of a circumstance can be categorized as uncertainty if:

---

[3] Hubbard, D. (2007), *How to Measure Anything: Finding the Value of Intangibles in Business*, John Wiley & Sons, Hoboken, NJ, pg. 46.

Definition:	The lack of complete certainty, that is, the existence of more than one possibility. The true outcome / state / result / value is not known.
Measurement:	A set of probabilities assigned to a set of possibilities. Example: There is a 60% chance this market will double in five years.

Otherwise, an event or a circumstance can be categorized as risk if:

Definition:	A state of uncertainty where some of the possibilities involve a loss, catastrophe, or other undesirable outcome.
Measurement:	A set of possibilities each with quantified probabilities and quantified losses. Example: There is a 40% chance the proposed oil well will be dry with a loss of $12 million in exploratory drilling costs.

Knight's and Hubbard's reasoning has a strong appeal, considering that the goal of managing threats confronting business organizations is to minimize the organization's exposure to potentially economically damaging events, or to support the attainment of stated strategic objectives. Uncertainty is undeniably ubiquitous and as such, very difficult—if not altogether impossible—to manage effectively. Risk, on the other hand, can be construed as a special case of uncertainty, further contextualized by the stated organizational strategic objectives.

It is also true, however, that much has changed since Knight published his insightful ideas. Most notably, the global economy is now leaning toward service, rather than manufacturing industries – in fact, according to the most recent figures available from the World Bank, of the twenty largest economies – i.e., the so-called G-20 – only three (China, Indonesia and Saudi Arabia) derive more than 50% of their gross domestic product from manufacturing. Hence it follows that a considerable number of business organizations are engaged in activities where the primary—meaning, of most concern—source of threat are events that both Knight and Hubbard would classify as uncertainty, rather than risk. For instance, a financial services organization, such as a bank or a mutual fund manager, can certainly be adversely impacted by natural catastrophes, but the potential peril would more than likely pale by comparison to the impact that mismanaged or miscalculated market or credit exposures would have on those organizations[4]. Secondly, in a methodological sense the notions of risk and uncertainty do not exhibit the necessary discriminant validity[5], as these two concepts are confounded and situation-dependent. For instance, two otherwise similar organizations could have considerably different analytical capabilities, so much so that what might appear to be un-measurable (and thus considered 'uncertainty') to one might be measurable (and thus considered 'risk') to the other.

In view of the above, what is the value of differentiating between risk and uncertainty, in the context of risk management? Are we getting too entangled in semantic considerations?

Let us go back to the basic definition of risk compiled by Merriam-Webster: Risk is a possibility of loss or injury. A loss can be a result of property damage caused by a natural disaster, it can be a result of a lawsuit brought by customers (product liability), shareholders (executive liability) or regulators (non-compliance), or it can stem from a decline in value of market securities. It can take on a number of other forms as well, but in all cases it will manifest itself as adverse impact on the organization's earnings. Furthermore, just because the outcome itself appears more tangible does not mean that the potential threat is more measurable. Each year, several hurricanes move along the Gulf Coast of the United States, and even though many follow very similar paths, their impact varies considerably. With that in mind, let us consider Hubbard's definitions of risk and uncertainty, presented earlier. The author defines uncertainty as '…the lack of complete certainty, that is, the existence of more than one possibility; the "true" outcome / state / result / value is not known'. At the same time, he defines risk as '…a state of uncertainty where some of the possibilities involve a loss, catastrophe, or other undesirable outcome'. Are these definitions meaningful, or sufficiently distinct, in the context of the aforementioned Gulf Coast hurricanes? Not at all and here is why.

Whether our focus is on hurricanes or any other type of a natural or a man-made threat, it is hard to envision a situation other than 'the lack of complete certainty', to use Hubbard's words. Short of being able to gaze into

---

[4] Two relatively recent events illustrate that point: The Financial Crisis of 2007-08 (also known as the Great Recession) and the Superstorm Sandy both directly impacted Lower Manhattan, home to some of the world's largest financial service organizations, yet only the former threatened the very survival of the said companies.
[5] A notion describing the degree to which a particular operationalization diverges from other, conceptually distinct, operationalizations – in other words, does it just sound differently, or is it indeed different?

the proverbial crystal ball, the lack of complete certainty is a ubiquitous property of future events, as prior to materializing the future state of any outcome is probabilistic in nature. Even if we know that the onslaught of a bad storm is unavoidable or the shareholder suit imminent – we do not have complete certainty regarding the ultimate consequence of either of these two, and countless other threats. The reason that Knight's and Hubbard's uncertainty vs. risk differentiation lacks operational clarity and definitional distinctiveness is because they do not expressly consider the *degree of knowability* of individual threats.

The key to being knowable, for a particular threat, is to be estimable using objectively sourced information. Furthermore, to be estimable a threat has to be assessed in the context of two key dimensions that jointly determine its expected consequences: 1. how likely is it to occur, and 2. how severe will be its impact. Recalling an earlier-made assertion that all future events are speculative (probabilistic), the distinction between the likelihood (#1) and the severity (#2) helps to illustrate why that is the case: From the standpoint of managing the organization's risk exposure, it is imperative to not only know the expected chances (likelihood) of a particular threat occurring, but it is also critical to know the force of its impact (severity). For example, if threats A and B have 90% and 10%, respectively, probability of occurrence, threat A appears to be clearly more worrisome – however, if A's severity is estimated at $10,000, while B's at $1,000,000 a different conclusion emerges[6].

Keeping the above in mind and turning our attention to the uncertainty vs. risk distinction and the notion of the degree of knowability, I define *uncertainty* to include all threats that have non-estimable likelihood and severity, and I define *risk* to include all threats that have estimable likelihood and severity. Furthermore, both likelihood and severity will be deemed non-estimable when the requisite data either do not exist or are insufficient, in view of an estimation methodology under consideration. Lastly, given the multiplicative nature of the two threat-defining dimensions of likelihood and severity, to be estimable a particular threat has to have the requisite data available for both dimensions.

Broadening the Scope of Risk

As discussed in the preceding section, the term "risk" denotes a *threat*, which is a reflection of certain amount of linguistic conditioning causing us to

[6] 0.9 * $10,000 vs. .1 * $1,000,000.

think of risk as a possibility of an undesirable event taking place. And certainly, every business organization faces a considerable amount of *downside*—defined here as asset damaging or loss-generating events—risk. The same organizations, however, also face a wide array of *upside risks*, defined here as an unrealized growth opportunity. For example, an electric utility with power generating plants located in the Gulf of Mexico region faces the downside risk of hurricane related wind damage, while at the same time it faces the upside risk associated with the decision to invest or not in renewable power generation assets. To truly appreciate the risk exposure of the said utility, it is necessary to assess both its downside as well as upside risks, hence our conception of risk needs to be framed in the context that includes both the avoidance of undesirable events, i.e., downside risks, as well purposeful pursuit of desired states, i.e., upside risks.

Downside risk is the possibility of asset-damaging or loss-generating events taking place, while *upside risk* reflects the chances of anticipated growth not materializing. Both can adversely impact the organization's earnings.

It follows that risk is not necessarily something to be avoided—in fact, good risk taking can have a very positive impact on the organization. Microsoft took a risk by tying its success, in terms of its core operating system, to the proliferation of personal computers, just as Google took a risk by deviating from an established practice of charging advertisers based on the actual visits to their websites, rather than total traffic (which was an established practice at that time). These are examples of companies that successfully increased their exposure to upside risks—of course, there are numerous examples of ineffective upside risk taking, such as the much-anticipated entrance of IBM into the personal computer industry in the 1980's (which turned out to be unprofitable for the company, ultimately causing it to exit out of that business) or the ill-advised decision by Gateway in the 1990's to vertically integrate by expanding into retail. Although the anecdotal evidence is mixed, the aggregate results overwhelmingly point to the desirability of increasing the exposure to the upside risk, as evidenced by the higher overall returns realized by investors (both individuals and organizations) who put their money in equities, rather than government and corporate bonds.

There is an important nuance, however, that needs to be addressed—risk taking recklessness. First reported by Bowman[7], and subsequently coined

[7] Bowman, E.H, (1980), 'A Risk/Return Paradox for Strategic Management,' *Sloan Management Review*, vol. 21, 17-31.

the Bowman Paradox, the positive risk-return relationship does not hold for organizations engaging in poor risk taking. Specifically, firms earning below average returns tend to exhibit negative risk-return relationship, while those earning above average returns tend to exhibit the (expected) positive risk-return relationship. In other words, good risk taking will advantageously increase the upside risk, while limiting the downside risk.

Overall, at any given time the organization-specific total risk exposure will be a sum of net present value of both the downside and upside risk, or

Total Risk Exposure → Present Value of Upside Risk
→ Present Value of Downside Risk

It is competitively advantageous to an organization to thoughtfully increase its exposure to upside risk, while systematically lowering the potential impact of downside risk. Increasing the spread between the two types of risks will systematically enhance the organization's competitive advantage. It follows that management of upside risk entails systematic evaluation of risks to be taken, while management of downside risk calls for systematic reduction of risk exposure.

Aside from considering what types of events should fall within our conception of risk, it is also important to explicitly estimate the possibility of both the upside and downside risks affecting the organization. It is intuitively obvious that risk potential is a function of two, usually independent dimensions of *likelihood/probability* and cost, usually referred to as *severity*. Risk is inherently probabilistic because it reflects uncertainty associated with the future. Events that have not yet occurred but whose future occurrence is known with certainty are not risks—they are more accurately described as either assets or liabilities. For instance, a lease payment that is to be made on a periodic basis is a liability, because its occurrence (or rather, its recurrence) and amount are known exactly ahead of time. On the other hand, future wind or flood related property damage is a risk because neither its occurrence nor the amount of damage are known ahead of time. Both good and bad outcomes, and upside and downside risks, respectively, can be expressed in terms of the likelihood of occurrence and the magnitude or severity of the resultant gains or losses.

Bowman, E.H, (1982), 'Risk Seeking by Troubled Firms,' *Sloan Management Review*, vol. 23, 33-42.

The third and final component of the definition of risk, in the organizational context, should the standardized impact estimation. This is most important when dissimilar risks are evaluated in a holistic, or enterprise-wide setting, and when resource allocation decisions are based on those evaluations. The most reasonable benchmark for cross-risk-types impact comparisons is the net earnings impact assessment. Stated differently, to adequately communicate the magnitude of an upside or downside risk, and to make rational (i.e., reflecting risk type-specific impact) resource allocations, the assessment of risk needs to be expressed in terms of the impact on the organization's revenues or earnings. Figure 4.1 summarizes the three key definitional components of risk.

Figure 4.1
Key Components of the Definition of Risk

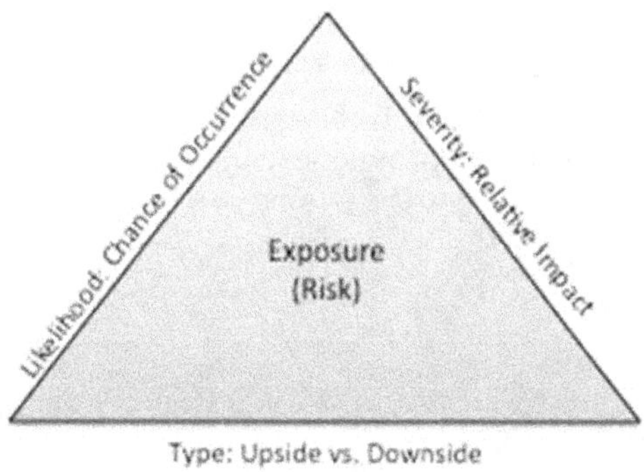

Although nominally the type of risk, the possibility of occurrence and the relative impact all play a role in framing individual risk types, their roles are not the same. More specifically, the type of risk and the possibility of the risk event materializing are both antecedents (i.e., they precede) the risk event, while its impact follows the risk event. Hence from a causal standpoint, it is more appropriate to express risk in the following manner:

Figure 4.2
Causal View of Risk

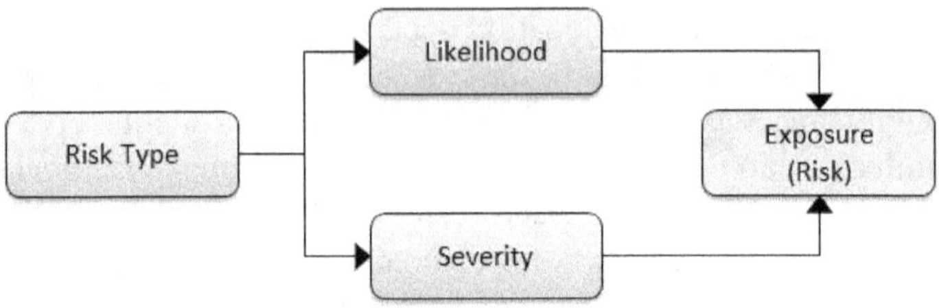

The causal view of risk is essential to the development of a holistic risk management approach, or active management of the organization's risk profile, because it draws attention to the distinctiveness of managing the underlying root causes of risk and the capitalization of the possible risk outcomes. To actively manage the organization's exposure to risk, explicit steps need to be taken to mitigate the possibility of unfavorable outcomes and to put in place economically optimal capital provisions.

Assessment of Risk

Accepting the dual face—upside vs. downside—of risk stretches the conceptual boundary of our conception of risk and so by extension, it also expands the requisite operationalization of it. Intuitively, there are considerable measurement differences separating risks as diverse as hurricanes, fraud, and cost of capital fluctuations or strategic missteps. The risk estimation process, however, will tend to follow a similar set of steps, as depicted in Figure 4.3.

Figure 4.3
Risk Estimation Process

First and foremost, individual risks need to be clearly identified. As detailed later, there is a long list of upside and especially downside risks that could potentially have a material impact on the organization's financial well-being. Once clearly delineated, the potential impact of each of the risks needs to be estimated, in terms of the probability of the event taking place as well as its severity. The *Estimation* stage is usually most readily associated with the notion of risk analytics, as it tends to be the most "analytical" part of the overall process, however, just presenting the likelihood and severity estimates outside of the earnings impact can be of limited utility to the decision makers because it does not expressly contemplate the net impact of risk on earnings.

Mapping of the individually identified and estimated risks is the next step in the risk analytics process. It is, in effect, putting together of a "risk puzzle", or a matrix of individual risks categorized in the context of estimated likelihood and severity. Figure 4.4 offers a generic example of a risk map.

Figure 4.4
Hypothetical Risk Map

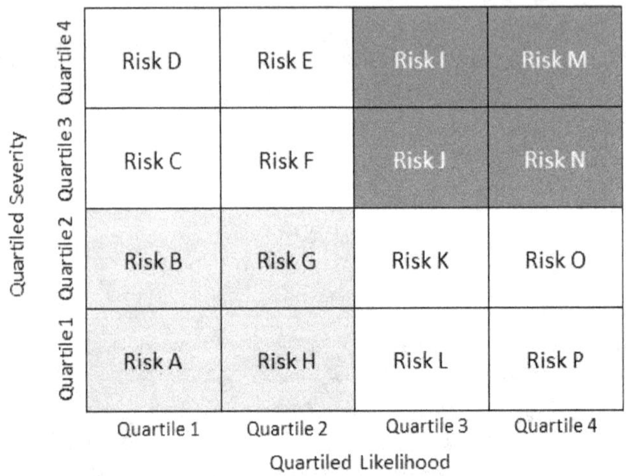

In the illustration shown above, each individual risk is plotted on the likelihood—severity grid, with each risk dimension being broken out into four magnitude-based quartiles. In effect, the probability and the estimated cost of each event are used as basis for placing individual risks into an appropriate cell. In the resultant 16-cell matrix used here, the four cells falling at the intersection of the top two likelihood and the top two severity quartiles are highlighted (in red) as the high risk region, while the four cells falling at the intersection of the bottom two likelihood and bottom two severity quartiles are highlighted (in red) as the low risk region. Using quartile-based likelihood and severity is somewhat of an arbitrary choice, as circumstances might warrant a more granular (such as decile-based) or coarser view—the important point here is that an single categorization schema should be applied to all risk to enable robust and objective side-by-side risk impact comparisons.

The next step in the risk analytics process is that of determining the most appropriate response. Consider Figure 4.5.

Figure 4.5
Response Selection

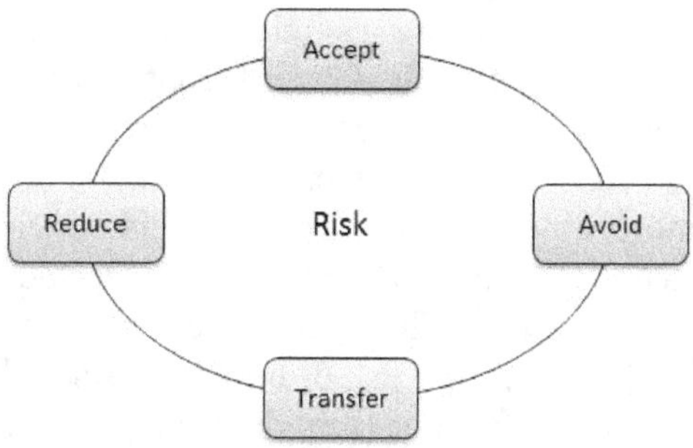

There are four distinct risk responses: *acceptance, reduction, transfer* and *avoidance* (more on each later in this chapter). The goal of this stage of the risk analytics process is to overlay the impact on earnings-adjusted efficacy of each of the four options onto the risk map develop in the previous stage, which leads to the final stage of the process: *Capitalization*. Virtually all non-zero likelihood risks, both upside and downside have capital implications ranging from setting aside funds for insurance coverage acquisition to contingent capital planning to product infrastructure investments.

Exposure

It is intuitively obvious that the degree of risk exposure will vary, at time significantly, across companies. Upon a bit more reflection, it also becomes intuitively obvious that cross-company risk exposure will depend primarily on the degree of business spread (the number of distinct product or service types offered) and geographic spread (the number of physical locations). A business entity that is comprised of multiple, dissimilar business units—i.e., a diversified conglomerate—will tend to be exposed to a wider array of risks than an entity operating a single business unit. For example, a vertically integrated electronics manufacturer (i.e., a company engaged in manufacturing and retail) will bear the risks associated with manufacturing as well as retailing, while a company engaged only in manufacturing will only bear the risks associated with manufacturing.

In a similar manner, an organization that operates in multiple geographic locations and/or jurisdictions will face more risks than a single location organization. For instance, a multinational firm is exposed to proportionally more regulatory, environmental, contractual and physical risks than an organization operating in a single location/jurisdiction.

Of course, that is not to say that it is more advantageous to only compete in a single product line or a single location as this type of concentration carries its own perils—the assumption of risk needs to be evaluated in the context of return it generates. In other words, the risk posture of an organization needs to be commensurate with the organization's economic returns. Furthermore, any incremental risk associated with the contemplated course of action needs to be contrasted with the expected incremental economic gain. For example, building an oil refinery in the coastal region of the Gulf of Mexico heightens the risk of hurricane-related wind damage, while at the same time it is advantageous from the standpoint of crude oil access and transportation costs. To make a rational build vs. not build decision, one has to be able to objectively estimate the incremental economic values of both sides of the risk—return relationship. Doing so, however, will amount to just a single step in the multi-step enterprise risk management process. In addition to wind damage related risk, what other risks need to be taken into account to make a more holistic risk assessment of this particular project. And what is the nature of any cross-risk type interdependencies?

Management of Risk

In 1956, Harvard Business Review published 'Risk Management: A New Phase of Cost Control', which posited that a professional insurance management should be the domain of a risk manager. Roughly two decades later, The American Society of Insurance Management changed its name to Risk and Insurance Management Society, and about a year later, in 1976, Fortune magazine published a seminal article titled 'The Risk Management Revolution', which discussed '…the coordination of formerly unconnected risk management functions with an organization with oversight by the board of directors'. In many regards, these events marked the rise of formal (i.e., department-based) corporate risk management functions. The creation of the first-ever Chief Risk Officer position by GE Capital in 1993 brought even a greater level of recognition of the importance of organization-wide, senior management level risk exposure oversight.

Risk management as an attempt at diminishing the exposure to risk, rather than a structured organizational function, has a far longer history. Interest rates, which started to emerge roughly 5,000 years ago in Babylon, are the earliest known form of a specific, definable way of treating risk. The Code of Hammurabi, circa 1755 BC, contains the first formal form of risk shielding, or insurance. By creating the concepts of 'bottomry' (i.e., ship bottoms) and 'respondentia' (or cargo), it laid the foundation for marine insurance which was built around the three key components: 1. a loan on a vessel or cargo, 2. an interest rate, and 3. a surcharge to cover the possibility of loss. In effect, ship owners were the insured and lenders were the underwriters. By about 750 BC, the concepts first introduced in the Code of Hammurabi were refined into the notion of 'general average', which became a fundamental notion underlying marine and other forms of insurance coverage.

Modern day insurance based risk management dates back to 12th century Italian ports, most notably, Venice (in fact, the term 'policy' is derived from Italian 'polizza', meaning a 'promise' or an 'undertaking'). Roughly five centuries later, insurance began to take hold in the Great Britain, with the Great Fire of London of 1666 giving rise to the first insurance company, The Insurance Office, formed a year later.

As noted earlier, however, risk management goes far beyond insurance coverage acquisition—more specifically, it encompasses the following set of activities:

Risk type identification.
Specific and distinct threats to the organization need to be singled out in an operationally clear manner.

Risk type impact estimation.
The two distinct and independent dimensions of risk—likelihood and severity—need to be estimated in terms of their potential impact.

Aggregate risk mapping.
Individual risks need to be pulled together into a single, coherent picture of the overall threat to the organization.

Response optimization.
Taking action is a logic consequence of the previous three steps.

These four sets of activities are causally related, as shown in Figure 4.6 below.

Figure 4.6
Interdependence of Risk Activities

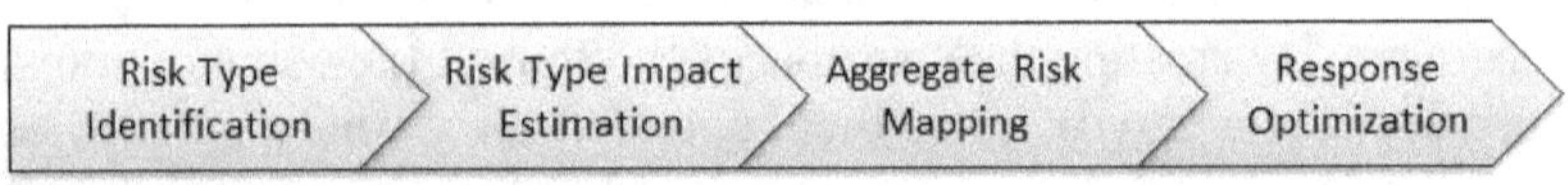

Risk Mapping

The delineation of individual risk types and the estimation of their impact should be framed in the context of *risk mapping*, which is simply the process of explicitly identifying and assessing specific areas of risk exposure. The most pronounced benefit of risk mapping is that it helps to pull together a variety of otherwise dissimilar aspects of the organization's overall risk exposure, thus yielding the first step in the enterprise-wide risk assessment process.

To yield thorough and credible outcomes, the risk mapping process should encompass two interconnected sets of activities: 1. Identification of all pertinent risks in the context of the known vs. knowable clarification, and 2. Meta analytic assessment.

Known vs. Knowable

All potential risks facing an organization should be clearly listed and for each, assess what is already known and what else might be knowable. The importance of the known—knowable dichotomy is primarily of methodological nature. More specifically, there are two, somewhat methodologically distinct approaches to risk quantification: 1. trend extrapolation-based outcome simulation, and 2. multivariate modeling. The goal of the former is to estimate the most likely outcomes by means of simulating a large number of potential outcomes and comparing the probabilities of different scenarios. The latter approach, on the other hand, is in principle a two-step process of explaining the past by means of identifying the key influencers and estimating their relative impact (step 1), followed by the construction of a forward-looking predictive function (step 2). Depending on the risk category, i.e., variability in known events vs. possibility of an unknown event, either of the two approaches may be more appealing or plausible. In general, the less manageable the risk, the lower the benefit of the explanatory approach, for the somewhat intuitive reason: Even if robust explanation is feasible, the return on the investment needed to craft an adequate explanation may simply not be there for risks over which the organization ultimately exercises little-to-no control. On the other hand, the return may be quite high for risks over which the management yields a meaningful degree of control.

Meta Analysis

Derivation-wise, the prefix 'meta' is a Greek-derived term meaning 'after', 'beyond' or 'adjacent'. Epistemologically, the term 'meta' is used to denote 'being about something'—such as *metadata* is data about data (i.e., description of informational contents of a particular data file) or metamemory refers to individuals' knowledge about whether they could remember something if they concentrated their efforts on trying to remember. Hence *meta analysis* is about knowledge extracted from the analysis of multiple other analyses. Sounds tautological, but the essence of meta analysis is to distil and summarize specific insights into a broader knowledge base.

Initially, meta analysis was used to circumvent sample size limitations for studies with sample sizes deemed too small to support broader generalizations; in that context, analyzing the results from a group of studies was believed to lead to greater reliability and generalizability of findings. According to Wikipedia, the first reported use of meta analysis dates back to

1904 and is attributed to Karl Pearson, one of the early pioneers of modern statistics; however, the term 'meta analysis' did not become formally recognized as a statistical term until the mid-1970's, as noted in Oxford English Dictionary. Interestingly, in contrast to the early goals of meta analysis, which was to overcome sample size inadequacies of individual studies, the current interest in meta analytic research is driven by the opposite problem—overwhelmingly large volumes of data and research studies necessitate the creation of higher order knowledge, which is the derivation of macro conclusions from more micro-focused research initiatives.

From the methodological standpoint, meta analysis imposes measurement uniformity in evaluating related, though somewhat dissimilar pieces of information. This is not a technique per se, but rather a loosely defined approach to distilling multiple sources of information into a singular, summary-like set of findings. The main benefit of meta analysis is that it draws attention to the key validity, reliability and generalizability related descriptors of individual sources of information or research studies. This is usually accomplished by cross-tabulating such a priori delineated evaluation criteria, followed by systematically assessing each source of information in terms of those evaluative dimensions. A more in-depth detailing of meta analysis is offered in later chapters.

How will meta analysis contribute to risk mapping? By bringing about two specific outcomes: First, it will result in the creation of an objective and robust evaluative template, which in turn will form the basis for consistent, risk type specific evaluation of the available information. Second, it will yield a summary of the available risk exposure information—in a sense, it will contribute an enterprise-wide summary of risk types and risk exposure, in the context of reliability of the current level of knowledge.

Risk Response

Establishing definitional and operational clarity with regard to risk types and risk exposure necessitates crafting an effective risk management plans. Stated differently, risks need to be dealt with, hence careful risk definition and cataloging needs to be followed by an equally thorough assessment of risk type specific response strategies. In general, an organization has four distinct risk response options available:

Avoidance.	In most situations, this translates into exiting out of activities that give rise to risks that are to be avoided.
Reduction.	Taking specific steps, often referred to as 'risk mitigation', to reduce the likelihood and/or severity of specific risk types.
Transfer.	Insuring, sharing or otherwise outsourcing specific risks.
Acceptance.	For the most part, it entails no action, either as a result of explicit cost-benefit analysis or because no other options are available.

Avoidance

'Don't do it' is often the easiest recommendation to issues and the hardest one to implement. As noted earlier, risk is a consequence of our, or in a broader sense, organizational actions, hence risk avoidance is ultimately directed at actions that precipitate risks to be avoided. Under most circumstances, risk avoidance is the most appropriate strategy for risks falling under the general umbrella of regulatory risks. An officer or a director of a company should not knowingly mislead investors or governmental officials; the same executives should not attempt to bribe foreign or domestic officials; a company should not engage in anti-competitive, price-fixing schemas, etc. As taxing, in terms of time and effort, as regulatory compliance can be (e.g., there is a mounting opposition to the reporting burden imposed by the enforcement of the Sarbanes-Oxley Act), it is nonetheless a relatively uncomplicated risk management task: Regulated behaviors are usually explicitly defined and penalties are equally clearly laid out. Contrasted with other types of business risks, such as the possibility of a hurricane damaging a particular facility, absolution of key technologies or the probability of a major product liability suit, identifying and avoiding regulatory risks is relatively easy. Why? Largely because unlike hurricanes or market forces, regulatory requirements are perfectly knowable (after all, that is the exactly the goal of governmental regulations), which also makes this a very atypical type of a threat.

Conceptually, there are other types of risks that can be avoided, to a larger or a greater degree, but are not knowable in advance, as is the case with regulatory threats. For instance, a decision to enter a particular geographic market or product category is generally under the company's control, though potential dangers that might be associated with those decisions are rarely, if ever, known in advance. Are those risks avoidable? In principle, yes, because they stem from the company-controlled factors.

To generalize beyond the above examples, there are two, mutually independent (i.e., either—or) prerequisites for avoidance being a viable risk management strategy: 1. a particular risk type is *knowable*, as is the case with regulatory risk, or 2. actions giving rise to a particular risk type are *controllable* by the company, as is the case with operational risks. If neither of the two conditions is true, avoidance is likely not a viable strategy.

In practice, how many risk types are then avoidable, at least in principle? Consider the earlier-delineated risk types shown below in Table 4.1.

Table 4.1
Sample Listing of Risk Types

Risk Type	Description
Market	Significant change in supply & demand function, including raw materials;
Competitive	Entry of new competitors;
Technological	Obsolescence of current technologies; cost of acquiring new ones;
Financial	Increase in the cost of capital; unfavorable exchange rate changes;
Operational	A broad category of threats relating to strategic and tactical decisions;
Regulatory	Changes in public policy and governmental regulation;
Environmental	Changing pollution, carbon emissions & disposal standards;
Supply Chain	Failure of contractor to deliver on time, schedule or for agreed price;
Physical/Property	Natural disasters, crime, vandalism or arson;
Socio-Cultural	Changes in the demographic makeup of the marketplace;
Reputational	Negative publicity adversely impact brand equity;
Professional	Changes in the ability to attract and retain skilled human resources;

The twelve different risk types listed and briefly defined in Table 4.1 can be considered in the context of the two key avoidance prerequisites named earlier: 1. being knowable, and/or 2. being controllable. Implicit in these two notions is the source of the specific actions giving rise to particular risk types. Hence the information presented in Table 4.1 can be further contextualized by expressly considering the source of each type of risk and ascertaining whether or not it is knowable and/or controllable. Consider Table 4.2.

Table 4.2
Contextualizing the Sample Listing of Risk Types

Risk Type	Source	Knowable	Controllable
Market	External	No	No
Competitive	External	No	No
Technological	External	No	No
Financial	External	No	No
Operational	*Internal*	No	*Yes*
Regulatory	External	*Yes*	*Yes*
Environmental	External	*Yes*	No
Supply Chain	External	No	No
Physical/Property	External	No	No
Socio-Cultural	External	*Yes*	No
Reputational	*Internal*	No	*Yes*
Professional	*Internal*	*Yes*	*Yes*

The risk type cross tabulation shown in Table 4.2 draws attention to several important conclusions. First, the idea of a risk type being knowable can be better understood in the qualifying context of *time* and *information.* Internally sourced risk types are knowable because the requisite information is readily available—at the same time, socio-cultural or environmental risks are knowable because these phenomena usually unfold very slowly, and though information may be imperfect, an interested observer will nonetheless be able to discern these trends by carefully studying their indicators. Second, the idea of risk creating actions being controllable can be further refined in relation to specific control mechanism, which can take the form of either policy-driven efforts, or risk profile management.

Policy-driven risk avoidance is the process of crafting, instituting and enforcing of rules of conduct expressly designed to avoid specific types of risks. For instance, putting in place and enforcing a clear, well-informed and compliance-minded hiring and promotion policies is one of the viable strategies for avoiding claims of unfair workplace practices. *Risk profile management* is a risk avoidance strategy built around purposeful analysis of key risk indicators (defined here as unambiguous and objectively measurable factors that are highly correlated with specific events), targeted at risk-adjusting the organization's decision-making processes. In contrast to highly deterministic, rule-based policy-driven risk avoidance, risk profile management is highly probabilistic in nature. For instance, thorough analysis of securities class action litigation might reveal that certain traits of organizational behavior, such as high frequency of financial restatement coupled with aggressive revenue accruing and highly volatile share price might be highly correlated with the risk of securities class action litigation. Active profile risk management efforts geared at avoiding the possibility of costly securities litigation would leverage this knowledge and use to risk-adjust decisions touching upon the above mentioned factors.

Turning our attention back to Table 4.2 brings to light the third key conclusion stemming from the analysis of risk type specific viability of risk avoidance. Roughly half of the twelve risk types listed above stem from external actions and are neither knowable nor controllable. In other words, for these risk types, avoidance is generally not going to be a viable strategy. In a broader sense, this suggests that a significant proportion of threats confronting organizations ought to be considered from the standpoint of financial management of risk exposure. This is saying that when it comes to some risks, the emphasis should be placed on objective assessment of the organization's exposure to those risk, expressed in terms of the probability of occurrence as well as the expected cost, and taking specific steps to either reduce or altogether transfer not so much the possibility of occurrence, but the resultant financial consequences.

Reduction

The distinction between risk avoidance and risk reduction is not always clear. Taking the regulation-mandated reporting steps does not guarantee regulatory compliance per se, most notably because the accuracy may be suspect. Similarly, a sound workforce practices policy will not immunize the organization from the possibility of discrimination or sexual harassment claims as rogue employees can willfully disregard the stated policy. The point is that risk reduction can, in many instances, be viewed as practical consequence of what might overtly be believed to be risk avoidance efforts. However, conceptually there are a number of distinctions separating these two risk response postures.

First and foremost, risk reduction does not necessitate risk type being knowable or controllable—it does, however, necessitate some degree of understanding of key risk indicators, which in turn necessitates the risk type being estimable. To be estimable, a risk type has to be operationally distinct and measurable, in a manner allowing cross-occurrence comparisons. In short, there has to be sufficiently sized and representative sampling of the event's occurrences to enable the estimation of the key dimensions of risk: likelihood and severity.

Risk reduction efforts need to be considered in the context of the two dimensions of risk—likelihood and severity. Stated differently, reducing the likelihood of a particular undesirable event might entail considerably different set of activities than reducing the severity of the same event.

Reducing Likelihood

There are two, briefly discussed earlier, broadly defined sets of activities that are available for reducing the likelihood of a particular risk type: 1. policy setting, and 2. risk profile management.

As implied in the name, *policy setting* is the creation, implementation and enforcement of specific rules of conduct aimed at diminishing the likelihood of undesirable events. Doing so is predicated upon the availability of appropriate knowledge regarding risk-increasing activities. More often than not, policy setting is prohibitive in nature, which is a direct consequence of the character of the policy-shaping knowledge. The risk estimation is in effect the analysis of historical occurrences of the event (i.e., risk type) which means that the resultant knowledge is going to be focused primarily on the event precipitating behaviors and other traits. As a result, the bulk of organizational policies designed to reduce the likelihood of specific risks are focused on prohibiting the undesirable event likelihood increasing behaviors and activities. This can be an effective tool for lowering the probability of certain types of risk, particularly those falling under the broad umbrella of reputational risks.

Risk profile management is an alternative likelihood lowering approach (discussed in the upcoming two chapters). It is rooted in the modern information theory[8], or more specifically, in multivariate probabilistic models leveraging large corporate and third-party (organizations maintaining large, usually national databases compiling behavioral, demographic, psychographic or attitudinal data) data sources. It is defined as the utilization of probabilistic, event predicting insights to risk-adjust organizational decisions. As implied in its description, risk profile management is not quite as 'cut and dry' as the policy setting outlined earlier. It generally does not produce prohibitive behaviors or activities—instead, it provides an objective, quantifiable method

[8] A branch of applied mathematics and electrical engineering concerned with the quantification of information. Its origins date back to the publishing of C. Shannon's seminal work 'A Mathematical Theory of Communication'.

of estimating incremental effects of actions or behaviors that have been shown to be associated with heightened likelihood of undesirable events. The informational basis of risk profile management is graphically depicted in Figure 4.7.

Figure 4.7
Informational Basis of Risk Profile Management

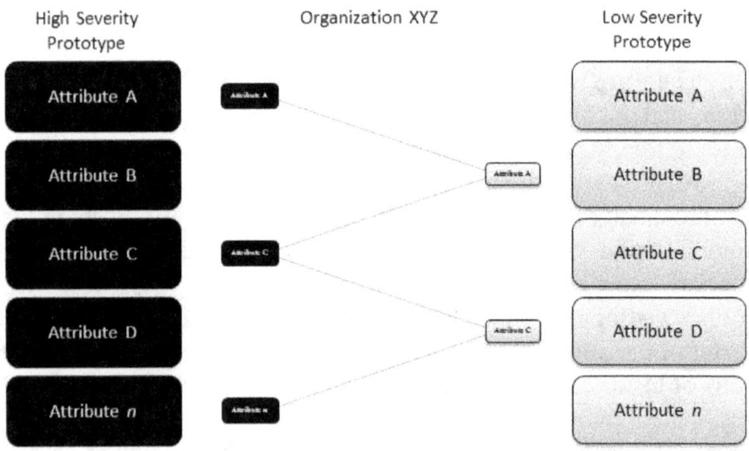

The High Likelihood of Undesirable Event represents a prototype of a high-risk organization, expressed in terms of specific, risk-increasing attributes, A thru *n*. The Low Likelihood of Undesirable Event represents a prototype of a low risk organization, expressed in terms of risk-reducing attributes. The line in the center of the chart shows the similarity of Company XYZ to either the high or low risk profile on each of the delineated attributes. The high and low risk profiles are expressed in term of probabilities, where the former exhibits significantly above average likelihood of the undesirable event taking place, while the latter embodies significantly below average chance. Active risk management entails a deliberate examination of the company's positioning on each of the risk exposure (likelihood) determining attributes, followed by making appropriate, informed decisions.

Transfer

Going back to Table 4.2, roughly half of the risk types identified there are externally driven events that are neither controllable, in terms of their likelihood or severity, nor knowable, at least no sufficiently ahead of their occurrence. The financial meltdown of 2007/2008 is an example of such a risk. On a more micro scale, a company can unexpectedly be confronted with a failure of a key supplier (supply chain risk), an introduction of a market-changing technological innovation by one of its competitors or the entry of a large, dominant organization into its product category. In short, there are multiple types of undesirable events that exhibit some, usually unknown probability of occurrence, possibly resulting in a wide range of economic losses. For those types of losses, the risk management efforts are—as they should be—focused almost entirely on the severity dimension, or the likely financial fallout. Stated differently, when confronted with unmanageable (i.e., those that cannot be either avoided or systematically reduced) risks, they seek to transfer all or some of those risks, largely with the goal of insulating their earnings from unexpected and potentially highly dramatic jolts. Insurance coverage is the most often sought remedy for dealing with unmanageable risks.

The acquisition of insurance coverage by an organization is often described as risk transfer. That is technically incorrect. Considering that any risk is defined in the context of two independent dimensions of likelihood and severity, transference of risk should be reflected in changes to both dimensions. In other words, in order for an organization to transfer a particular of risk to another entity, the recipient, or transferee, has to assume both the likelihood of the threat materializing as well as the severity of the risk type being transferred. That is not the case with insurance coverage, which affects only the severity aspect of risk, while having no impact on likelihood. This leads to an obvious conclusion that commercial insurance should not be described as risk transfer, but rather as a post-event compensatory mechanism. This line of reasoning is intuitively obvious to most of us: Buying flood insurance, for instance, does not remove the possibility of our homes getting flooded—it only offers financial compensation in the event that threat materializes.

Definitional issues notwithstanding, let us accept the conventional notion that insurance coverage does indeed constitutes risk transfer. Broadly speaking, an organization considering procuring insurance has two basic options: 1. to buy specific type and amount of coverage from a commercial insurance provider, or 2. In the case of the first of the two options, the decision amounts to selecting the type of coverage, the amount of coverage (i.e., the 'limits') and the attachment point, also called self-insured retention. Having made those decisions, all that is left is to shop around for the best terms (i.e., price) and conditions (coverage inclusions, exclusions, etc.)[9]. The key advantage to using commercial insurance is that, under most circumstances, it is readily available, which means that a desired amount of protection can be put in place relatively quickly. The key disadvantage to relying on commercial insurance coverage is that it represents, from a financial standpoint, an expense yielding no residual value[10]. And although an insurance policy is technically an asset, as it represents a contingent form of capital, purchasing it creates a drag on earnings.

An alternative to commercial insurance is the so-called 'captive insurance'. *Captive insurance* companies are insurance companies established with the specific objective of financing risks stemming their parent company, or a group of companies. In essence, it amounts to a particular organization choosing to establish its own insurance company, rather than relying on commercial coverage. The term 'captive' was coined by F. Reiss in the 1950's. Working (as a consultant) with Youngstown Sheet & Tube Company, Reiss was looking for a risk financing solution which would enable his client to put in place the required coverage, but in a more financially economical manner. His client company had a series of mining operations and its management referred to the mines whose output was put solely to the corporation's use as 'captive mines'. When Reiss helped them incorporate their own insurance subsidiaries, they were referred to as captive insurance companies because they wrote insurance exclusively for the captive mines[11]. The key advantage to owning a captive is financial—unlike commercial insurance premiums which are paid to an outside entity, payments made into a captive stay within the parent organization, which means that if the captive's operating costs combined with incurred losses are less than the paid premiums, the effective cost of coverage is reduced by the amount of residual value. The key

---

[9] Obviously, this is a bit of an oversimplification, as the coverage limits, the attachment point, terms & conditions and price are often jointly determined.

[10] Under certain, limited set of circumstances, insurance coverage could yield some residual value; perhaps the best example of that are the so-called 'membership credits' available to policy holders of industry mutuals, such as those formed by electric utilities.

[11] This is an example of a 'pure' captive; a captive can also serve the needs of multiple entities, in which case it will be broadly referred to as a group captive. The latter can still take on different forms such as industry captive, association captive, or risk retention group captive, in addition to rent-a-captive. Recently, a yet another form of a captive started to take hold, the so-called program business captive, which is structured expressly as a profit center for the parent company.

disadvantage to owning a captive is twofold: 1. Added complexity to the risk management (or more specifically, financing) function, and 2. Increased risk exposure—captive, after all, is an insurance company, which means it too faces the possibility of incurring abnormally large losses[12].

Turning our attention back to more broadly defined risk transfer considerations, in a true risk transfer, the other party assumes both dimensions of risk, either by means of a contract or a hedge. A *contract,* in the context of risk transfer, is defined as a voluntary, deliberate and legally binding agreement between two or more competent parties, while a *hedge* is defined as an investment made by taking a trading position in a futures or options market to minimize the impact of adverse changes in interest rates or in the prices of commodities or securities[13].

Contractual risk transfer shifts the responsibility for claims, loss and damages to the other party, with the goal of shielding the organization from any responsibility relating to the risk being transferred. Risk transfer contracts are relatively common in construction, where the owner of the project being constructed may transfer all responsibility to the project's manager, or in supply chain management, where the risk may be transferred to a major vendor. Conversely, these types of arrangements are rarely seen in the realm of professional liability (e.g., professional malpractice or directors' and officers' liability).

Unlike the explicit and somewhat tangible contractual risk transference, *hedging* is more of a broad risk transfer strategy aiming to minimize, rather than altogether eliminate exposure to certain types of business risks. There are different types of hedges available, reflecting varying amounts of speculative decision-making. One of the most straightforward and least speculative types is the so-called 'natural hedge' which is based on pairing of naturally co-existing phenomenon. For instance, one of the safest methods of limiting a multinational company's exposure to currency exchange fluctuation is to establish production facilities in a country in which a given product is being sold (doing so, of course, may expose the organization to other risks, such as socio-political or regulatory ones).

---

[12] With that in mind, the majority of captives purchase re-insurance to protect against that possibility. Furthermore, that particular risk should be considered in the context of counter-party risk associated with the procurement of coverage from a commercial carrier, best illustrated by the liquidity crisis at AIG in the latter part of 2008 and early 2009.

[13] Sourced from BusinessDictionary.com

There are a number of alternatives to the above outlined traditional risk transfer approaches; as a group, these fall under the umbrella of *alternative risk transfer*, or ART. Given the proliferation of those methods, it is worthwhile to take a closer look.

The ART of Risk Transfer

Perhaps the first known alternative risk transfer mechanism was Tanker Insurance Company Ltd., which was the first captive insurance company formed in 1920. Self-funded insurance, as exemplified by captives, became more widely spread following Douglas Barlow pioneering the notion of "cost-at-risk" (introduced in 1962) which offered an objective method of comparing the total cost of insurance to the total cost of risk self-funding. Many of the alternative risk transfer mechanisms in use today grew out of series of insurance capacity crises in the 1970's through the 1990's. As a group, most of the ART techniques allow investors in capital markets to play a more direct role in providing insurance-like protection, effectively contributing to the blurring of the distinction between insurance and financial markets. The most frequently used alternative risk financing alternatives are shown below.

Table 4.3
Alternative Forms of Risk Financing

Form	Description
Self-Funded Insurance	Frequently taking the form of captive insurance or financial reinsurance; both captives and financial reinsurance come in a variety of different forms, such as single parent, association, group, agency or rent-a-captive; or finite, surplus relief, funded (for reinsurance).
Risk Securitization	Exemplified by the so-called special purpose vehicles best known for offering catastrophe & reinsurance bonds.
Non-Indemnity Trading	Best exemplified by industry loss warranties.
Insurance Hedge Funds	Investment vehicle which function like fully collateralized reinsurance but take the form of hedge funds.
Fronting Arrangements	Under most circumstances, these are a specialized form of reinsurance where a commercial insurance company which is licensed in a particular jurisdiction to issue a policy acts as a front, but the risk is then fully transferred to a captive insurance company through a reinsurance agreement.
Loss Portfolio Transfer	Negotiated arrangements which mitigate accrued liabilities by converting future liabilities to present day fixed price.
Reciprocal Insurance	It represents an interchange among subscribers of reciprocal agreement of indemnity thru a common attorney-in-fact.
Finite Risk Reinsurance	Built around matching of current and potential liabilities against assets over an appropriate length of time; if a company ends paying most of its losses over time, but if it has a favorable loss experience it also shares in the underwriting profit, inclusive of investment income).
Contingent Capital	Often used to provide financial coverage for statistically improbable losses without incurring the cost of maintaining excess (over and above realized severity) insurance limits; it is a form of securitized capital based on option contracting.
Retrospective Ratings	A mechanism for adjusting insurance premium, retrospectively, on the basis of losses incurred during the insurance period.

On average, about 40% of the total cost of risk in North America is handled by the variety of alternative risk financing solutions outlined above.

Naturally, in view of the combination of buyer-specific risk transfer needs, the prevailing marketplace conditions (most notably, the availability of capital) and the risk transfer mechanism specific characteristics, the 'best' alternative risk transfer solution will be highly situational. That said, expressly considering the available ART options should be a standard risk management practice.

Acceptance

Not everything that is worth knowing is knowable. And similarly, not every imaginable potential threat should be acted on. It is simply not economically feasible to "do something" about each and every conceivable threat. But how does the organization decide which risks it should actively manage (i.e., avoid, reduce or transfer) and which it should, in effect, do nothing about? The answer can be found in the nature of the impact of a given risk type, specifically, the *competitive parity* of impact. In essence, the key determining factor governing the risk acceptance decisioning is whether or not a particular risk type is expected to have a disproportionately large impact on the organization, or can the expected impact be assumed to be proportionate to the impact on other organizations?

Consider the threat of a large asteroid striking Earth. According to the scientific community, the likelihood of it happening is far less than 1-in-1,000,000, but nonetheless, it is a possibility and hence it poses a potential threat to an organization (and obviously all life on our planet, but I shall only consider the impact on organizations). If it materialized, would it be significantly more damaging to Company A than to Company B? Obviously, nobody really knows, but as far-fetched as it may seem, the fate of dinosaurs can give us a hint. The dominant, at this point in time, theory explaining the relatively sudden disappearance of dinosaurs points to a large asteroid colliding with Earth, which resulted in a huge dust cloud being kicked up shutting off much of solar radiation needed for plant photosynthesis, ultimately resulting in cutting off the dinosaurs' food supply. Of interest to us is that it was not just one, two or a few dinosaur species that disappeared—essentially the entire dinosaur ecosystem vanished. The risk associated with this particular event (i.e., an asteroid colliding with Earth) was essentially the same for all species of dinosaurs, hence accepting that risk did not disadvantage any of the individual species.

In the context of (human) risk management, financing threats that do not expose the company to a disproportionate, vis-à-vis the competitors, amount of risk amounts to unnecessarily reducing the firm's earnings, in effect imposing an excessive risk tax on shareholders. Hence the decision to accept certain risks should be based on comparative exposure assessment, rather than the often-recommended cost-benefit analysis[14]. Comparative assessment analysis examines the potential impact of a risk type in the context of the organization's set of competitors to determine if the potential impact, in term of its consequences, would vary across individual companies. The analysis itself is highly contextualized, shaped largely by the nature of specific types of risk and industry characteristics. For instance, the potential impact of global warming driven changes in carbon dioxide emission standards (a type of regulatory risk) would be far more pronounced in large emission footprint industries, such as electric utilities or manufacturing, than in (relatively) low emission footprint industries, such as financial services or healthcare.

More so than in the case other three risk response modalities (avoidance, reduction and transfer), risk acceptance can be a reflection of the organization's culture. A conservative, risk-avoiding entity might have a significantly different view of a particular risk, such as carbon emission related potential regulatory changes, than an aggressive, risk-taking organization. Neither view is inherently better or worse than the other, though expressly taking it into account is an important part of the due diligence process. It is important to note that the character of an organization tends to be a reflection of natural biases of the key decision makers. According to the cultural theory[15], there are four major perceptual biases relating to the perception of risk: individualist, egalitarian, hierarchist and fatalist. *Individualists* are those whose decisions are generally unconstrained by the demands of the organization at large; *Egalitarians* are those favoring a more democratic decision making;

---

[14] The view expressed in this book is that cost-benefit analysis is not an adequate evaluation framework for making risk acceptance decisions. Philosophically, the widely used cost-benefit technique tends to give undue prominence to quantifiable manifestations of risk, which are not necessarily the most significant. Practically, even focusing on the overtly quantifiable aspects, the validity of estimates of what constitutes costs and benefits is often suspect. What is the cost of accepting the regulatory risk of stricter carbon emission standards? What is the benefit of this course of action? Given that the majority of risks that organizations tend to accept are those that are hard to measure, both in terms of likelihood and severity; it is borderline naïve to believe that traditional cost-benefit analysis can yield objective and robust conclusions.

[15] Thompson, M., R. Ellis and A. Wildavsky (1990), *Cultural Theory*, Westview Press, San Francisco, CA.

Hierarchists tend to ascribe value and importance based on the input-provider's position in the organization; *Fatalists* tend to believe that little can be done to mitigate risks. In the somewhat subjective assessment of hard-to-measure risks, the evaluation of the type of risk that is deemed acceptable will be influenced by the bias of the key decision makers.

Not Either Or

It is common to think of the alternative risk responses in the context of one or the other choice. That is not correct. As shown in Figure 4.2, the causal view of risk shows a clear line demarcation between the antecedent causes and the resultant outcomes, which suggests that risk mitigation and risk transfer efforts should proceed concurrently. To a large degree, that is because it is not reasonable to believe that risk mitigation alone will eliminate the possibility of an undesirable event taking place, while on the other hand, it is unwise and economically reckless to forego risk mitigation efforts once some financial protections have been put in place. An ideal risk management approach, which is also at the heart of the risk profile management framework presented in this book, calls for combining risk mitigation and risk capitalization efforts in such a way as to deliver the greatest possible earnings' protection, at the least cost. Conceptually, the framework borrows from some of the key tenets of enterprise risk management (ERM), a broad outline of which is offered next.

Enterprise Risk Management Typologies

The continuing maturating of risk management as a distinct organizational function prompted a number of organizations to start to think in terms of the overall, or organization-wide risk exposure, a notion that has come to be known as *enterprise risk management*, or ERM. The impetus behind ERM is twofold: First, as the scope of risk management efforts continued to grow, it became progressively more and more important to develop a coherent organizational framework to organize the overall efforts in terms of the decision making processes. Second, as the cost associated with organizational responses to individual risks grew, it became progressively more challenging to make sound financial decisions concerning risk management expenditures. Hence, the imperative to systematically evaluate the organization's exposure to clearly delineated threats and to identify the most effective remedies prompted many organizations to consider a more holistic view of risk.

The emerging discipline of enterprise risk management is being shaped by the forces of the evolving regulatory environment, the ongoing development of internal control standards and the growing informational/analytic efficacy. Those forces, in turn, are themselves driven by the seemingly never-ending succession of corporate scandals and—by extension—risk management failures. The collapse of the savings-and-loan sector in the late 1980's and early 1990's, the 1991 Salomon Brothers bond scandal, the Bearings derivatives fiasco of the mid-1990's, the Enron, WorldCom and other corporate governance scandals of the early 2000's, the stock option back-dating that following shortly after, the subprime lending disaster that already racked up over half a trillion of U.S dollars of financial institutions' write-offs (as the writing of this book) and it is still believed to be far from over…

It is hard to pinpoint a specific time when ERM entered the corporate stage. In fact, it is probably more appropriate to look at its emergence as a gradual phenomenon, a product of evolution of the corporate conception of risk and risk management practices. The emergence of the modern portfolio theory, marked by Markowitz's seminal work on portfolio allocation under uncertainty[16] is generally believed to mark the starting point of modern, corporate risk management efforts. The subsequent introduction of the Capital Assets Pricing Model (CAPM) as a tool for determining a theoretically

[16] Markowitz, H. (1952), 'Portfolio Selection', *Journal of Finance*, 7 (1), 77-91.

appropriate required rate of return of an asset[17] and particularly, Black and Scholes' options pricing model[18], laid the foundations for major risk transfer jump-started systematic risk evaluation and management efforts. The passing of the Foreign Corrupt Practices Act in 1977[19] acted as yet another force prompting organization to consider more formal risk management efforts. Initially, that led to strengthening of focus on compliance and internal controls, but eventually, starting in the mid-1980's companies began to form risk management departments.

The 1985 formation of COSO (Committee of Sponsoring Organizations[20]) tasked with sponsoring the National Commission on Fraudulent Financial Reporting opened a new chapter in structured risk management efforts—a formal study of causal factors precipitating fraudulent financial reporting. Several years after its formation, COSO published its first official risk management framework: *Internal Control – Integrated Framework* (1992). Several waves of corporate scandals later and on the heels of the 2002 Sarbanes-Oxley Act, which established new or enhanced standards for all U.S public company boards, management and public accounting firms, COSO published a broadened and significantly revised version of its original framework, described in more detail in the next section.

Though many of the ideas imbedded into it are universal in nature, the inner-logic of the COSO framework primarily reflects North American regulatory priorities and marketplace realities, all of which makes this framework less applicable outside of North America. The *ISO 31000 Standard*, published by the International Organization for Standardization[21] in 2009, is both more universal and more contemporary (the aforementioned revised COSO framework was released in 2004), which means it explicitly considers

---

[17] Sharpe, W. F. (1964), 'Capital Asset Prices: A Theory of Market Equilibrium under Conditions of Risk', *Journal Finance*, 19 (3), 425-442.

[18] Black, F. and M. S. Scholes (1973), 'The Pricing of Options and Corporate Liabilities', *Journal of Political Economy*, 81(3), 637-654.

[19] Which came on the heels of SEC investigations which concluded that over 400 U.S. companies admitted to making questionable or illegal payments (in excess of $300 million) to foreign officials.

[20] Sponsored jointly by: The American Accounting Association, the American Institute of Certified Public Accountants, Financial Executives International, The Institute of Internal Auditors and the Institute of Management Accountants (formerly, the National Association of Accountants)

[21] An international standard-setting body founded in 1947 and composed of representatives from various national standards organizations.

threats accentuated by more recent events, such as the financial crisis of 2008. Thus, even though North American risk management community might be more familiar with the COSO framework, the ever-accelerating globalization trend points toward the ISO 31000 standard as a more universally appropriate conceptualization.

Although some components of the enterprise risk management may reflect binding governmental regulations (e.g., Basel II capital requirements for financial institutions or Sarbanes-Oxley Act's Section 404 imposing risk assessment and reporting requirements for publicly traded companies), enterprise risk management is fundamentally a self-governing endeavor. In other words, beyond adherence to applicable regulations, companies are in essence free to embrace – or not – an enterprise approach to risk management and for those that do, to design their own ERM infrastructure. An organization interested in instituting sound ERM practices should seek the guidance of one or more of the established frameworks: 1. Committee of Sponsoring Organizations, or COSO, *Enterprise Risk Management – Integrated Framework* (2004); or 2. International Organization for Standardization, or ISO, *Standard 31000*, commonly referred to as ISO 31000: 2009. I should point out that the latter of the two frameworks is a replacement to the Australian/New Zealand Standard (*Risk Management, AS/NZS 4360*: 2004, itself a revision of AS/NZS 4360: 1999 standard), so although some literature might cite three distinct general ERM conceptualizations, effectively there are only two current ones. In addition, financial organizations might also want to refer to the Bank for International Settlements: Basel II standard (*International Convergence of Capital Measurement and Capital Standards: A Revised Framework*[22]), which addresses systemic risks that are unique to financial intermediaries, such as liquidity or capital adequacy (given the idiosyncratic character of the Basel II standard it will not be covered here).

[22] Issued by Basel Committee on Banking Supervision, based at the Bank of International Settlements in Basel, Switzerland. Committee consists of representatives from central banks and regulatory authorities of the G10 countries, plus others (specifically Luxembourg and Spain). The committee does not have the authority to enforce recommendations, although most member countries (and others) tend to implement its policies.

COSO Framework

In September of 2004, the Committee of Sponsoring Organizations of the Treadway Commission issued an expanded version of its 1992 framework (*Internal Controls – Integrated Framework*), under a new heading of *Enterprise Risk Management – Integrated Framework.* The *COSO ERM Framework*, as it is commonly known, has since gained wide acceptance among U.S-based companies, but not so outside of the United States.

COSO defines enterprise risk management as '…a process, effected by an entity's board of directors, management and other personnel, applied in strategy setting and across the enterprise, designed to identify potential events that may affect the entity, and manage risk to be within its risk appetite, to provide reasonable assurance regarding the achievement of entity objectives'. Among the most noteworthy notions put forth in the aforementioned definition is the emphasis of the role of ERM as a strategic tool, rather than a mere means of demonstrating compliance. In other words, risk management should be viewed—and more importantly, practiced—as a contributor to the organizational value creation. To do that, ERM needs to be able to deal effectively with potential future events that could be a source of economically impactful uncertainty, and it needs to provide means of reducing the likelihood of negative and increase the likelihood of positive outcomes.

Application-wise, the COSO framework attempts to help organizations accomplish four risk management related core organizational objectives of strategic planning, operational management, reporting and compliance. As expressly noted in the language of the framework, those objectives need to be evaluated at all levels of the organization, inclusive of division, business unit or subsidiary. In more explicit terms, COSO defines those as follows:

- *Strategic planning.*
  Those aligned with and supporting attainment of the organization's high level goals; it is focused on the question of 'What we are trying to accomplish?'
- *Operational management.*
  More tactically oriented outcomes, such as performance or profitability; it is focused on the question of 'How are we going to accomplish our strategic goals?'

- *Reporting.*
  Communication means and processes; it is focused on the question of 'How are we going to communicate with our internal and external stakeholders?
- *Compliance.*
  The organization's adherence to applicable laws and regulations; it is focused on the question of 'What are we going to do to make sure we comply with all laws and regulations affecting us?'

Regardless of the organizational level of analysis (i.e., entity-wide vs. division, etc.), the assessment should be built around a portfolio view of risk, in a sense in which 'portfolio' is used in the Modern Portfolio Theory (MPT) in finance. (Very briefly, MPT describes how rational investors can use diversification to optimize their portfolios and how risky assets should be priced.) The basic provisions of the Modern Portfolio Theory yield two key, ERM-related implications: 1. portfolio risk is not the simple sum of the individual risk elements, and 2. to understand portfolio risk; one must understand the risks of the individual elements and their interactions.

Stated differently, each risk needs to be evaluated independently of all other risks, in addition to which, cross-risk interrelationships need to be estimated. In other words, one of the basic provisions of the COSO framework is to estimate, at the level of individual business units as well as entity-wide, the impact of individual risks and the interdependencies among those risks. Having done so, the organization is then in position to explicitly consider its overall risk exposure vis-à-vis its risk appetite and make appropriate risk type specific decision: to avoid, reduce, share or accept.

The overall enterprise risk management process is embodied in the following eight components (see Figure 4.8 for a visual depiction):

- *Internal Environment.*
  Goal: To set a philosophy for how risks and controls are viewed and addressed by the organization; also, to expressly call out the management's risk appetite.
- *Objective Setting.*
  Goal: To delineate the entity's business goals, as an essential prerequisite to identifying events that may potentially impede reaching of those objectives.
- *Event Identification.*

Goal: To single out specific factors, both internal and external, that may affect strategy implementation and the attainment of stated organizational objectives.

- *Risk Assessment.*
  Goal: To estimates the likelihood and impact of identified risks.
- *Risk Response.*
  Goal: To select actions aligning organizational treatment of individual threats with its risk appetite.
- *Control Activities.*
  Goal: To select and deploy policies and procedures for ascertaining that the selected risk responses are adequately carried out.
- *Information Sharing.*
  Goal: To develop a process for capturing and dissemination of pertinent information.
- *Monitoring.*
  Goal: An ongoing oversight of the risk management process, inclusive of any modifications that may be deemed necessary.

Figure 4.8

COSO Enterprise Risk Management Framework

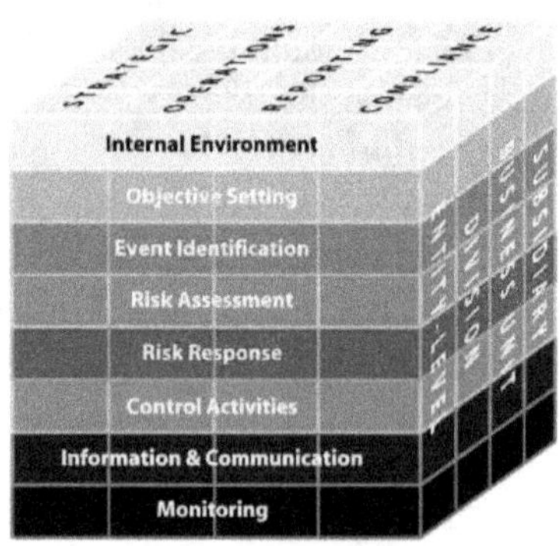

The COSO framework presents a compelling depiction of how the otherwise amorphous goal of managing the totality of an organization's risks can be broken down into a set of discrete, more operationally oriented tasks. At the same time, it also paints a relatively methodologically complex picture. If risk portfolio cannot be assumed to be a simple sum of its parts, enterprise risk management measurement has to encompass the means of empirically estimating the nature of cross-risk interdependencies. To be informationally complete, these estimates ought to be framed in the context of risk-specific likelihood and severity assessment.

Impact of the COSO Framework

The vast majority of organizations that embrace the idea of enterprise risk management also embrace the COSO framework as its primary conceptualization. In view of that, the COSO framework should have had a considerable impact on the practice of risk management; yet, the evidence does not necessarily support that assertion.

An informal survey conducted among risk managers representing a cross section of energy, hospitality and entertainment, healthcare and technology organizations suggests that, on the one hand, COSO-expressed ERM initiatives garnered a lot of attention and interest, but, on the other hand, to-date tangible benefits are far and few in-between. The findings suggested two key reasons behind the lack of noticeable business impact of the COSO framework:

- *The combination of the framework's complexity and its breadth.* The implications of the Figure 4.8 are intellectually compelling, but equally operationally daunting. In theory, it is hard to argue with the vision where the totality of the organization's risks is systematically evaluated at all levels of the organization and results communicated to the appropriate stakeholders – however, the framework offers no clear analytical 'how-to' guidance. As a result, the ambitious all-risks encompassing vision is typically reduced to a far smaller subset of risks exhibiting known mathematical properties (e.g., workers' compensation and like casualty or property risks). Furthermore, the combination of its all-encompassing scope and reductionist approach means that, for a large, multi-SBU company, implementation of the COSO framework represents a gargantuan undertaking. Even though, if executed successfully such an undertaking would be potentially quite beneficial to the organization, the sheer complexity of the task at hand, coupled with the lack of clear operational guidance render the framework's promise simply inaccessible to many, if not most, large business enterprises.

❖ *The lack of clear measurement guidelines.*
The COSO's framework is surprisingly mute on the topic of measurement. While going into considerable depth regarding the desirability to explicitly measure individual risks, the framework offers no appreciable guidance regarding how that is to be done. The lack of risk measurement guidance is likely a consequence of the combination of the multiplicity of distinct threats to be measured and their situational character, in view of which it appears reasonable (at least to the architects of the framework) to push that responsibility onto the users of the framework. The underlying reasoning notwithstanding, the paucity of risk measurement details lead to a fairly predictable outcome of low framework implementation rate. Furthermore, as shown graphically in Figure 4.9, the very conceptualization of risk measurement might be too broad, as the framework defines the scope of measurement to include not only the expected element of 'assessment', but also 'control' and 'communication', which in eyes of many (including this author) represent distinct and different activities.

Figure 4.9
COSO Risk Measurement Conceptualization

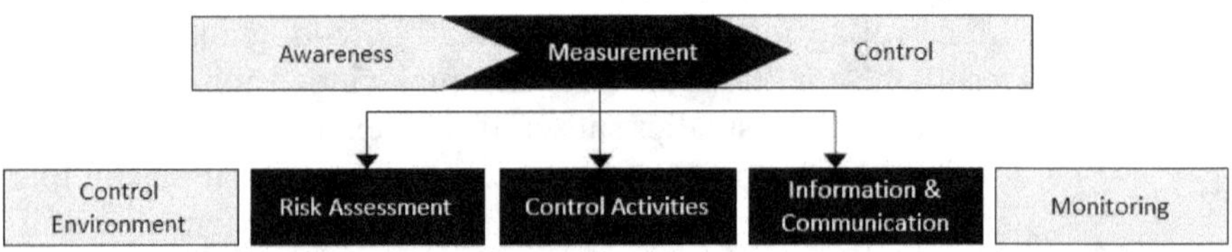

As shown in the above, COSO-derived conceptualization, measurement plays a pivotal role in the efficacy of the overall framework—after all, control activities are predicated upon objective assessment of the viability of risk events. It is simply hard to understand why risk measurement is given so little attention in the context of the overall framework, unless this silence can be taken as an implicit admission of intractability of the ideas embodied by the COSO process. Or perhaps in its drive to be all-encompassing, COSO failed to take into account the issue of risk type specific measurability. As it is intuitively obvious, some risk types are much prone to being estimated than some others. For instance, the probability of an organization incurring securities class action litigation can be more precisely estimated than the probability of its technology becoming obsolete. Specific reasons notwithstanding, the efficacy of the enterprise-wide risk assessment promoted by the COSO framework is suspect as a direct consequence of its failure to take into account inherent measurement differences separating individual risk types. So while it puts forth some very worthwhile conceptual ideas, the COSO ERM framework is not likely to become the agent of change for the risk management practice.

Beyond the insights revealed by the aforementioned survey, the COSO framework suffers from a couple of additional, somewhat more subtle limitations. First, it implicitly anchors risk in the possibility of an adverse event taking place or not. In other words, risk is viewed as having either a negative (an adverse event materializes) or a neutral (an adverse event does not materialize) outcome—i.e., it equates risk with downside risk. As discussed earlier, a complete definition of risk needs to also include upside risk, such as those exemplified by introducing a new product, new technology or venturing into a new market. Just as storms or civil litigation, both examples of downside risk, can have costly consequences, investing in a new product launch can have equally (or even greater) significant negative consequences. Hence both downside and upside risks can negatively impact the organization's earnings, in addition to which, upside risk can have a positive impact on earnings. This is to say that in order to be truly "enterprise-wide", a risk assessment framework needs to encompass both the downside as well as upside risks.

Secondly, COSO invites a certain amount of reductionism. More specifically, there is a tendency to use it a 'check the box' tool for internal reporting or compliance-related needs. In some way, this is yet another consequence of the framework's complexity, coupled with lack of clear operationalization. Nonetheless, there is a temptation to reduce the risk investigatory power of the framework to that of superficial compliance. Stated differently, in order to be truly effective, a risk assessment framework cannot be reduced to a superficial compliance tool.

ISO 31000 Standard

The current Standard traces its origin to the *AS/NZS* (Australia / New Zealand) *4360, Risk Management* framework published in 2004, itself a third revision of the framework bearing the same designation originally released in 1995 (and subsequently revised in 1999). The overall goal of the Australian /

New Zealand Standard is to outline a rational context for identifying, analyzing, evaluating, treating, monitoring and communicating risk in a manner geared toward reaching a balance between the pursuit of growth and avoidance of losses. The risk management approach the Standard promotes is built around an iterative process consisting of sequentially ordered steps that encourage continuous improvement in risk-related decision-making efficacy. The process is intentionally generic, so that it can be applied to a wide range of activities or decisions in public, private or community (e.g., not-for-profit) enterprises.

Continuing the AS/NZS 4360's spirit of universal applicability, the ISO *Standard 31000*: *2009* outlines a framework for implementing risk management, rather than a framework for supporting the risk management processes (which is the case with the earlier discussed COSO framework). Overall, the intent of the Standard is to enable individual organizations to shape their own risk management-supporting frameworks by way of expressly defining their risk architecture, risk strategy and risk protocol related preferences, as graphically depicted in Figure 4.10.

Figure 4.10
ISO 31000 Risk Management: The Building Blocks

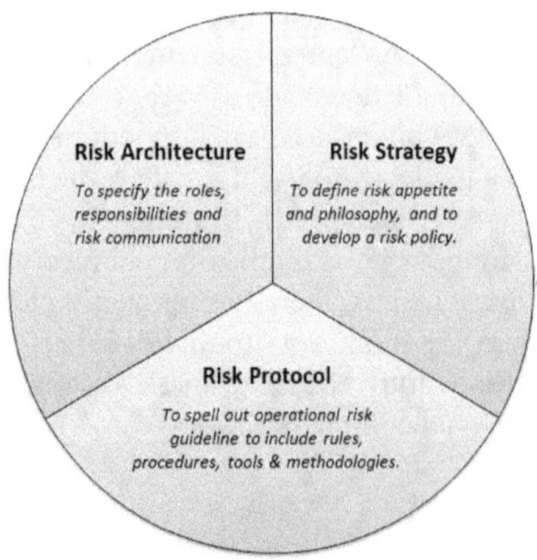

Understandably, the greater (than COSO) ambiguity of the Standard can be unsettling, but there is wisdom in it that should not be missed: To be universally applicable, which is to say to be meaningful to public, private or community enterprises, across types of endeavors and/or industries, a framework has to be devoid of any specifics that are meaningful in one context but not in another. At the same time, to be useful, an approach has to offer insights or guidance that would otherwise not be available, which raises an obvious question: What specific guidance does ISO 31000 Standard offer?

First and foremost, the Standard makes it clear that to yield material gains, the embrace of ERM by an organization has to be rooted in a leadership (board of directors and executive management) mandate and an express commitment. Once that has been secured, the next step is to design a framework tailored to the specifics of the organization's circumstances, with a particular emphasis on its risk philosophy and risk appetite. Once designed, the framework needs to be operationalized, or implemented, which has wide ranging implications from the, somewhat intangible process design to more concrete rules, procedures, tools, techniques and methodologies. Once implemented, the effectiveness of those processes and the framework as such, needs to be monitored and, periodically, reviewed. Inevitably, the ongoing monitoring is likely to produce framework enhancement ideas, thus the next step suggested by the Standard is that of improving the framework, at which point the risk management process loop starts anew…Figure 4.11 shows the schematic of the process.

Figure 4.11
ISO 31000 Risk Management Process: High Level View

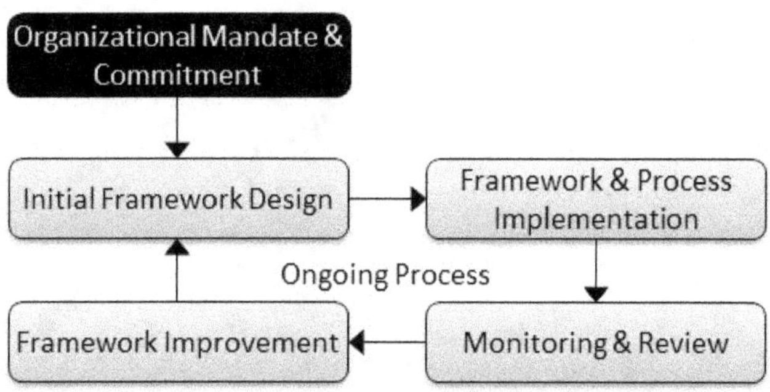

Perhaps one of the more controversial aspects of the ISO 31000 conceptualization is that it departs from a traditional definition of risk which defines it as the probability of loss – using the Standard's terminology (ISO Guide 73), risk is '…the effect of uncertainty on objectives'. In doing so, the Standard explicitly incorporates the earlier discussed notions of upside and downside risk, which is an important consideration in establishing the view of risk management as a function which aids the attainment of organizational objectives, rather than merely contributing to the minimization of the impact of adverse developments.

The heart of the ISO 31000 process outlined in Figure 4.11 is the process geared at objective, ongoing and systematic risk assessment, treatment and response. Using the Standard's terminology, the process – which takes place within the risk management context of the organization (i.e., is adapted to the uniqueness of the organization) – is comprised of two main elements: 1. Risk assessment, and 2. Risk treatment. The former entails *risk identification*, which establishes the exposure of the organization to identifiable (upside and downside) risks, all in the context of uniqueness of the organization's legal, political, social, cultural and economic circumstances, *risk analysis*, the goal of which is to produce a risk profile of the organization to aid in the risk prioritization and treatment efforts, and *risk evaluation*, the goal of which is to map individual risks to the part of the organization effected by those exposures and to describe the available control mechanisms. The latter of the two key elements of the process – risk treatment – is conceptualized as an activity of selecting and implementing the appropriate response mechanism, which encompass the earlier-discussed options of risk avoidance, mitigation, transfer and financing. Lastly, the ISO 31000 process acknowledges the importance of feedback, for which it suggests two distinct mechanisms: 1. communication & consultation, and 2. monitoring & review. Figure 4.12 shows a graphical depiction of the ISO 31000 process.

Figure 4.12
ISO 31000 Risk Management Process

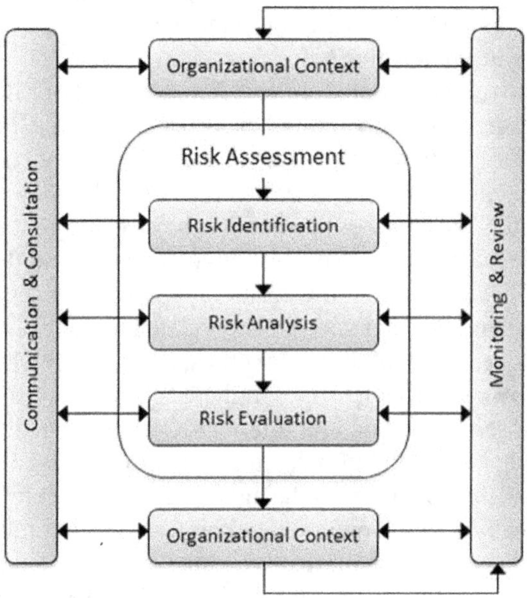

ERM and Debt Ratings

One of the major rating houses, Standard & Poor's (S&P), recently announced that it was planning to expand its current assessment framework to also include an evaluation of the state of enterprise risk management. The outside commentators, such as various consultancies and auditors, had a generally positive reaction to S&P's announcement, as at least on the surface it appears to be a formal acknowledgement of an important aspect of organizational management. Again, it is a compelling argument—that said, there are serious questions surrounding the efficacy of such assessments.

To start, I should point out that Standard & Poor's embraces the COSO framework as the model for ERM construction and implementation. Naturally, the earlier noted operational shortcomings of the COSO model need to be taken into account while contemplating the efficacy of S&P's assessment of corporations' ERM practices. Given the considerable operational ambiguity characterizing the COSO framework, and more specifically the framework's largely undefined measurement specifics, what exactly will be the target of

S&P's assessment? Stated differently, if the COSO conceptualization does not offer tangible guidelines spelling out the specific steps and actions that an ERM-implementing organization is to take, what exactly will the S&P (or any other entity) assess? How valid and reliable will such an assessment be and what will be its ultimate value?

Secondly, it seems obvious that being an assessor requires a considerable degree of demonstrated expertise in the area. What qualifies Standard & Poor's to be the evaluator of the adequacy of companies' ERM adequacy? A skeptic would say that being a baseball umpire does not make one a qualified football referee—why should it be any different in this context? Furthermore, has Standard & Poor's demonstrated a great deal of proficiency in mastering its core skill set, to warrant it venturing into becoming the evaluator of yet another, not very closely related dimension of organizational efficacy? Consider the 2008 financial crisis, an event which, to a large degree, was triggered by catastrophic losses in the US markets connected to a broadly defined area of securitized debt obligations. S&P, as well as other major rating agencies put what amounted to a 'stamp of approval' on billions of dollars of debt obligations that, contrary to the agency's ratings, were built on dangerously shaky foundations…To be fair, there were multiple other entities, both private and governmental, that were just as blindsided by the said collapse – of course, it is also fair to say that S&P is in the business of knowing and the mere fact that their failure was accompanied by failures of others does not make it any less of a failure. All of this goes to say that healthy skepticism seems warranted when it comes to an organization which seeks to broaden its evaluative scope, while manifestly still has not perfected its core capabilities.

Thirdly, the COSO framework embraced by S&P is skewed toward North American considerations while more and more companies are operating globally. Although a number the North American regulatory philosophies and practices have been adapted in other parts of the world, considerable cross-market differences endure, which means that an assessment of a particular company's enterprise risk management practices ought to be carried out in the context of a more universal framework, which in this case is ISO 31000 Standard discussed earlier.

All considered, is an assessment of the organization-specific enterprise risk management embrace and implementation feasible, regardless of what entity is doing it? I believe so, provided a more explicit operationalization of the conceptually sound ERM ideas spelled out in the aforementioned Standard, especially the notion of *risk profile* addressed by the ISO 31000 guidelines.

5

Measuring Risk

Much like individuals, organizations are bundles of individual attributes. An organization can be described in terms of its business (i.e., products or services and it produces and markets), size (revenue, market capitalization, number of employees), the degree of diversification, location, growth, means of ownership (private vs. public), etc. The resultant description can be relatively broad or quite specific, which means that the list of descriptors can be relatively short or quite long.

A special type of a description is *profiling*. Although 'profiling' and 'describing' are often used interchangeably, these two activities are considerably different. The main thrust of this difference is the idea of distinctiveness, or the degree to which a particular entity stands out. Generally speaking, to describe means to paint a complete picture, without regard to whether or not the individual components making up the description give rise to distinctiveness of individual entities. For instance, a description of an organization will include traits that are unique to it, as well as those it shares in common with other organizations. On the other hand, to profile means to assemble a sub-set of all available characteristics, specifically, those that are unique to a given entity, thus enabling cross-entity differentiation. In that sense, a profile is almost comprised of a sub-set of traits making up a broader description.

An obvious benefit of profiling is that is focuses on a smaller number of difference-communicating metrics. An equally important, though somewhat less obvious benefit of profiling is disambiguation.

Let us consider a business organization. We can provide a very general description of our hypothetical organization in terms of the type of business, size, products/services, number of locations, and means of ownership. At the same time, we can create a far more detailed description by including specific financial, accounting, governance and other details, which quite conceivably (especially for a public company) can entail hundreds of individual metrics. Although relatively simple operationally, the task of compiling an adequate description can be somewhat complex in the sense of deciding just how much detail to include.

Profiling offers a natural solution to the above problem by re-redirecting the efforts away from informational completeness and toward the aforementioned distinctiveness. It amounts to asking: In the universe of all available descriptors, which ones make this organization stand out? In other words, all available descriptors can be grouped into distinctive and non-distinctive traits. The former are those that give rise to differences, while the latter are a source of similarities. Of course, being classified in one group or the other is context-dependent, as under one set of circumstances a set of attributes can be a source of differences, while in a different situation it can be a source of similarities. It sounds a bit confusing, but it is quite straightforward: Since information—and ultimately, knowledge—is compiled for a purpose, it stands to reason that its efficacy is tied to context, meaning that all worthwhile information is necessarily contextualized.

Risk Profiling

Profiling is ideally suited to the analysis or risk because it helps to focus attention on the most pertinent areas of the organization's exposure to risk. This may not seem very clear at first, but let us consider another important concept briefly discussed in the opening chapter, namely the notion of *competitive advantage.*

The vast majority of business organizations have competitors and thus the vast majority of business decisions are, to some degree, shaped by competitive considerations; risk management related decisions are certainly not an exception to that rule. Let us consider the decision process of choosing the amount of directors' and officers' insurance coverage to purchase: It is almost a matter of habit for organizations to expressly consider the amount of coverage purchased by their peers, as most insurance buyers do not want to materially deviate from the peer-defined norm. Similarly, when evaluating the efficacy of their risk mitigation efforts, organizations tend to benchmark their results against peer groups, again, to make sure their outcomes compare favorably to those of their competitors.

Risk Profile

Although the vast majority of risk-related decisions are made in the context of a particular exposure – such as physical damage to buildings and equipment, supply chain or cyber related business interruption or regulatory investigation – from an organization-wide perspective, the basic tenets of the earlier discussed enterprise risk management are suggestive of the need to simultaneously consider the totality of the organization's exposures to all identifiable threats. Conceptually, from the standpoint of risk management any business organization can be viewed as a 'bundle of risks'; hence, the totality of risk exposures facing a firm can be thought of as its *risk profile*, defined here as a composite of the organization's exposures to identifiable and meaningful threats. Risk profiling of organizations has a wide range of goals, some of the most common of which include clearly, objectively and unambiguously compiling and communicating the totality of the organization's exposures to all knowable and material threats; drawing comparisons among individual threats; and suggesting optimal risk management choices.

Risk profiling is implicitly selective, insofar as its intent is to draw attention to organizational characteristics that are capable of materially impacting shareholder value. Manifestly, the overt goal of compiling and focusing on the organization's risk profile is to reduce the complexity of managing risk at the enterprise level by narrowing the focus to what matters the most. The rationale behind *risk profile management* is as follows: In order to ensure an operational feasibility of the holistic management of the totality of the organization's threat exposures, the analytical scope has to be reduced to a manageable set of factors. To be manageable, a particular threat has to be knowable, which is to say that it has to be estimable (recall the earlier made distinction between uncertainty and risk). To be estimable, both the likelihood and the severity of a threat have to be objectively quantifiable, which means that a statistically adequate past occurrence and outcome data has to be available[1]. Lastly, the magnitude of earnings impact ought to be strong enough to have a measurable impact on the organization's competitiveness, which in this context is operationalized as the impact on the firm's earnings. Hence, the management of the organization's risk profile is ultimately focused on the identification and estimation of specific factors that are capable of materially affecting the organization's competitiveness.

Figure 5.1
Hypothetical Risk Profile

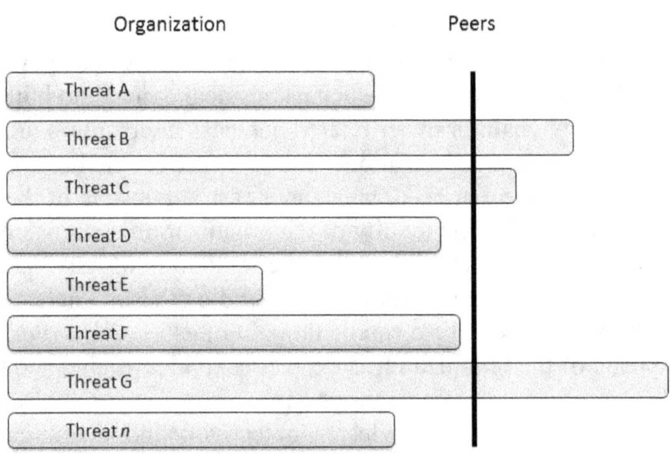

[1] *Statistical adequacy* is a function of numerous considerations which include the type of estimation methodology used, the desired precision of the resultant estimates and the type of data; those and other considerations are discussed in more detail in later chapters.

As graphically illustrated in Figure 5.1, there are two key components of a risk profile: 1. a peer group average, and 2. the organization-specific assessment, which imply two points of comparison. The first is the threat-by-threat assessment of the organization vs. the peer group defined average, which offers insights into which of the individual exposures could be deemed abnormal. In the hypothetical example shown in Figure 5.1, Threat B, C and G all could be deemed abnormally large, as their organization-specific levels are noticeably greater than the peer-wide average. The second point of comparison is the within the organization threat-by-threat assessment, the goal of which is to provide an objective threat response / management prioritization. Again referring to Figure 5.1, Threat G, followed by B and C should be place at the top of the 'need to manage / determine appropriate response' list. More on that in later chapters.

The Economics of Risk

It is important to note that the economics of risk necessitates carefully considering the costs (e.g., insurance premiums) and the benefits (e.g., loss protection) of each of the four risk response options discussed in the previous chapter. In that sense, the organization's risk profile can be viewed as one of the key influencers of that organization's competitiveness, as each of the four risk response alternatives discussed in the previous chapter have either near-term and definitive (e.g., insurance premium) or longer-term and speculative (e.g., unexpected and high loss) cost consequences. For instance, assuming a greater amount of risk can effectively enhance the firm's near-term profitability (by foregoing the expense of insurance premiums), and thus its competitiveness; at the same time, however, will expose the firm to the possibility of a larger future loss and a resultant erosion of competitiveness. Transfer of a greater amount of risk will have an opposite effect, which underscores the key risk transfer interdependence: The cost of risk transfer is definitive—its benefits are speculative, but the latter tends to be considerably greater (by, on average, about 50:1 ratio) than the former. And therein lies the challenge: In order for a business organization to have a competitively advantageous risk profile, it has to find an optimal balance between near-term earnings dampening risk transfer or mitigation efforts (e.g., commercial insurance coverage, the use of outside risk mitigation advisors, etc.) and potential longer-term earnings volatility increasing risk acceptance. The remainder of this book is focused on providing specific analytical insights into how to effectively balance these opposing considerations.

The RPM Typology of Risk

Einstein believed that '…solutions should be simple, but not too simple.' According to that line of reasoning it is important to properly balance the desire to simplify our explanation of a phenomenon, but not to the point of foregoing to communicate the degree of intricacy of a system. This is a very true of risk analytics, where two, often opposing considerations need to be balanced: 1. the desire to simplify the explanation to make it more 'workable', and 2. the need for it to be sufficiently complete to be beneficial. Hence the challenge lies in finding the optimum tradeoff between the completeness of the estimation process, which is necessary to yield valid and reliable likelihood and severity of impact estimates, and the explanatory simplicity, which is needed in order to formulate and implement risk reduction or avoidance strategies. Echoing Einstein's belief, I am convinced that the best solution is to meet halfway: Analysts should strive to de-mystify the often-esoteric risk modeling methodologies, while at the same time, risk management practitioners should strive to gain a base level of proficiency in risk quantification methodology.

With that in mind, let's turn our attention to risk categorization. As noted in the previous chapter, from the standpoint of an organization, risk encompasses the possibility of asset-damaging or loss-generating events taking place, and the chances of the anticipated growth not materializing. The former is called *downside* risk, primarily because it is associated either with loss or the absence of it, but no gain. The latter, on the other hand, is called *upside* risk because it is associated with the possibility of a gain. In many regards, these two types of risk are quite different, but ultimately, both can be expressed in terms of their expected impact on earnings. Hence the efficacy of upside and downside risk assessment, in terms of the likelihood of occurrence and the severity of impact, will have a pronounced impact on the overall financial well-being of the organization. That said, the manner in which upside and downside risks impact the organization's earnings are quite different.

Upside risk is, to a large degree, a reflection of an organization's strategic posture. It is well known that the earning power of even the most successful products will tend to diminish with time due to competitive forces, changing tastes and other factors. In other words, an organization that wants to not even grow, but just maintain its earnings level simply has to bet on new products and other growth-spurring initiatives. These bets represent upside risk; these are decisions involving choices among competing resource allocation options and the risk is a measure of likelihood and degree of success. It follows that growth is a function of successfully increasing the organization's upside risk, which means selecting options boasting the greatest likelihood of success and the greatest payout.

When looked at from the standpoint of financial well-being, downside risks are a potential drag on earnings. In general, that is a result of either actual losses and damages or inefficient risk capitalization structure. The former is relatively self-evident: A damaging event such as a hurricane can cause a considerable amount of wind and flood related physical damage to factories, offices and other structures, in addition to business interruption costs. Somewhat less visible, but potentially also quite costly are financial losses related to high accident-related injury rates.

The second of the two downside risk related sources of earnings drag, an inefficient risk capitalization structure, is considerably less obvious. The essence of the impact of risk capitalization structure on earnings is as follows: An organization that is lacking effective downside risk assessment functionality is usually forced to adapt a conservative—meaning, costly—capital structure, which amounts to using equity as a cushion against possible financial distress. On the other hand, an organization with more robust risk assessment functionality is able to adapt a more financially aggressive and less costly capital structure. More specifically, by using debt to finance specific risks, the organization will be able to lower its weighted cost of capital[2].

Putting the two together—the potential revenue/earnings gains associated with placing thoroughly considered upside bets, coupled with systematically reducing the potential downside costs of risk—will result in improving the organization's overall competitive position. Stated differently, the goal of risk profile management is to systematically increase the upside risk (i.e., to maximize the organization's growth opportunities), while, simultaneously systematically reducing the downside risk (i.e., minimizing the likelihood of loss generating events). In such broadly defined role, risk management becomes a direct contributor to the organization's competitiveness, as shown in Figure 5.2.

---

[2] The various frictional elements, such as taxes (which favor debt, because interest payments on debt are not taxable), imperfect information and transaction costs all add up to a conclusion that an optimal financial structure of an organization contains a mixture of debt and equity. This is the general rationale used by equity firms when evaluating public companies as possible targets for buyouts.

Figure 5.2
Risk and Competitive Advantage

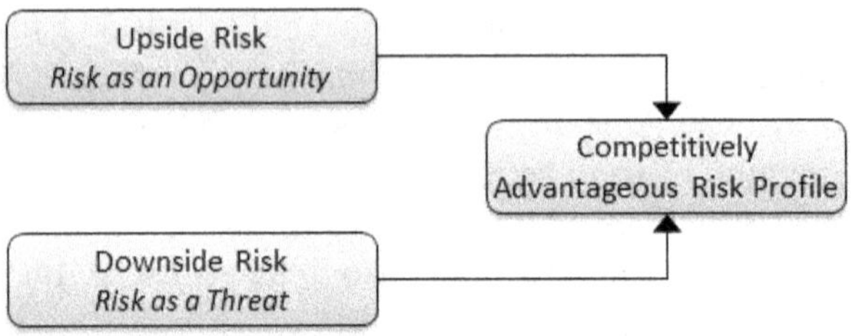

Upside Risk

Perhaps the best way to frame the notion of "upside risk" is to relate it to the well-known economic concept of opportunity cost, which is the amount of foregone value associated with choosing one alternative over another. Opportunity cost suggests the choice between two mutually exclusive, but desirable options—in a sense, it is a measure of efficiency, as it assures that scarce resources, financial, human and other, are deployed against the most beneficial of multiple alternatives. The scope of opportunity cost stretches beyond the explicit financial expenditure focused notion of accounting cost, insofar as it attempts to take into account monetary as well as non-monetary (or at least, hard to express in monetary terms) costs associated with different alternatives. The rationale imbedded in the idea of opportunity cost is an essential component of the marginal theory of value, which captures the amount of change associated with competing alternatives. In that sense, it is one of the key considerations underpinning the strategic decision making process.

Broadly speaking, strategic planning can be viewed as the process of evaluating competing capital investment decisions geared toward identifying the courses of action that will result in the greatest increase in shareholder value. A key part of the strategic planning process is the assessment of risk and return associated with each alternative being considered. In more operationally-clear terms, strategic risk has been defined (by the U.S Office of the Comptroller of Currency) as '…the risk to earnings or capital arising from adverse business decisions or improper implementation of those decisions…it is a function of the comparability between an organization's strategic goals, the business strategies developed to achieve those goals, the resources deployed against those goals and the quality of implementation'. According to a recent

Booz Allen Hamilton's Shareholder Value Destruction study which analyzed 1,200 global companies with market capitalization greater than $1 billion, strategic failures (such as poor brand or customer relationship management, emergence of disruptive technologies or industry cannibalization) accounted for approximately 60% of the reasons behind the loss of shareholder value[3]. These findings are in keeping with another research conclusion, a 2002 Academy of Competitive Intelligence survey of 140 corporate strategists which concluded that about two out of every three organizations have been surprised by as many as three high impact events in the preceding five years, which does not seem surprising given that 97% of the surveyed organizations indicated having no 'early warning' systems in place.

Not surprisingly, issues relating to strategic risk assessment have been receiving increasingly more attention, both from academics and practitioners alike. In their 2005 Harvard Business Review article[4], Slywotzky and Drzik identified seven distinct classes of strategic risk:

- *Industry*: Margin squeeze, overcapacity, commoditization, deregulation, etc.
- *Technology*: Patent expiration, process obsolescence or shifts in technology.
- *Brand*: Erosion of value or outright collapse.
- *Competitors*: Emergence of global rivals or one-of-a-kind competitor.
- *Customers*: Shifting preferences or over-reliance on a few customers.
- *Project*: R&D, M&A or IT failures.
- *Stagnation*: Flat or declining sales volume, unfavorable shift in volume-price relationship.

Is strategic risk synonymous with upside risk? In effect, yes. Simply put, *upside risk* is a strategic failure relating to the assessment of the available courses of action and the resultant plan of action. More specifically, it represents the possibility of failing to achieve revenues or earnings growth due to misalignments of strategic goals, external forces impacting those goals, the

---

[3] Of the remaining 40%, 27% was attributed to operational failures (such as cost structure, poor project delivery or channel/supplier challenges) and the last 13% to compliance failures (e.g., SOX, SEC violations, fraud).

[4] Slywotzky, A. J. and J. Drzik (2005), 'Countering the Biggest Risk of All', *Harvard Business Review*, April, 78-88.

strategies developed to achieve them, the resources deployed against them and the quality of implementation.

One of the more striking characteristics of upside risk is that it does not lend itself to easy objective (i.e., numerical) codification. In other words, one should not expect to be able to devise a robust rule-based strategic risk evaluation schema. On the one hand, that certainly contributes to the complexity of evaluating strategic risks; however, it has the positive benefit of removing the temptation of transforming risk analytics into a box-checking set of activities. Instead, the assessment of upside risk needs to take an interdisciplinary view combining the traditional risk quantification approaches with the real options framework and the cultural theory rooted assessment of revealed or expressed preferences. More on that later.

Downside Risk

Although it is intuitively obvious as an idea, the notion of downside risk can be operationally amorphous and highly context dependent, as it encompasses a seemingly infinite number of threats, while also being subject to evolving regulatory and broader societal forces. Still, it is possible to arrive at a general risk typology by systematically moving down the level of threat generalization. In that sense, downside risks can be either external or internal; the former can be sub-divided into controllable and not controllable, while the latter fall under the general umbrella of managerially controlled activities. Each of the resultant risk categories is made up of multiple, more narrowly defined risk types, briefly defined below:

- *Economic*: The effect of global economy on localized (i.e., of interest to a particular organization) economy.
  Risk type: External—Not Controllable.
- *Market*: A significant change in supply and demand functions, including prices of raw materials and other production inputs.
  Risk type: External—Not Controllable.
- *Competitive*: Entry of new competitors.
  Risk type: External—Not Controllable.
- *Technological*: Obsolescence of current technologies / costs of acquiring and instituting new technologies.
  Risk type: External—Not Controllable.
- *Financial*: Cost of capital and exchange rates.
  Risk type: External—Not Controllable.

- *Operational*: A broad category of risks arising out of the organization's implementation of its strategy and tactics.
  Risk type: Internal—Controllable.
- *Regulatory*: Changes in public policy and governmental regulations.
  Risk type: External—Controllable.
- *Environmental*: Changing pollution, carbon emission or disposal standards.
  Risk type: External—Not Controllable.
- *Supply Chain*: Also known as contractual risk, this pertains to contractor failure to deliver on time, schedule or for agreed upon price.
  Risk type: External—Controllable.
- *Professional*: Change in the firm's ability to attract and retain skilled human resources.
  Risk type: Internal—Controllable.
- *Natural*: Natural disasters, such as wind and flood dangers; crime, such as theft, vandalism or arson.
  Risk type: External—Not Controllable.
- *Socio-Cultural*: Demographic changes affecting the demand for the organization's goods or services.
  Risk type: External—Not Controllable.
- *Reputational*: Negative publicity in media, word-of-mouth and other sources, potentially adversely affecting the firm's brand equity.
  Risk type: Internal—Controllable.

This is a relatively long list—and quite varied. However, upon a closer examination, these risk types can be grouped into a more coherent downside risk typology shown below in Table 5.1.

Table 5.1
Typology of Downside Risks

External		Internal
Not Controllable	**Controllable**	**Controllable**
Financial	Regulatory	Compliance
Market	Supply Chain	Operational
Political		Reputational
Economic		Professional
Natural		
Socio-Cultural		
Environmental		
Technological		

All downside risk types are either *external* or *internal* in terms of their source. The former represent outside ongoing forces, such as regulatory frameworks, or isolated events, such as natural catastrophes, affecting the organization and potentially causing financial distress (i.e., adversely impacting earnings). The latter represent the failures of management to exercise proper control, as exemplified by failure to comply with applicable laws or regulations. External risk types, which are far more numerous and diverse, can be further subdivided into *controllable* and *not controllable*. As implied by the label, controllable external risks are those whose possibility of occurrence or adverse impact can be actively managed either by adapting organizational behavior or contractually. Conversely, not controllable external risks are those over which an organization exercises little-to-no control.

What is a common thread connecting all of these diverse types of risk? There are several: First, regardless of type, all risks are probabilistic in nature. In other words, the cost of capital will not definitely increase (it could stay the same or decrease), new regulations are not necessarily imminent or competitively unfavorable, nor is natural disaster-rooted property damage guaranteed. Second, risk refers to negative outcomes—e.g., changes in competitive, technological, market or financial circumstances that may benefit the organization are a source of opportunity, not risk. Third, risk has tangible economic consequences, usually expressed as a loss of monetary value. For instance, an unfavorable (to a US firm) change in the U.S dollar—euro exchange rate does not constitute a risk for a company with no European market, production or asset exposure. And fourth, and perhaps the most obvious communality is that risk refers to the future. Stated differently, risk is a reflection of uncertainty stemming from a lack of control over future developments.

Tying these three common threads together yields the following, generic definition: Downside risk reflects a probability of a negative outcome stemming from a future event and relating to something that is of value. In the context of competitive advantage, downside risk represents the probability of an adverse impact on the level or the stability of earnings.

Risk Quantification

As noted in the previous section, what is broadly defined as 'risk' represents the possibility of occurrence of an undesirable event or an outcome. Furthermore, the possibility of occurrence is itself a function of likelihood and severity of the individual undesirable events and outcomes. Hence, risk quantification should be viewed as a task of estimating the said two dimensions of risk—likelihood and severity—for each event or outcome that is of interest or concern.

The typology of risk outlined in the previous section stressed the importance of evaluating the individual risk types as potential sources of drag on earnings, which means evaluating risk in the context of its potential impact on the organization's competitive advantage. Put another way, it is important to consider the relative (to competitors, or otherwise defined peer group) impact of risk types, which calls for estimating the average impact and organization-specific deviation from that average. This adds a yet another aspect to the evaluation of risk, namely the notion of volatility.

The next few pages are dedicated to a general overview of measurement aspects of concepts of *volatility, likelihood* and *severity*. The goal of this overview is to bring to light the most important measurement considerations associated with each of these concepts.

Measuring Volatility

A concept of considerable important to the quantification of both the likelihood and severity dimensions of risk is *volatility*, which is defined as the degree of unpredictable change in a variable over a period of time. In finance, volatility captures the essence of risk, or fluctuations in returns generated by financial instruments. In statistical analysis, volatility is expressed through the notion of *variance*, which is a measure of statistical dispersion, computed by averaging the squared distance of possible (i.e., observed) values of a random variable from the expected value, or mean. Consider Figure 5.3.

Figure 5.3
Variance

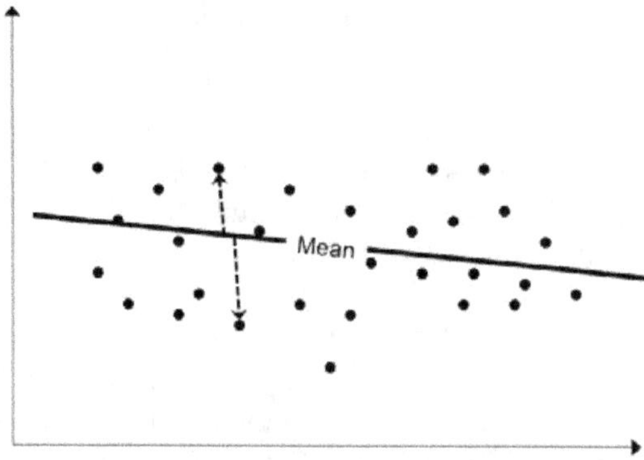

The above diagram shows a scattering of data points casted in the context of a 2-dimensional space. Let us say that these points represent monthly generation output of a hydroelectric utility, with the vertical axis capturing the magnitude of the said generation. The 'mean' line drawn through the middle of the distribution represents the average production for a particular time period (e.g., the past five years) and each 'dot' denotes monthly output. The points, or dots, falling both above and below the mean line, can be expressed in terms of relative deviation from the average, as shown by the two dotted arrows.

In the above illustration, variance is the total or combined—i.e., above as well as below the mean—amount of deviation from the expected, or mean, value. Mathematically, variance can be expressed as follows:

$$Variance = \sum_{i=1}^{n} (x_i - \bar{x})^2$$

where,

n is the number of observations
x_i is an observed value i
$\bar{x}$ is the mean value

Although mathematically useful, variance has relatively little practical informational value, as it confounds the unit of measurement with the total amount of variability in a given data set. However, once standardized, variance can be a very telling indicator. Standardizing variance simply amounts to taking a square root of it; its derivative is known as 'standard deviation' and it is computed as follows:

$$Standard\ Deviation = \sqrt{\frac{\sum_{i=1}^{n}(x_i - \bar{x})^2}{n}}$$

where,

n is the number of observations
x_i is an observed value i
$\bar{x}$ is the mean value

The key advantage of standard deviation (over variance) is that it standardizes the measurement of volatility by factoring out the magnitude of the unit of measurement, while retaining the proportional aspect of the assessment. The net effect of this simple transformation is the enablement of direct cross-variable comparisons.

Just standardizing the measurement scale is not enough, as in the analysis of risk it is usually not the total, but directional volatility that matters. Consider the example of a hydroelectric utility mentioned earlier. The generation of hydroelectric power is highly dependent on the level of river flows—in particular, it is impacted by declining flows. In other words, as the amount of water in a particular river diminishes (which might be a result of a relatively dry winter resulting in a diminished amount of snow to be melted) the hydroelectric output will fall. Since electricity is generally consumed as it is being produced, diminished output may necessitate gap purchases in the electricity marketplace, which not only requires the availability of funds, but itself is also a subject to potential market price volatility. In short, the same amount of gap electricity purchase can carry a different cost, depending on the spot market prices at the time of the purchase. Hence a hydroelectric utility is faced, in this scenario, with two distinct and directionally different risks: The possibility of diminished flows-related generation <u>decrease</u> and the potential <u>upward</u> volatility in electricity market prices. Clearly, the worst-case scenario is a simultaneous decline in generation and an increase in market prices.

As illustrated by the above example, the notion of variance and its derivative the standard deviation can be too general to capture the true amount of risk-related volatility in an outcome of interest, because these measures do not expressly differentiate between the upward and downward variability. Hence in situations where risk is reflected in either upward or downward deviation from the base, or mean, values, it might be more applicable to consider only a part of the overall variability, as shown in Figure 5.4.

Figure 5.4
Downside vs. Upside Variance

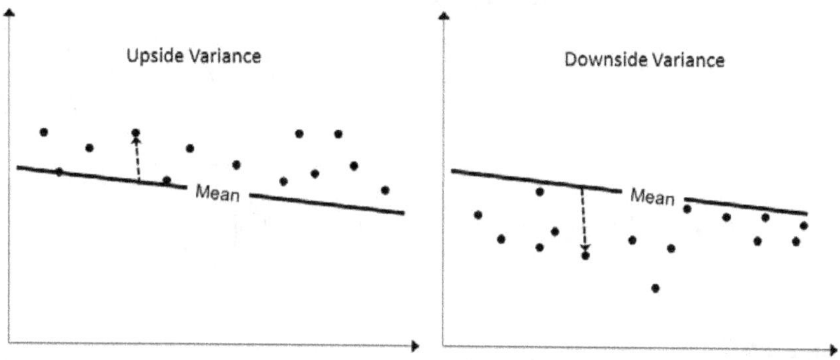

If that is the case, *semi-variance* should be used in place of variance. More specifically, *positive semi-variance* should be computed when risk is reflected in an increase over the mean baseline, which is computed as follows:

$$Positive\ Semi - Variance = \frac{1}{n}\left(\sum_{x_i > \bar{x}}^{n} (x_i - \bar{x})^2\right)$$

where,

n is the number of observations above the mean
x_i is an observed value i
$\bar{x}$ is the mean value

Alternative, *negative semi-variance* should be computed in situations where risk is reflected in a decrease below the mean level:

$$Negative\ Semi\ Variance = \frac{1}{n}\left(\sum_{x_i < \bar{x}}^{n} (x_i - \bar{x})^2\right)$$

where,

n is the number of observations below the mean
x_i is an observed value i
$\bar{x}$ is the mean value

As is the case with variance, both the positive and negative semi-variance can be standardized to enable direct cross-variable or cross-effect comparisons. The resultant measures, positive and negative semi-standard deviations, respectively, are computed as follows:

$$Positive\ Semi\ Standard\ Deviation = \sqrt{\frac{1}{n}\left(\sum_{x_i > \bar{x}}^{n} (x_i - \bar{x})^2\right)}$$

$$Negative\ Semi\ Standard\ Deviation = \sqrt{\frac{1}{n}\left(\sum_{x_i < \bar{x}}^{n} (x_i - \bar{x})^2\right)}$$

where,

n is the number of observations above or below (for positive or negative semi-standard deviation, respectively) the mean
x_i is an observed value i
$\bar{x}$ is the mean value

The above shown operationalizations of semi-variance and semi-standard deviation are uniquely suited to the analysis of risk, because they underscore the fact that risk, in the sense of a possible loss, is usually a manifestation of directional volatility. Specifically, in situations where risk increases as a function of negative deviation from the mean, negative semi-variance and its derivative, the negative semi-standard deviation should be used. On the other hand, in situations where risk increases as a function of positive deviation from the mean, positive semi-variance and its derivative, the positive semi-standard deviation should be employed.

Variance estimation is a mean to an end, which, in the context of risk is the estimation of the probability[5] of an adverse event, which is discussed next.

---

[5] It has become a matter of common practice to use the terms 'probability' and 'likelihood' interchangeably. I will adhere to this practice in discussing the topics relating to probability estimation, however, I would like to point out that, technically, those two concepts are somewhat distinct. According to R. A. Fisher, the father of modern statistical analyses, probability is the inference of sample occurrences drawn from assumptions regarding the population; likelihood, on the other hand, is inference of population characteristics from sample characteristics (see 'Statistical Methods for Research Workers', R. A. Fisher, 1st edition, 1925). In applied business analytics we are concerned with the latter, as we typically use the knowledge derived from analysis of a sample to make projections regarding the larger population.

Probability as a Business Tool

In the everyday language of business, likelihood is synonymous with probability, which is simply an attempt to predict unknown outcomes based on known parameters. Weather forecasters strive to predict (unknown) outcomes such as the future air temperature, the amount of precipitation or sunshine, based on known parameters, which are historical trends and interdependencies. In a more technical sense, the deployment of statistical likelihood estimation techniques allows us to estimate the unknown parameters based on known (i.e., historical) outcomes. In other words, by leveraging historical data, likelihood estimation enables us to create empirical bases for making forward-looking predictions. In the context of risk, the probability dimension reflects an attempt at quantifying the chance that a particular undesirable event will take place.

In business analyses, we are concerned with three basic types of probability: marginal, joint and conditional. *Marginal probability* is the probability of a given variable assuming a specific value, irrespective of the values of other variables. In the context of the automotive insurance claims example cited earlier, marginal probability could be computed to estimate, for instance, the probability of the total accident cost exceeding $5,000. Marginal probability, along with the equimarginal principle discussed later, forms the foundation for the approach for estimating the unique amount of total risk exposure to a specific factor, or the notion of 'effect attribution'.

Joint probability is the probability of two or more events occurring together. Consider the probability of an automotive accident, in inclement weather conditions, involving three of more vehicles. In the statistical modeling context, joint probability forms the basis for estimating interaction effects, which is a co-occurrence of two or more events.

Conditional probability is the probability that a given event (such an automotive accident) will occur given that one or more other events (such as inclement weather or speeding) have occurred. The notion of conditional probability provides a conceptual rooting for the area of business analytics that has come to be known as predictive analytics, which focuses on making forward-looking estimates of outcomes of interest based on an a priori assessment of causal interdependencies.

Probability Estimation: Divergent Philosophies

According to Jeffrey[6], '…before the middle of the seventeenth century, the term 'probable' (derived from Latin *probabilis*) meant approvable, and was applied in that sense, univocally, to opinion and to action. A probable action or opinion was one such as sensible people would undertake or hold, in the circumstances'. The more formalized, or mathematical treatment of probability (i.e., the Probability Theory) can be traced as far back as the sixteenth century and the first attempts to analyze the games of chance[7]. Hence initially the probability theory focused almost exclusively on discrete events, later expanded to include continuous variable, largely in response to the growth of calculus-rooted analytical applications[8]. The seminal work of Kolmogorov[9] laid the foundation for modern probability theory.

Risk analyses historically made a heavy usage of one of the key contributions of the probability theory: probability distributions. It has been observed than the occurrence of numerous natural or physical phenomenon and processes can be described with the help of a range of probability distributions. A probability distribution captures a range of possible values that a random variable can attain and the probability that the value of the random variable is within a measurable subset of that range. Some of the more frequently used (in actuarial analyses and elsewhere) discrete variable distributions include binomial, negative binomial, Poisson and Bernoulli, while the most frequently utilized continuous distributions include normal, exponential, gamma and beta.

Interpretation-wise, there are two somewhat distinct (and dissimilar) approaches: *Bayesian* and *frequentist*. The basic tenets of these competing approaches are briefly summarized in Table 5.2.

---

[6] Jeffrey, R. C. (1992), *Probability and the Art of Judgment.* Cambridge University Press, New York, NY, 54-55.

[7] The earliest known contribution in this area is attributed to an accomplished Italian Renaissance mathematician and…gambler, Gerolamo Cardano (1501-1576).

[8] *Analytical Theory of Probability*, published by Pierre Simon de Leplace in 1812 is believed to be the first major work blending calculus with probability theory.

[9] Kolmogorov, A. N., *Foundations of the Theory of Probability*, 1950. (Originally published in German in 1933.)

Table 5.2
Competing Likelihood Quantification Approaches

Approach	Description
Bayesian	Named after Thomas Bayes, who derived what is now called Bayes' Theorem; it relates conditional and marginal probabilities of two random events, which is often used in estimating the likely underlying causes of an observed outcome (or posterior probabilities). Broadly speaking, Bayesian Probability treats likelihood as measure of a state of knowledge; in other words, probabilities are a function of beliefs and uncertainty. However, that interpretation can be further segmented into two somewhat distinct schools of thought: the objective school, which relies on logical interpretation, akin to Aristotelian logic; and the subjectivist school, which promotes the view that the state of knowledge should correspond to personal belief. Needless to say, the former is easier to codify, hence it is used extensively in data mining applications.
Frequentist	As implied in the name, this is a strictly observation-based, empirical approach. Relying on objective data collected by means of experiments or recorded historical occurrences, the probability of random variable reflects the relative frequency of occurrence of the observed outcome. Under the Frequentist view, if 2% of publicly traded companies end up entangled in securities class action litigation on annual basis, on average, a given publicly traded company faces 2% chance of incurring this type of litigation.

Both the Bayesian and frequentist approaches have quite a bit to contribute to the risk management efforts. For risk types of which robust historical event data is available, the frequentist approach can provide a good approximation of the average, expected future probability of a particular event taking place. For example, an insurance company writing automotive coverage will almost always have ample historical accident data, which will enable to empirically estimate the likelihood of different types of accidents, etc. Not surprisingly, the Frequentist approach has been used extensively in the insurance industry.

At the same time, there are a number of important risks for which transaction-type quantitative data is not readily available. Avian flu, terrorism, ransom and kidnapping, reactor meltdown at a nuclear power plant are among the examples of such risks. Even if data on such events is available, it is usually too sparse to be generalizable for forecasting purposes. In those situations, Bayesian approach, combining expert knowledge and uncertainty can yield estimates superior to pure guessing.

The analytic framework outlined in this book aims to incorporate the elements of the two competing probability approaches—the frequentist method is used with (relatively) high frequency risks for which robust quantitative data is available and the Bayesian approach is employed when risk types lack the requisite objective data.

The above discussion focuses on likelihood as a single measure problem. A particular event of interest, such as hurricane, an automotive insurance claim or the availability of capital, is viewed more-or-less in isolation from everything else. For instance, a frequency distribution of automotive accidents of single, male drivers between ages of 18 and 25 shows a cumulative frequency counts in the context of their probability of occurrence. It offers no insights regarding the underlying causal factors—in other words, it is a descriptive tool showing what-is, without providing any explanation as to why-it-is.

Multivariate Probability

In business analyses, we often try to understand the inner-workings of a particular micro-system, many of which are comprised of multiple variables and a web of interdependencies. The behavior of each of the elements of such a system can be described in terms of its (univariate) probabilities; however, to understand the system as a whole requires the assessment of the combination of all component probabilities, or multivariate probability.

Conceptually, *multivariate probability* is a generalization of a univariate probability to higher dimensions, where 1 variable = 1 dimension. It means that unlike a single variable (i.e., univariate) probability which entails an assessment of a single value frequency distribution, multivariate probability entails a single-value assessment of a product of multiple frequency distributions. Consider the sample contrast: The economic cost associated with auto accidents can be expressed as a frequency distribution, where different dollar intervals represent different frequency of occurrence, as shown in Figure 5.5 below.

Figure 5.5
Univariate Frequency Distribution

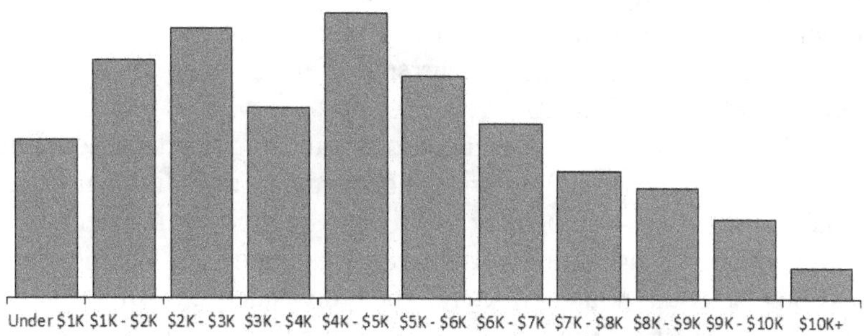

Utilizing the frequentist approach outlined earlier, the above frequency distribution can be easily converted into probabilities associated with each cost interval (e.g., under $1K, $2k - $3k, etc.) by computing relative frequencies, which is a given interval's share of the total frequencies.

The picture becomes a lot more complex when the above example is extended to jointly consider a couple of additional measures, such as the age of the driver and the time of day. The resultant multivariate distribution can no longer be depicted in the context of the familiar Cartesian (i.e., X-Y) coordinates used in figures 5.3 and 5.4; instead, it needs to be presented as a far harder to visually interpret response plane or a multivariate density function, exemplified in Figure 5.6.

Figure 5.6
Response Surface

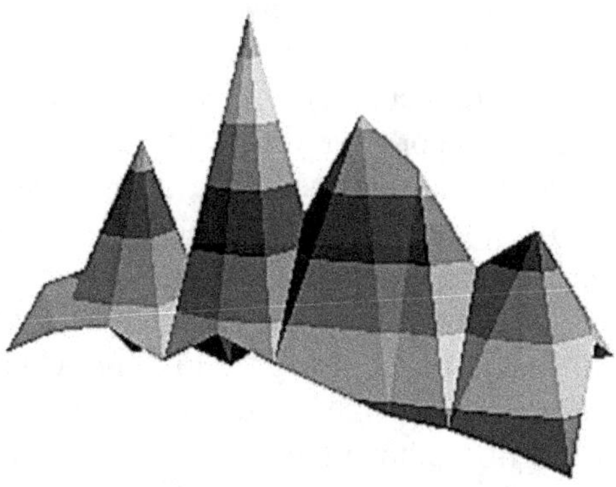

An important notion associated with multivariate probability is that of *dependence vs. independence* of the constituent variables. In a technical sense, any two (or more) variables are considered to be independent if their conditional probability is equal to their unconditional probability. Or stated differently, when the occurrence or non-occurrence of one of the variables does not affect the occurrence or non-occurrence of the other(s), the variables can be considered to be independent.

This is an important consideration, both from the data modeling and practical standpoints. Modeling-wise, independence of individual measures is a reflection of their non-redundancy and it is among the requirements of some of the more commonly used multivariate statistical modeling techniques, such as regression discussed in later chapters. The independence assumption, as an attribute of multivariate probability, carries some very real implications for risk management practices. Risk mitigation efforts can be greatly enhanced by the delineation of drivers of risk, or factors that have been shown to either heighten or lower the organization's exposure to specific risks. In order to establish actionable and effective risk mitigation efforts, the organization must be able to estimate factor-specific impact, or the degree to which pulling a specific lever (i.e., acting upon an individual risk factor) is going to have a desired impact.

Severity Estimation

In many respects, severity is a far simpler notion than likelihood. In essence, *severity* is an estimate of the magnitude of economic impact associated with a particular risk; it is typically expressed in terms of cost.

Much like probability, severity estimates are highly dependent on the availability of historical loss data. Depending on the type of risk, historical losses can come in the form of (relatively) exact insurance claims and the resulting payouts (e.g., securities litigation claims), internal company records (e.g., workers' compensation claims), coverage provider (e.g., automotive accidents) or outside private or governmental sources (e.g., terrorism). Consequently, the accuracy of the resultant estimates may vary quite widely.

There are three important considerations that need to be addressed in the context of severity estimation: attribution, recency and projectability. *Attribution* is a measure of accuracy of the cause—effect linkage. Is the particular loss figure attributed, or assigned to a correct cause? It is intuitively obvious that attributing correct amounts to correct causes is essential to making reliable forward projections, though the available data may not necessarily exhibit the requisite coding discipline.

Recency reflects the newness of the historical loss data. For some types of risks, such as operational risks falling under the umbrella of general liability or workers' compensation, an organization might have 10, 15 or even 20 years of data available, which poses the question—how far back should an analyst reach to make reliable forward-looking projections? This issue is further complicated by the notion of *claim development*, which is a measure of the maturation of individual losses[10]. All considered, what constitutes appropriate, from the practical standpoint, and adequate, from the data modeling standpoint, recency will vary across situations.

Projectability addresses the fundamental question of usability—is the available historical cost data going to form a valid foundation for making future projections? There are numerous reasons for why the available data may not be projectable. First, it could be non-generalizable. In other words, while the data may reflect a particular sub-set of the overall population, the goal might be to make population-wide projections (or vice-versa). Second, it could be too sparse. A case in point is the growing threat of pandemic risks (such as avian flu) and terrorism, neither of which has enough data points to substantiate robust projections (a potential qualitative remedy, the Delphi method, is discussed later). Third, it could be either too specific or too broad. For example, the much talked about global warming patterns and the supporting numerical evidence might form an appropriate background for setting global CO_2 emission standards, but would likely be too coarse to help a single utility organization risk-adjust considerations surrounding the construction of a new power plant.

A Note on Likelihood vs. Severity Independence

For methodological and practical purposes, the two risk dimensions—likelihood and severity—are almost always estimated individually. At times, it might be beneficial to combine the two sets of estimates into a single "expected value of risk" figure. The ability to do that hinges on the degree to which the two sets of estimates are mathematically independent of one another.

In a data analytical sense, independence = additivity, which in turn supports computing of a product of likelihood and severity, i.e., the

[10] While some events are characterized by a single point in time loss, others entail multi-year payment streams comprised of amounts that may not be known ahead of time. For example, a workers' compensation claim which includes ongoing medical treatment may take a number of years to "fully develop" (i.e., account for all costs) and there is generally no way of knowing the costs of medical treatment in advance.

aforementioned expected value of risk. As used in this book, the notion of likelihood—severity independence is a binary consideration, meaning that the two risk dimensions either are or are not independent. Measurement-wise, that determination is based on computing of a correlation coefficient and the corresponding statistical significance testing (both concepts are discussed at length in later chapters). A lack of statistically significant correlation between likelihood and severity is taken as an indication of likelihood—severity independence. On the other hand, the finding some degree of interdependence between the two attests to interdependence between the two risk dimensions, with the magnitude of the correlation coefficient providing an estimate of the strength of the said relationship. Since that points to an informational overlap between likelihood and severity (i.e., some degree of redundancy), combining of the two dimensions into the aforementioned expected value of risk estimate should not be undertaken.

6

Risk Profiling Organizations

The ideas outlined in this book are rooted in the belief that analyses of business data in general—and risk analytics in particular—are most effective when framed in the context of *explanation-based prediction* and *entity- specific estimation.* To appreciate the importance of former it is important to consider it from the standpoint of epistemology, which is the study of nature of knowledge and processes that create it, while the latter of the two considerations is a reflection of the unit of analysis, or the level of aggregation of analytic conclusions. In a more applied sense, the informational benefits of entity-specific, explanation-based predictions are most evident when contrasted with the widely used, in the analyses of risk, alternative, which is the extrapolation of past trends into the future. Commonly used in actuarial analyses, this broadly considered approach generalizes past patterns without expressly considering any underlying causes – for instance, insurance loss reserving is based on past, aggregate outcomes such as past losses and loss development factors to estimate the value of future liabilities. While such approaches yield adequate insights for some information seekers (e.g., insurance carriers), they fall short in other contexts where deeper knowledge is needed to support activities such as risk mitigation.

Risk Profile Management

Estimation is, generally, a mean to an end. The point made repeatedly throughout this book is that objectively derived, robust information increases the quality of decisions, ultimately positively impacting the organization's competitiveness. In the context of risk management, objectively estimated likelihood and severity of individual threats are the foundation of risk profile management (note the distinction between "management" and "measurement"- the latter can be considered an enablement of the former).

Risk Profile Management (RPM) was first briefly discussed in the preceding chapter, in the context of risk reduction. It represents an application of multivariate modeling (a family of statistical techniques for simultaneous analysis of multiple metrics) to the problem of likelihood and/severity estimation. Although I initially talked about it in the context of reducing downside risk, RPM should in fact be generalized to a broader definition of risk, which includes both downside as well as upside risks.

Recall the earlier discussed risk response alternative, graphically summarized in Figure 6.1 below.

Figure 6.1
Risk Response Alternatives

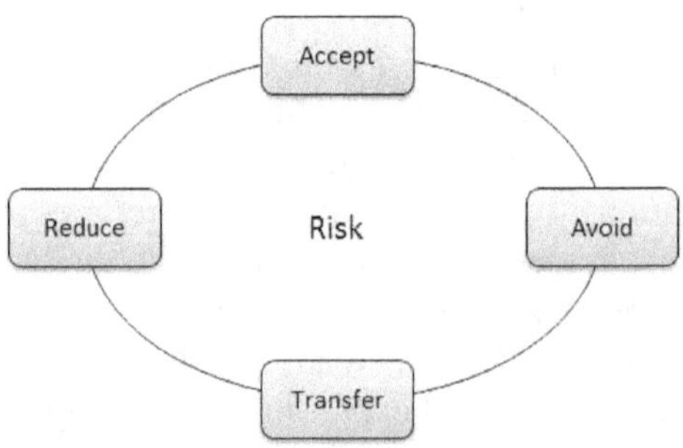

The essence of RPM is to minimize the adverse impact on earnings stemming from the organization's exposure to identifiable and measurable risk types. Each of the four broad responses, acceptance, reduction, transfer and avoidance, entails a different set of risk management activities. That should be intuitively obvious. Somewhat less obvious, however, might be an assertion that the type of information that is available will also play a role. Of course, in order for that effect to be discernable, the continuum of possible informational inputs needs to be broken out into a manageable number of discrete, non-overlapping categories. The proposed information type categorization schema is shown in Figure 6.2.

Figure 6.2
Informational Inputs and Their Impact

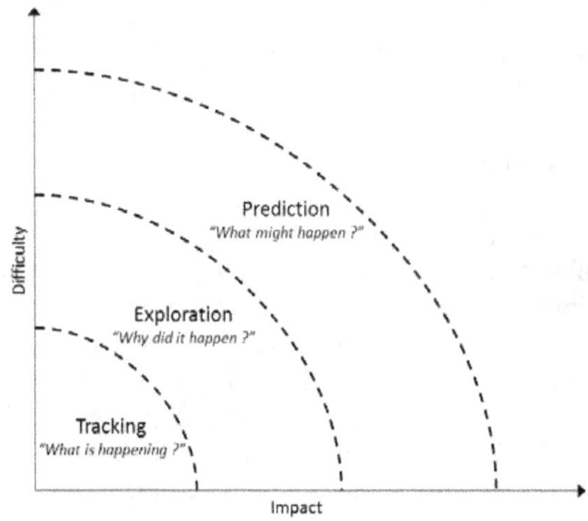

There are three distinct types of informational inputs: tracking, exploration and prediction. Their relationship can be captured in terms of analytical difficulty and business impact, which comprise the vertical and horizontal dimensions, respectively. *Tracking*, which entails actively capturing information regarding a phenomenon of interest, is analytically the least involved of the three, but it also delivers the least amount of business value or impact, because it focuses on generic (i.e., not a source of competitively advantageous insight) information, which is also rarely suggestive of the underlying root causes. *Exploration*, which is the conduct of analysis the goal of which is to discern the root causes of the observed (i.e., tracked) outcomes, is more analytically involved, but it also delivers greater impact to the organization, in the form of knowledge of factors influencing the phenomenon of interest. Lastly, *prediction* is the most analytically involved of the three types of informational inputs, while also delivering the greatest amount of impact on the organizational decision-making. It entails making forward-looking predictions regarding the outcomes of interest, built on the foundation of rigorous cause-effect analysis.

The importance of the above outlined continuity of informational inputs to RPM is paramount, as it provides the informational basis for an ongoing monitoring and adjustment. Information is not uniformly distributed across risk types, which means that the type of assessment—i.e., tracking vs. exploration vs. prediction—will vary across the types of risk. That said, it is the goal of Risk Profile management to gather the best available information, on ongoing basis and in a format that contributes to shaping risk response decisions.

Ultimately, any risk response decision should be considered in the context of a risk-return tradeoff. At least in theory, it is possible for an organization to enter into a large number of financial contracts which would either outright transfer the risk or provide post-event compensatory mechanisms, so much so that the said organization would be shielded against a vast majority of loss causing events. However, the overall cost would be more than likely prohibitively high, so that from the economic standpoint, that would not be a plausible scenario. Hence basic economics, in effect, force organizations into deciding which risks to transfer, which ones should be considered avoidable, or at least mitigatable, and which ones simply need to be accepted. In order to not imperil the organization, this decision needs to be rooted in the explicit analysis of clearly defined risk type—risk response conjoints, such as storm damage—transfer vs. storm damage--accept. It is another way of saying that organizations need to make economically rational decisions regarding the most economically appropriate response to each delineated risk. Insurance coverage offers protection against certain types of insurable events, but it can be costly, which means that buying large amounts of insurance can be a drag on earnings. At the same time, an un-insured adverse loss can be a source of even a greater shock to earnings. Hence an objective and reliable evaluation of the aforementioned risk type—risk response conjoints is at the heart of Risk Profile management.

Risk Acceptance

The willingness to participate in a competitive marketplace implies willingness to accept a certain amount of risk. More specifically, it entails the acceptance of the upside component of the overall risk (see the *Defining Risk* section in the previous chapter), which is a set of risks surrounding the organization's strategic decisions. For instance, an auto manufacturer developing (i.e., investing in) an electricity-powered automobile implicitly assumes the (strategic) risk associated with future viability of this particular alternative fuel approach. In other words, the organization makes a strategic decision and then it implicitly assumes the risk of that being the "wrong move".

At the same time, a successful business organization will also actively hedge against a number of other risks, discussed earlier under a broad umbrella of downside risks. As a whole, downside risks are events or outcomes threatening to bring about an economic loss or otherwise defined cost, which means that, true to their name, there are no potential benefits to downside risks. Storm related damage either occurs or not; employment practices or securities class action either happens or not; unfavorable (to the organization) legislation is either enacted or not, etc.

In addition to upside risks, there is a handful of downside risks that an organization may choose to accept. Consider the 'external, not controllable' risk types delineated earlier in Table 5.2—virtually all of those broadly defined risk types fall outside of the organization's sphere of control. Of course, it does not mean that the organization should accept all of those risks, in the sense of assuming a "do nothing" posture; in fact, by doing so, it would have likely increased the potential adverse impact (of those exposures) on earnings. At the same time, some of those exposures, such as socio-cultural, political or economic present very few, if any, real options.

Well, that is not entirely true. Just because certain types of risk exposure are not "manageable", in the sense of being changeable likelihood or severity-wise, does not mean that the organization needs to become a victim of its circumstances. Aggressive intelligence gathering and incorporating the so-collected insights into decision making can be an effective risk reducing mechanism. The essence of Risk Profile Management is that every delineated risk—without regard to whether or not internal or external, controllable or not—needs to be actively managed in a way that is most appropriate, given the risk type's inherent characteristics. It means that while an organization may have to accept certain types of risk, it should actively track important and knowable manifestations of those risks with the goal of adjusting its decisions, as appropriate.

Recall the Figure 6.2 shown earlier: In the context of the three types of information inputs outlined in that illustration, risk acceptance entails that—at a minimum—the organization puts in place a process to track and disseminate (to the appropriate stakeholders) information pertaining to risk types it chooses to accept. In essence, this amounts to saying that there are external factors, which are not controllable yet pose a potential threat to the organization; if the organization chooses or is otherwise forced into accepting those risks it should actively track them and incorporate those insights into its overall risk management process.

Risk Transfer

This is probably the most intuitively obvious risk response mechanism. At the same time, it is also the costliest, in terms of near-term financial cost, risk response alternative. Essentially, risk transfer entails the use of a wide range of financial tools to provide protection against , ranging from traditional insurance coverage to an array of alternative risk transfer mechanisms, such as captive insurance, hedge funds, contingent capital, securitization and other, discussed in more depth in the previous chapter (even though, as pointed out earlier, insurance coverage is technically not a risk 'transfer' but a post-event compensatory mechanism, since it affects the severity, but not the likelihood dimension of risk, it is commonly thought of as a risk transfer tool).

In the event-tracking sense, risk transfer is the most involved risk response decision, as it involves a two-part consideration: 1. Is it economically desirable to transfer a particular risk? and, 2. What specific monetary value should be pursued?

The ultimate determinant of the extent of the potential damage associated with a given risk type is its estimated impact on earnings. In terms of the three broad types of informational inputs, the risk transfer decision calls for the prediction of risk type-specific likelihood and severity. This is, of course, one of the key difficulties associated with effective risk transfer, namely, the availability of quantitatively sound, rational informational basis. For some types of risk, such as physical, i.e., property, damage, the needed information may be easier to obtain than for other types, where objective valuation is not plausible. Let us consider two typical cases: physical damage and executive liability to illustrate the difference.

In the case of physical damage, such as the threat to physical structures (e.g., manufacturing plants, office buildings, hotels, etc.) posed by wind, flood or earthquake, the extrinsic value of the property provides a key set of objective inputs into severity estimation, while historic event occurrence records will yield another set of inputs, namely the frequency estimates. Obviously, the extent of damage is a range in itself (i.e., it could range from very minor damage to complete destruction of a property), and the historical trend-derived frequency estimate represents an average of past occurrences, nonetheless, the appropriateness of entering into a risk transfer contract (question #1 above) and the value of the said contract (question #2 above) can be estimated from a sound informational basis.

That is not the case for executive liability considerations. The core executive liability risk is that faced by directors and officers of the organization who might stand accused of 'causing' financial losses to investors by virtue of improper or inadequate communications. The result can be a securities class action, which is a legal action taken by shareholders against directors and officers of the company[1]. Although the basis for those suits is a decline in the company valuation, the ultimate cost (which typically takes the form of a settlement for non-dismissed cases) is not very closely tied to settling companies' market capitalization, so much so that a large company may end up with a relatively modest settlement, while a significantly smaller company may end up with a considerably larger one[2]. Hence in contrast to the physical damage example, when it comes to less tangible threats organizations do not necessarily have readily available informational input that could be used to substantiate the appropriateness of their risk transfer decisions.

Risk Avoidance & Reduction

From the informational standpoint, the essence of Risk Profile Management is the notion of 'prediction thru explanation'. The centerpiece of that approach is the process of delineation of threat-heightening factors, the totality of which can be construed as a hypothetical 'high risk organization'. Measurement-wise, the individual risk indicators can assume one of two distinct forms: 1. categorical, which indicate discrete states, such as presence vs. absence or a group membership, or 2. continuous, which capture the level of a particular quantity or quality. Some threat-heightening factors can only be measured using a single form (e.g., a company being public vs. private), while others can be measured using both forms (e.g., filing of net income restatement can be captured as a 'yes or no' categorical event, but if 'yes', then the magnitude of the restatement can be measured as a continuous quantity. Consider Figure 6.3.

---

[1] On average, there are about 200 of securities class action suits filed in federal courts annually (following the passage of the Private Securities Litigation Reform Act of 1995, these claims can no longer be filed in state courts).

[2] Of the nearly 3,000 securities class action claims filed since the PSLRA of 1995, only seven were resolved by a jury; the rest were either dismissed or settled.

Figure 6.3
Informational Basis of RPM: Likelihood

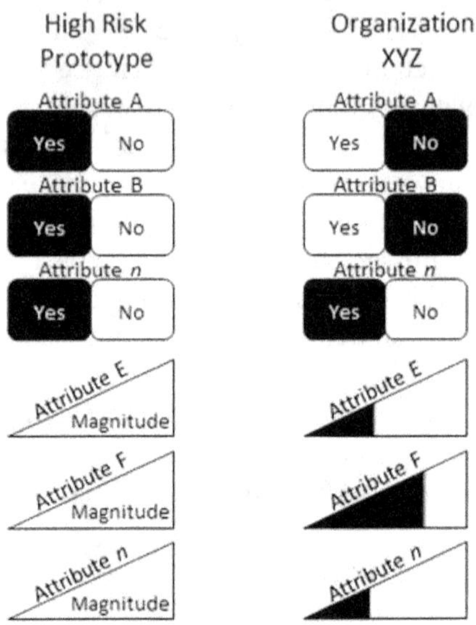

The *High Risk Prototype* represents an agglomeration of threat-heightening organizational traits, measured either as distinct states (Yes-No attributes A and B) or continuous quantities (attributes E and F). The *Organization XYZ* illustrates a sample application of the threat-heightening prototype to an actual organization – the more commonalities exist between the prototype and the organization, the higher the risk exposure of the organization being evaluated. RPM entails a deliberate examination of the company's positioning on each of the risk exposure (likelihood) determining attributes, followed by making appropriate, informed decisions.

There are two key aspects of risk profiling that define active profile management: 1. identification of actionable attributes, and 2. assessment of partial, or attribute-specific impact.

Actionable Attributes

Just as every one of us has multiple characteristics over which we have little-to-no control, there are aspects of organizations that are not subject to their direct control. A publicly traded company controls the number of shares of its stock that it sells to the public, but it has virtually no control over the trading price of its shares. Similarly, an organization has quite a bit of control over the direct or absolute pricing of its products, but it has considerably less control over relative prices of its products, as the latter are heavily influenced by competitors' prices (and ultimately, most organizations are constrained by their input prices). As a result, some aspects of the organization's risk profile will not be directly controllable, which means that a critical part of RPM is the identification of specific risk-related traits over which the organization does have a reasonable degree of control.

Attribute-Specific Impact

As noted earlier, risk profile is a mix of risk exposure-effecting organizational traits. To the degree to which risk profiling is based on similarity (to prototypical high and low risk exposure entities) analysis, some of those attributes will be those that are shared with high-risk prototype, while some others will be shared with low risk prototype. Hence it follows that some of the organization's characteristics will increase its risk exposure, while some others will lower it. Furthermore, both the risk heightening and risk lowering attributes will vary in terms of the strength of their impact. Consider the following generic example:

Figure 6.4

Sample Attribute-Based Assessment

EFFECT TYPE	KEY RISK INDICATORS									
	Metric A	Metric B	Metric C	Metric D	Metric E	Metric F	Metric G	Metric H	Metric I	Metric J
Contribution to probability change: *Magnitude*	11%	8%	22%	77%	23%	60%	15%	1%	10%	5%
Contribution to probability change: *Direction*	▲	▼	▼	▲	▼	▲	▼	▲	▲	▲
Company-Level Assessment on Key Risk Indicators										
Organization XYZ			■	■				■		■
Peer 1		■								
Peer 2		■	■		■			■		
Peer 3		■	■		■			■	■	
Peer 4		■		■						
Peer 5				■			■			
Peer 6							■			
Peer 7				■	■		■			
Peer 8		■		■						
Peer 9		■		■			■		■	
Peer 10		■		■	■		■			
Peer 11			■							
Peer 12	■						■			
Peer 13		■		■						
Peer 14					■		■			
Peer 15		■		■	■					
Peer 16		■		■	■		■			
Peer 17				■		■	■			
Peer 18										

DEFINITIONS:

Contribution to probability change: Magnitude. Percent change in the likelihood associated with 1-unit change in the level of attribute.

Contribution to probability change: Direction. ▲ Heightens Risk ▼ Reduces Risk

Key risk indicators (Metric A, Metric B, etc.) are presented in the context of two effect types: 1. Contribution to probability change: *Magnitude*, which shows the standardized impact of individual attributes on likelihood (shown above) or severity, and 2. *Contribution to probability change: Direction*, which depicts the nature of impact of a metric on a particular risk dimension. The former is a measure of elasticity, or responsiveness of either likelihood or severity to the level, in changes in it, of a particular predictor of risk, such as Metric A, Metric B, etc. The latter encapsulates the direction of change, where each predictor of risk can either heighten or reduce the probability of its occurrence or its severity.

The second part of the assessment illustrated in Figure 6.4 above is focused on contrasting the focal company's metric-by-metric exposure with that of a set of pre-selected peers. This part of the evaluation attempts to pinpoint specific aspects of the company's risk profile that contribute unfavorably to its risk exposure. There are two distinct aspects to that assessment: First, each organization (i.e., the company as well as each of the peers) are compared to the overall size and industry type adjusted average to determine whether each entity is above, below, or within the average, across all metrics that have been identified to be predictive of a particular risk (jointly labeled as Key Risk Indicators above). Second, if a particular attribute (e.g., Metric A) heightens the company's risk exposure, it is beneficial to be below average on that metric; hence if any of the entities evaluated is above average on that attribute. The reverse logic applies to all predictors of risk which lower the exposure to risk, such as Metric B: It is advantageous to be above average on a measure which reduces risk, while the instances where an entity is below average.

Process & Methods

Taking a closer look at the issues relating to epistemology, it is important to keep in mind some of fundamental differences between the purely scientific goal of theory creation and testing and the focus of applied risk analytics, which is that of estimating the likelihood and severity of specific outcomes (i.e., individual risk factors) along with the delineation and parameterization of key risk drivers. Hence, the goal of risk analytics is not to search for universally true and longitudinally invariant (i.e., unchanging over time) generalizations, but rather, to make reasonably accurate estimates in relation to future states of certain outcomes that are of interest to us. In fact, it is usually assumed that much of what we find today is going to change in the future given the dynamic nature of market behaviors. Process-wise, the logic of risk analytics can be depicted as follows:

Figure 6.5
Generic Process of Risk Modeling

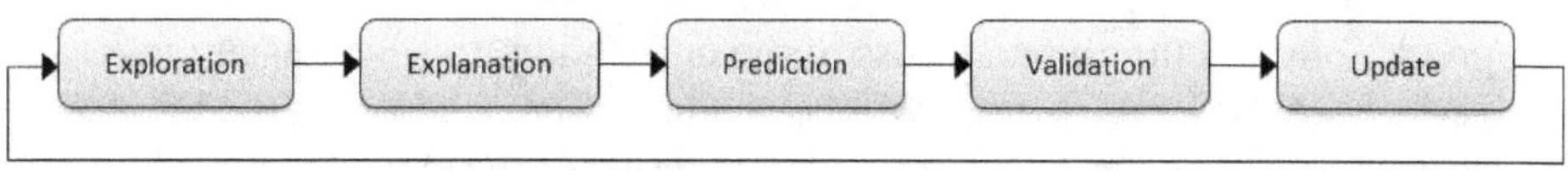

The process depicted in Figure 6.5 illustrates the notion of explanation-based prediction: Exploratory analysis-generated prediction gives rise to a prediction, which is followed by validation. In practice, exploratory analyses will yield a causal model which in turn forms the basis for a scoring equation which generates forward-looking (likelihood and severity) estimates, which are validated against the known outcomes. Once the new batch of behavioral data is available, the analytical process is re-started to take into account any changes in (data-contained) behavioral patterns. This process is inherently reductive, which is to say it analyzes individual risk types into their constituent, lower level components, all with the goal of identifying specific indicators that can be used to estimate future outcomes and to mitigate their likelihood and/or severity, when possible.

Somewhat more hidden is the second of the two previously mentioned characteristics of the risk analytical approach described in this book is the notion of entity-specific estimation. This might seem self-evident, but there are many aspects of risk management where that is not the case. For instance, when assessing exposure to executive liability, which is one of the major components of compliance risk, it is common to make use of group attributes such as industry membership, size (i.e., its market capitalization or revenue) and a handful of somewhat more esoteric characteristics, such as accounting accruals. Companies with shared communalities on those attributes form risk clusters which may include as few as several dozen and as many as several hundreds of individual organizations, all of which are assumed to exhibit essentially the same exposure to, in this example, executive liability (or other threats). In the absence of more specific information, these types of approximations might be deemed reasonable—and indeed they are, but only to the extent to which the available data does not support more detailed, entity-specific analyses[3].

Methods

The two framing aspects of the risk analytics approach described in this book—explanation-based prediction and entity-specific estimation—carry a number of implications. First, the estimation of the likelihood and severity of outcomes of interest will encompass the use of multiple metrics, both quantitative and qualitative, to enhance the accuracy of future states' predictions and the completeness of the underlying causal explanation. Second, analytic conclusions will be geared toward improving the business efficacy of future decisions, measured in terms of the expected impact on earnings. Third, the interrelationships among the individually estimated risk types will be assessed in the context of a dynamic system capable of propagating future changes. Method-wise, these translate into the following considerations:

- *Focus on multi-source, multivariate analyses.*
  Risk types vary widely in terms of their nature, the overall frequency of occurrence and the availability of ready-to-use data. Frankly, some risks are significantly easier to measure than some other ones, a fact which obviously contributes to very uneven enterprise risk operationalization landscape. The approach outlined in this book is expressly focused on developing all-inclusive, in terms of the individual risk types, risk assessment capabilities. In more operational terms, the risk analytic methodology presented here is built around multivariate, or multi-

[3] In the example used here, there is adequate data to support entity-specific analyses, which means that the belief that group-level analyses are adequate is unwarranted.

variable, analyses of dissimilar sources of data. Multi-source analyses are a necessary prerequisite to a simultaneous assessment of the totality of the organization's risk exposure. Multivariate analyses, on the other hand, are necessary to the development of reliable explanation-sourced forward-looking prediction of likelihood and severity of individual risk types. The basic tenets of modern measurement theory[4] stipulate the use of multiple indicators in situations where the phenomenon of interest is illusive in nature (i.e., the so-called "latent" or unobservable constructs) or when no single indicator is a perfect predictor of the outcome of interest. With that in mind, multivariate statistical analyses can be thought of as a family of mathematical techniques designed to simultaneously estimate the effects of multiple measures, in such a way as to allow to: 1. take into account possible cross-variable interdependencies, and 2. quantify the net effect that can be attributed to each measure. In a context of a specific risk type, such as exposure to securities class action litigation, multivariate analyses will yield insights that are both maximally complete (given data limitations), while containing minimum amount of explanatory redundancies. Hence extended over a number of different risk types, i.e., multi-source data analysis, multivariate analytical techniques will yield maximally explanatory and the most accurate predictive capability. In this book, multivariate statistical modeling will be jointly referred to as *Predictive Analytics* (PA). Figure 6.6 offers a graphical summary of generalized predictive analytical risk estimation processes.

---

[4] *Measurement theory* is a branch of applied mathematics, often used in data analysis. Its basic premise is that measurements (defined as a process of assigning numbers or other symbols to entities in such a way that relationships of those numbers or symbols reflect relationships of the attributes of entities being measured) are not the same as attributes being measured, thus in order to draw conclusions about attributes one must take into account the nature of the correspondence between attributes and their measurements.

Figure 6.6
Predictive Analytical Process

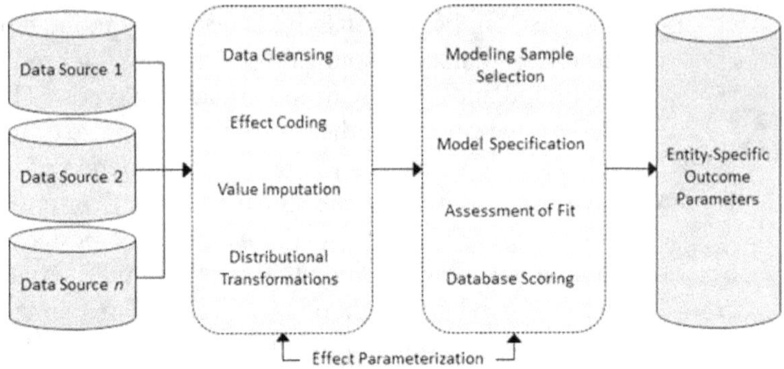

- *Qualitative estimation of risk types for which no reliable quantitative data exists.*
  Recently, a number of organizations became increasingly concerned with a threat of pandemic, which is an outbreak of an infectious disease, infecting humans and causing serious illness that spreads easily across a large area, such as a continent or worldwide. There is very limited, at best, data available to use as basis for estimating likelihood and severity of a major epidemic, such as the much talked about avian flu, yet to a number of organizations (particularly healthcare providers who would incur a heightened inflow of patients while facing their own staffing shortages) this is a risk worth considering. In situations such as that and similar, the requisite likelihood and severity estimates need to be derived via alternative means, the most appropriate of which is the Delphi method. Also known as 'jury of expert opinion', this approach takes advantage of a cross-section of subject matter experts by funneling their judgment and experience into stress-tested set of qualitative estimates. Hence in this book, qualitative risk assessment will be referred to as *Delphi Approximations* (DA), graphically depicted in Figure 6.7.

Figure 6.7
Delphi Approximations

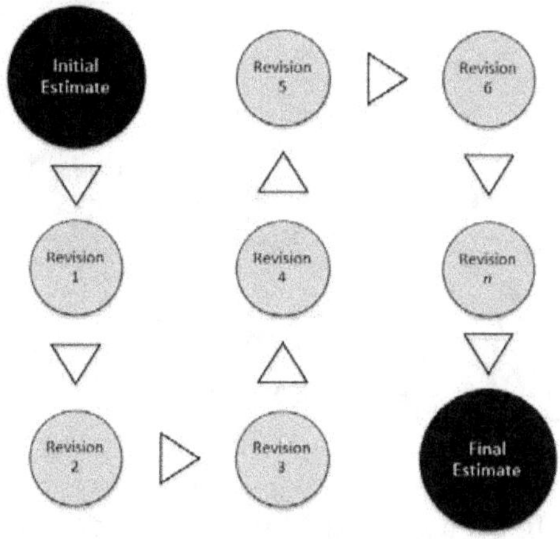

❖ *Estimation of cross-risk interrelationships, supporting system-wide propagation of future changes.*
As noted earlier, the individually estimated risk types are subsequently integrated into an overall system combining risk type impact enumeration with the assessment of interdependencies among the individual risks. Furthermore, in order to be able to accommodate the ongoing updates called for by the analytical approach discussed in this book, the risk assessment system needs to be capable of propagating changes to one or more "connections" onto the entire network. Consider Figure 6.8.

Figure 6.8
Hypothetical Bayesian Risk Network

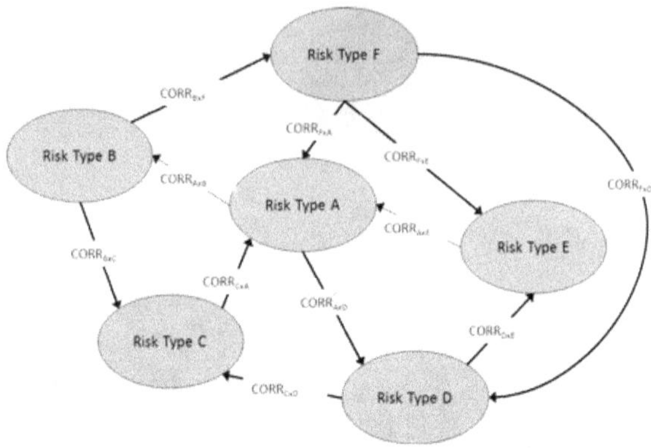

In the hypothetical risk network depicted above, the individual risks—Risk Type A, Risk Type B, etc.—are connected by lines showing their interdependencies, along with magnitudes of those interdependencies ($CORR_{AxB}$, etc.). The interdependencies are measured in terms of bivariate correlations, which are non-directional. The arrow-expressed directional cross risk type connections denote future propagation of changes to any of the bivariate relationships onto the entire network. This is a basic outline of a Bayesian belief network, which is the methodological foundation of the cross risk type integration framework discussed later. Consequently, the overall risk type integration methodology will be referred to as *Bayesian Networks* (BN).

Process vs. Method

The overall risk analytical process discussed earlier (see Figure 5.1) suggests a deterministic lock-step progression of *exploratory analysis* being followed by *explanation*, then *prediction* and then *validation*. However, in view of considerable differences separating Predictive Analytics (PA), Delphi Approximations (DA) and Bayesian Networks (BN), the meaning of each of the analytical stages will take on a significantly different meaning for each of the three methodologies.

Figure 6.9
Predictive Analytics vs. Delphi vs. Bayesian

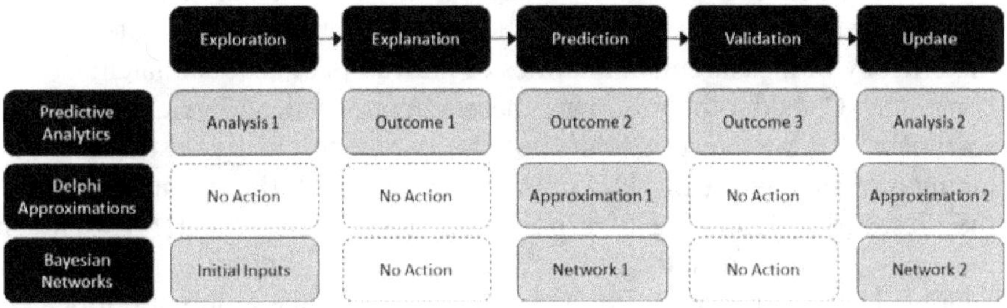

As highlighted in Figure 6.9, the fundamental difference between PA, DA and BN, in the context of the data analytical process, is that Predictive Analytics is a continuous endeavor while Delphi Approximations and Bayesian Networks are in essence discrete events. More specifically, within the realm of PA, data and the analysis of it are two separate entities, where externally sourced data is gradually transformed into evidence and knowledge, with the help of data analytical techniques. Stated differently, data and data analytic techniques are independent of one another, which is in contrast to DA and BN, where data and the analysis of it are indistinguishable from one another. In the case of Delphi Approximations, there is no external data—instead, it is created by the technique itself. In fact, DA is synonymous with outcome parameterization by means of subjective estimates, while PA is synonymous with parameterization of external outcomes based on objective, past frequencies.

Bayesian Networks' development structure follows yet a different pattern. As an integrative framework amalgamating outcomes of Predictive Analytics and Delphi Approximations, it becomes "active" when either PA or DA make appropriate inputs—or more specifically, likelihood and severity estimates—available. The initial network (Network 1 in Figure 6.9) is completed when either evidence-based, or objective (Predictive Analytics) or belief-based, or subjective (Delphi Approximations) probabilities are made available.

Considering the substantial differences in the development paths separating PA, DA and BN, it is important to ascertain their respective validity and reliability. The next section considers these notions in more detail.

Validity & Reliability

The concepts of validity and reliability are often used somewhat interchangeably, mostly because both are tools that are useful in ascertaining the efficacy of measurement qualities of indicators of abstract, latent constructs. Consider the following measurement challenge: A group of political scientists is trying to estimate the possibility of a politically destabilizing event taking place at a particular part of the world in the next 12 months. What are their respective definitions of a 'politically destabilizing event'? Restated in more operational terms, the problem at hand can be phrased as follows: What tangible benchmarks or indicators could be used by the group of political scientists to estimate the probability of a politically destabilizing event taking place in the part of the word of interest, in the next 12 months? Graphically, this can be expressed as follows:

Figure 6.10
Latent Construct Measurement

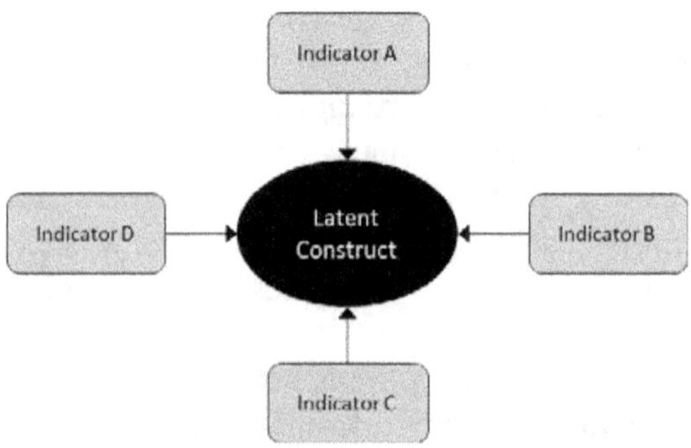

In essence, the challenge of quantifying the likelihood or the severity of somewhat abstractly expressed events is twofold: First, it is of identifying the right indicators (Indicator A, Indicator B, etc., in Figure 6.10), which are the tangible, easier to assess proxies for the event in question. Second, it is that of ascertaining the accuracy of those indicators—in other words, how good a proxy Indicator A is the latent construct of interest. These considerations are of considerable importance to the informational robustness of Delphi Approximations.

There are two distinct dimensions characterizing the quality of measurement of the Latent Construct depicted in Figure 6.10—reliability and validity. *Reliability* captures the repeatability or consistency of a particular operationalization. A measure (such as Indicator A or Indicator B) is considered reliable if it gives us the same result over and over again, of course assuming that what we're measuring (Latent Construct) is not changing. Conceptually, reliability can be thought of as a ratio of true level of the measure" to the "entire measure. In practice, however, the 'true' measure is rarely known hence in an applied sense the best way of estimating reliability is to express it as a correlation among multiple observations of the same measure. There are several different types of reliability—internal consistency, test-retest reliability, parallel forms and inter-rater reliability—however, in the context of risk measurement it is the inter-rater reliability that is of greatest importance.

In the context of Delphi Approximations, the *inter-rater reliability* is operationalized by correlating single item responses across responders. Responses of all experts to Indicator A would be correlated to estimate the reliability of Indicator A, responses of all experts to Indicator B would be correlated to estimate the reliability of Indicator B, and so on. Computationally, this would be accomplished as follows (the following assumes that individual expert's responses are continuous—if not, an appropriate non-continuous measure based coefficient of correlation, such as Kendall's tau or Spearman's rho, should be used):

$$IRR = \sqrt{\frac{\sum_{i=1}^{n}(X_i - \bar{X})^2}{n-1}}$$

where,

IRR is Inter-Rater Reliability
X_i is response of expert 1
$\bar{X}$ is the mean

As a general rule, to conclude that there indeed is a sufficient level of inter-rater reliability, the following decision rule can be employed:

$$|IRR| \geq \frac{2}{\sqrt{n}}$$

where,

n is the number of individual experts/opinions

For example, if IRR = 0.80 and there are 15 individual experts, then the measurement can be deemed reliable if IRR is 0.52 or higher.

The other of the two key aspects of latent construct measurement is *validity*, which captures the degree to which the construct's conceptualization and operationalization are in agreement. Simply put, it is the quality of measurement. Conceptually, validity is both broader and a somewhat more elusive idea, hence it can be looked at from a number of different angles, which reflect two key underlying questions: 1. Is the operationalization a good reflection of the construct? 2. How will the operationalization perform? These two broad questions can be broken down into several, more specific question-expressed types of validity considerations:

Table 6.1
Types of Validity

Type	Description
Face Validity	On their face value, are the indicators (Indicator A, Indicator B, etc., in Figure 3.5) as a whole a good reflection of the latent construct?
Content Validity	Is the informational content of individual indicators in keeping with the meaning of the latent construct?
Discriminant Validity	Are these measures of the latent construct operationally different from other sets of measures?
Predictive Validity	Will the operationalization be able to predict the outcome of interest with a reasonable degree of accuracy?
Convergent Validity	Do predictions generated by the operationalization converge with other, related predictions?
Concurrent Validity	Can the operationalization distinguish among types of outcomes?

Clearly, validity-related considerations represent a mix of qualitative and quantifiable considerations. The goal behind the assessment of Delphi Approximations related validity considerations is not necessarily to attempt to provide a numeric assessment of the different faces of validity outlined above. Rather, it is to draw attention to potential pitfalls and thus to invite a thorough due diligence of the measurement approach.

In terms of more tangible outcomes, a thorough consideration of the two key aspects of latent construct measurement—validity and reliability—will contribute to more accurate estimates. More specifically, the measurement of risk types for which no readily available quantitative data is available will be expressed as an additive composite of two components: a true estimated value and an error associated with that estimate. Formally, that can be expressed as follows:

Risk Type Estimate = True Value + Random Error

More specifically, the likelihood and severity of occurrence of an event of interest can be expressed as:

$$\text{Likelihood Risk Type}_A = \text{variability}(\text{Risk Type}_A\ \text{Frequency}) + \text{error}$$
$$\text{Severity Risk Type}_A = \text{variability}(\text{Risk Type}_A\ \text{Cost}) + \text{error}$$

Organizational Resilience

Resilience as an Emerging Organizational Competency

Any organization that operates fixed physical facilities needs to be prepared to mitigate the potentially destructive effects of environmental factors, such as severe storms, earthquakes, fires, floods and other natural disasters. Some of those events are fairly predictable, in the sense of expected occurrence – for instance, each year several hurricanes typically threaten some parts of southeastern United States. Some other events, however, might be somewhat less expected – for instance, although about 83% of Nepal is covered by mountains, the occurrence of floods in that country is about 2.5 times the occurrence of landslides. In addition, organizations also need to be prepared to respond to manmade crises, which can include events such as major labor disputes, corruption or corporate governance scandals. Some of the likely consequences of natural and manmade catastrophes can be managed by processes discussed in the previous section (Risk Management), but the potential scale and duration of some such events dictates that organizations develop means to 1. absorb those disturbances, and 2. return to normal (operating conditions). The economic importance of developing a sound organizational resilience 'buffer' are clearly illustrated by the aggregate costs of 2012 natural catastrophes which totaled about $140 billion, of which only $45 billion were insured. Stated differently, roughly ⅔ of the economic cost of those events had to have been absorbed by the effected entities. Organizational Resilience (OR) is the emerging capability of business and other organizations which encompasses planning, preparation, control and recovery processes and means aimed at enabling an organization to 'bounce back' from a large scale natural disaster or manmade crisis.

As discussed in Chapter 1, OR is a relatively new organizational competency representing the coming together of originally distinct fields of 'disaster risk reduction' (which includes 'emergency management') and 'business continuity planning'. When considered as either a subject of academic inquiry or a practical application OR is still in its infancy, thus it is important to look at that aspect of organizational threat management through the prism of the two distinct fields of 'business continuity' and 'emergency' management. These two 'component areas' of OR fully capture the scope and the depth of that important organizational function: the former addresses the full range of planning that is essential to assuring the continuity of organizational functioning in the face of a disabling event, while the latter details the mechanisms, skills and processes organizations need to develop in order to effectively manage emergencies.

Practicing Resilience

As a new and still evolving field, Organizational Resilience (OR) is a product of gradual maturing and coalescing of several disciplines driven and shaped by numerous standards-minded professional organizations. Summarized below are the leading professional organizations that contribute to the ongoing development of different elements of comprising the broad field of OR.

Business Continuity Institute (www.thebci.org)
The Business Continuity Institute (BCI) was established in 1994 to enable members to obtain guidance and support from fellow business continuity practitioners. Through its certification scheme, the Institute recognized professional status to its members by attesting to the members' competence to carry out business continuity management (BCP) to a consistent high standard. The BCI has over 4,000 members spread over 85+ countries.

DRI International (www.drii.org)
DRI International was founded in 1988 as the Disaster Recovery Institute in order to develop a base of knowledge in contingency planning and the management of disaster related threats. In a manner similar to BCI, it offers recognized professional status to its more than 3,500 individuals throughout the world, through its four levels of professional certification.

International Association of Emergency Managers (www.iaem.com)
The International Association of Emergency Managers (IAEM) is a non-profit educational organization dedicated to promoting the goals of saving lives and protecting property during emergencies and disasters.

International Consortium for Organizational Resilience (www.theicor.org)
The International Consortium for Organizational Resilience (ICOR) was founded in 2005 with a mission to integrate the many silos, industries or separate bodies of knowledge that together support resiliency into one profession entitled organizational resilience; in a sense, it was meant to supplant the more narrowly focused BCI, DRI and IAEM. The Consortium provides a multi-level credentialing program that is meant to address every career level: from entry level to existing practitioners to senior business and government leadership.

7

Business Continuity Planning

The vast majority of business organizations are characterized as 'going concerns', which is a basic declaration of a firm's intention to keep running its operations without the threat of liquidation for the foreseeable future, usually regarded as at least within 12 months. At its core, *going concern* is primarily a financial accounting consideration as it is a basic assumption underpinning the preparation of financial statements, reflecting the conceptual framework of the International Financial Reporting Standards[1].

When considered from a broader, ecological perspective, remaining a going concern can be seen as an expression of the most fundamental of business needs: to survive. Threats to organizational survival encompass a wide spectrum of factors ranging from broad economic, market and competitive forces to distinct dangers stemming from disruptive events. While it is the responsibility of an organization's strategic planning function to craft and implement plans that will materially reduce the threat of economic, market and competitive forces, attenuating threats posed by disruptive events is the responsibility of organizational resilience management. Business continuity planning is an important part of that critical organizational function.

---

[1] A set of international accounting standards stating how particular types of transactions and other events should be reported in financial statements, issued by the International Accounting Standards Board; the standards were established in order to have a common accounting language, so business and accounts can be understood from company to company and country to country.

Business Continuity Primer

As a starting point, let us define *business continuity planning* as the capability of an organization to plan for and respond to incidents and disruptions in order to continue business operations at acceptable, pre-defined levels. Although originally focused on electronic infrastructure, now that scope encompasses a wide variety of incidents and disruptions, not just those involving computer hardware systems, software applications and data. *Business continuity planning* (BCP), on the other hand, are those management and governance processes which allow this capability to be fully developed and incorporated into an organization's management fabric. At its core, BCP encompasses an enterprise-wide program that identifies potential threats to an organization as well as their associated impacts, and provides a framework for building organizational resilience.

One of the operative words in the above definition is 'program'. Business continuity needs to be a *program* and not just a project or a plan. The initial design and implementation effort can certainly begin as a project, but needs to evolve into an ongoing and sustainable *business continuity program* (BCPM). It is understood that the BCP should be properly supported by senior management, appropriately positioned within the organization, and adequately resourced.

As briefly pointed out in the opening section, the totality of threats confronting an organization is very broad and diverse as it encompasses economic factors, such as the general 'health' of the economy, strategic choices and actions of competitors, in addition to a wide array of disruptive events. Given that, it is important to note that business continuity planning, and the broader organizational resilience efforts are focused explicitly on managing the impact of disruptive events. Although a broad category in itself, *disruptive events* represent only a subset of the totality of efforts geared toward assuring that an organization will continue as a going concern. That is an important distinction to keep in mind to assure proper contextualization of the notion of 'business continuity' as used here. Figure 7.1 offers a graphical representation of the scope of business continuity as a part of organizational resilience efforts, set in the broader context of organizational survival. As shown there, though organizational resilience, and strategic efficacy, and systemic contributors (and possibly other broad factors) all play a role in ascertaining organizational survival, business continuity addresses only those threats that fall within the scope of organizational resilience.

Figure 7.1
Business Continuity as Organizational Survival vs. Resilience

Keeping the distinction illustrated in Figure 7.1 in mind, now consider Figure 7.2 below. That summary diagram provides a good overview of where business continuity fits into the enterprise risk management equation. In this chapter and next, our focus will be on the right side or 'managing abnormal threats' portion of the road map depicted in Figure 7.2. We will spend time reviewing the best practices and operational application associated with some key business continuity, emergency management and crisis communication concepts. However, we need to make sure that we do not lose sight of the left side, or 'managing everyday threats' portion of the road map. Integration of these two components is essential for both an effective ERM (discussed in Chapter 4) and business continuity programs.

Figure 7.2
ERM Road Map Diagram

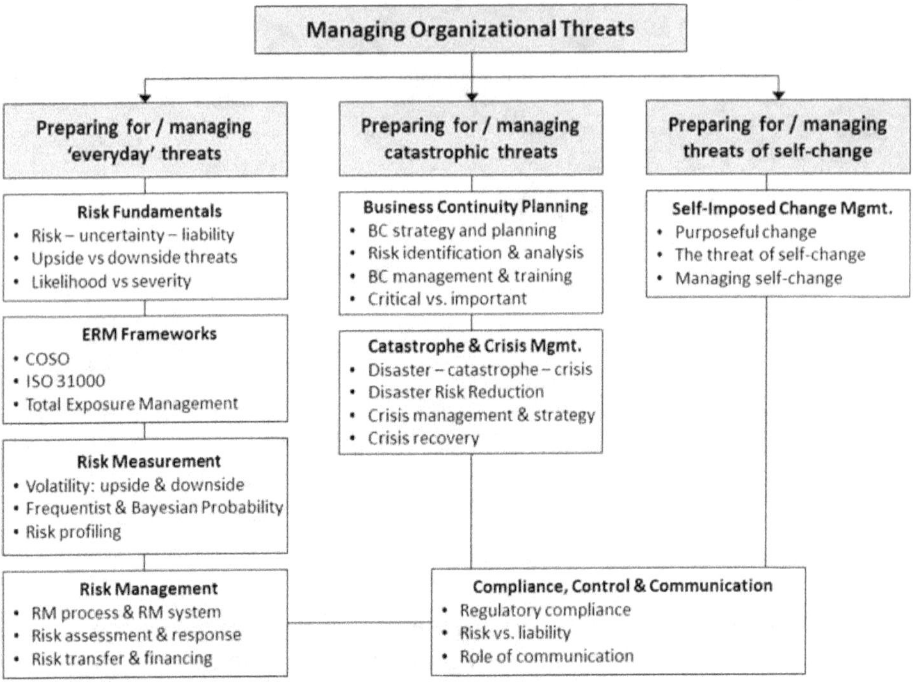

The Historical Perspective

Business continuity has its roots in the early to mid-1970s when companies began taking on the challenge of protecting their major investments in expensive mainframe computer systems. The focus was initially placed on data backup and then on the recovery and restoration of entire computer systems. These early developments provided the foundation for what would later become disaster recovery, or technology recovery.

During the mid-to-late 1980s several professional groups were created to support and formalize the disaster recovery activities. These included the Association of Contingency Planners (ACP) and the Disaster Recovery Institute International (DRII), referenced above. Later on, the Business Continuity Institute (BCI) was established to primarily support the activities of the international community. To this day, the DRII and BCI continue to be the main professional institutions for business continuity and disaster recovery.

Also during this period, companies such as IBM, EDS (Hewlett-Packard) and Comdisco (SunGard) began offering disaster recovery services to their customers. These services continued to be concentrated in the recovery and restoration of systems and data. It was not until the 1990s at which point companies began to focus on the response, recovery and restoration of the entire business to include people and processes and not just the technology infrastructure. This change in focus was underscored by several significant events including the economic developments of the 1990s and 2000s, the September 11th tragedy, the avian/swine flu outbreaks, as well as several major hurricanes.

The Need for Business Continuity

A discussion of business continuity is not complete without introducing statistics on the number of business failures that result from disasters. An online sampling of websites and white papers includes the following statistics for 2012[2]:

- In the past two years, over 50% of businesses experienced an unforeseen interruption, and the vast majority (81%) of these interruptions caused businesses to be closed one or more days.
- For those businesses without detailed plans, 80% suffering a major disaster go out of business in three years, while 40% of businesses that experience a critical IT failure go out of business within one year. In the case of suffering a fire, 44% of enterprises fail to reopen and 33% of these failed to survive beyond 3 years.
- For companies that lost their data center for 10 days or more due to a disaster, 93% filed for bankruptcy within one year of the disaster.
- Companies that are not able to resume operations within ten days (of a disaster hit) are not likely to survive.

While a number of industry experts debate the validity of the disaster failure statistics referenced above, one factor does remain conclusive. That is, disaster-related failures for businesses without contingency plans are significant.

---

[2] Sourced from Pivotal IT (2012), *10 Backup and Disaster Recovery Statistics You Must Know*, an industry research report.

In a 2014 report[3] published by the Business Continuity Institute (BCI) and the British Standards Institute (BSI), a number of business leaders were polled to identify what they felt were the top ten threats to their business. Not surprisingly, the list included unplanned IT and telecom outages, cyber attacks, data breaches, adverse weather, interruption to utility supply, fire, security breaches, health & safety incidents, acts of terrorism, and new laws or regulations. The BCI/BSI study went on to indicate that over three quarters (77%) of business leaders said they fear the possibility of an unplanned IT and telecom outages, while 73% worry about the possibility of a cyber-attack or data breach. The report has also identified long-term trends, with 73% seeing the use of the internet for malicious attacks as a major threat that needs to be closely monitored, and 63% feeling the same way about the influence of social media. Adverse weather also moved up the list of threats with 57% of respondents expressing concern or extreme concern. According to Howard Kerr of the BSI, 'At a time when changing climatic, social, political and economic situations are forcing organizations to be nimble in adapting to novel threats, it is essential to learn from others experience and best practice. Developing the resilience of networks, services and business critical information must be an integral part of an organization's wider business resilience strategy. By putting in place a framework based on risk standards, you will be able to identify, prioritize and manage the range of threats to your business more effectively and keep your stakeholders reassured.'

There are then a number of factors in play that combine to justify the corporate investment in a BCP. Providing a more resilient operational infrastructure allows for the:

- Protection of employees, property, equipment and other organizational assets;
- Compliance with legal and regulatory requirements;
- Continuation of market share and revenue during a disabling event;
- Maintenance of the corporate brand and reputation.

Business Continuity Program – A General Outline

On a macro level, the business continuity program (BCPM) in most organizations is comprised of three major components: *emergency management*, *technology recovery* and *business resumption*. Companies may

---

[3] Horizon Scan (2014), *Business Continuity Institute and British Standards Institute.*

have different names for these components; however for consistency purposes I will use this terminology throughout this and the next chapter. A high-level summary of some of the primary responsibilities that fall within each of the three components is shown in Table 7.1.

Table 7.1

Components of a Business Continuity Program[4]

Emergency Management	Technology Recovery	Business Resumption
Evacuation & Accountability; Availability & Tracking; Emergency Notification System; Incident Management Plans; Special Scenario Plans; Building D/R Infrastructure; Live Incident Response Process; Recovery Workspace; Command / Control / Communication; Emergency Agency Integration; Testing; Training & Awareness	Systems Mapping; Systems Criticality Assessment; SDLC Process; Technology Recovery Strategy; Technology Recovery Plans; Data Center D/R Infrastructure; Live System Response Process; Vendor D/R Integration; Cyber Security / Data Breach; Testing	Corporate D/R - BCP Strategy; Corporate D/R – BCP Governance; Workforce Mobility Program; Business Impact Analysis; Hazards / Vulnerability Analysis; Corporate Policies; Corporate Plans; Business Area Plans; Vendor D/R Integration; Testing; Client RFPs; External Program Assessments; Training & Awareness

It is important to note that for a continuity program to be effective, each of these three program components must be fully developed and integrated, which brings up an important question: How and where does it fit within the corporate Enterprise Risk Management (ERM) structure?

The answer to the question is not as simple as one might expect. The initial response is that the BCPM should roll up under the Chief Risk Officer (CRO) function or its equivalent in the organization. However, some

---

[4] Sourced from Hiles, A. (2014), *Business Continuity Management: Global Best Practices*, 4th ed., Rothstein Publishing.

companies have yet to establish a CRO position. In these organizations, the de facto CRO may be the COO or the Chief Auditor so it's fairly common for the business continuity function to report to one of these entities. Adding to that disarray, there are elements of the overall business continuity program that may be subject to oversight by heads of Legal, Finance, Facilities or IT departments.

In 2014, Continuity Insights in partnership with audit firm KPMG performed a global business continuity benchmark study[5] involving over 400 publically and privately held companies/organizations. One of the survey questions asked was focused on what C-level (e.g. Chief Executive Officer, Chief Financial Officer, etc.) executive had the ultimate responsibility for the business continuity program. The responses were as follows:

- CEO/President ≈ 17%
- COO ≈ 14%
- CIO ≈ 13%
- CRO ≈ 11%
- CFO ≈ 10%
- Other ≈ 35% (Legal, Compliance, Security, etc.)

One of the observations from this survey is that the BCP can have a wide variety of nesting spots within the corporate hierarchy. However, to be effective and ultimately successful, it should:

- Be enterprise-wide in scope with senior-management level accountability;
- Have direct access to senior management;
- Be fully supported with financial and operational resources;
- Incorporate emerging disciplines in addition to IT and facilities, such as security and communications.

[5] Continuity Insights and KPMG (2014), *Global BCM Benchmarking Study*.

Designing an Organizational Continuity Function

Earlier, I made the point that business continuity needs to be an ongoing, sustainable program and not just a project or a plan. The development of that function can certainly start out as a project; however it is essential that the end product be continuously evaluated, enhanced and exercised. As is the case with other organizational functions, there are numerous frameworks that can be used to guide the process – one such widely used Business Continuity Program (BCPM) function development process[6] is as follows:

- Clearly communicate the need for establishing of a business continuity program.
- Secure organizational agreement and commitment.
- Plan the BCPM project.
- Establish the BCPM organization.
- Identify critical processes and infrastructure
- Identify options for continuity and recovery and defining continuity strategy.
- Craft the business continuity plan.
- Develop and implement BCPM maintenance and audit procedures.
- Develop and implement training and testing programs.

The DRII and the BCI have expanded upon the elements in the above cycle to come up with a 'common body of knowledge' in the form of professional practices for their respective business continuity practitioners. Since these professional practices are relatively similar, we have selected the ten DRII principles for use and reference as follows[7]:

1. *Program Initiation and Management.* Establish the need for a business continuity planning process, including resilience strategies, recovery objectives, business continuity and incident management plans; obtain management support and organize and manage the formulation of the function.

---

[6] Hiles, A. (2014), *Business Continuity Management: Global Best Practices,* 4th ed., Rothstein Publishing, p. 9.

[7] DRI International (2012), *80 Professional Practices for Business Continuity Planners,* version 1.

2. *Risk Evaluation and Control.* Identify the risks/threats and vulnerabilities that are both inherent and acquired which can adversely affect the organization and its resources, or impact the organization's image. Assess these threats and vulnerabilities as to the likelihood that they would occur and the potential level of impact that would result. Recommend additional controls, mitigations or processes to increase the organization's resiliency from the most commonly occurring and/or highest impact events.

3. *Business Impact Analysis.* Quantify financial and other impacts on the organization and its business processes resulting from disruptions and disaster scenarios; identify critical activities and functions, their recovery priorities, and inter-dependencies. Establish time sensitive processes and the requirements to recover them in the timeframe that is acceptable to the organization.

4. *Business Continuity Strategies.* Identify available continuity and recovery strategies for the entity's operations and technology from the data collected during the BIA and Risk Evaluation. Approve and fund these strategies to meet both the recovery time and recovery point objectives identified in the BIA. Perform a cost benefit analysis on the recommended strategies to align the cost of implementing the strategy against the assets at risk.

5. *Emergency Response and Operations.* Develop and implement procedures for response and stabilizing the situation following an incident or event, including establishing and managing an incident command center. Document how the organization will respond to emergencies in a coordinated, timely and effective manner to address life safety and stabilization of emergency situations.

6. *Plan Implementation and Documentation.* Develop and implement a set of plans that cover the processes and procedures associated with the organization's continuity strategies and detailed response and recovery activities.

7. *Awareness and Training Programs.* Create a program to establish and maintain corporate awareness about Business continuity

planning and train staff so that they are prepared to respond during an event.

8. *Business Continuity Plan Exercise, Audit and Maintenance.* Establish an exercise, testing, maintenance and audit program. The tracking and documentation of these activities: provides an evaluation of the on-going state of readiness, allows for continuous improvement of recovery capabilities, and ensures that plans remain current and relevant. Establish an audit process that will validate the plans are complete, accurate and in compliance with organizational goals and industry standards as appropriate.

9. *Crisis Communications*. Provide the framework to identify, develop, communicate, and exercise a crisis communications plan. A crisis communications plan addresses the need for effective and timely communication between the organization and all the stakeholders impacted or involved during the response and recovery efforts.

10. *Coordination with External Agencies*. Establish policies and procedures to coordinate response, continuity and recovery activities with external agencies at the local, regional and national levels while ensuring compliance with applicable statutes and regulations.

All of these DRII principles probably deserve their own chapters and in fact, the next chapter of this book will focus on Emergency Response and Operations. For now, let us focus on three of the foundational principles of business continuity planning: 1. Risk Evaluation and Control, 2. Business Impact Analysis, and 3. Business Continuity Strategies.

Risk Evaluation and Control

As previously mentioned, risk evaluation involves the identification of threats to an organization and the estimation of the likelihood of their occurrence, as well as the determination of those mitigating controls that are or should be in place. This includes risks that are under an organization's control and those that are not. By identifying and ranking disruptive events, it is easier to understand the exposure to those threats and develop mitigation strategies where necessary, or to make a conscious decision to accept threats for which mitigating actions are not deemed necessary. In that sense, threat assessment represents due diligence that enables an organization's management team to safeguard the assets and operations of the company.

The DRII-recommended[8] macro level threat assessment approach that many organizations follow includes:

- Working with senior management to establish the organization's risk appetite/tolerance levels and to agree upon a standardized risk assessment methodology;
- Developing and implementing information gathering activities across the organization to identify threats/risks and the entity's vulnerabilities;
- Determining probabilities and impact of the threats/risks identified;
- Evaluating the effectiveness of the current controls and safeguards in place;
- Identifying business resiliency strategies to control, mitigate, accept or take advantage of the potential impact of the risk/threat or reduce the organization's vulnerabilities;
- Documenting and presenting risk/threat/vulnerability assessment and recommendations to senior management for approval.

Risk evaluations can take several different shapes and forms. One particular type of risk evaluation that is common in the business continuity world is the Hazards and Vulnerability Assessment, or HVA.

The purpose of an HVA is to identify the many types of physical incidents and emergencies that could affect an organization, the projected impact of each type of event and the resources that are available to respond to the emergency. The HVA focuses primarily on natural hazards as well other threats to security and health, be they natural or man-made.

For instance, a healthcare company in the northeastern United States initially took a siloed, insurance-based approach to risk evaluation and control. The landscape began to change with some of the regulatory and legislative developments relative to healthcare, both on the local and national level, beginning first with regulatory demands imposed by the US Health Insurance Portability and Accountability Act of 1996, commonly known as HIPAA.

---

[8] DRI International (2012), *Professional Practices for Business Continuity Planners,* version 1.

During this time period, the company transitioned to more of an ERM-based approach, although this continues to be a work-in-progress. Part of this transition process is how they identify and assess risks, which is now being done on two levels summarized in Table 7.2 below:

Table 7.2
Sample Risk Evaluation – Health Insurance

Description	Risk Evaluation Methodology	Scope
Corporate – Level Threat Categories	Own Risk and Solvency Assessment (ORSA)	Account Pricing; Investment Portfolio; Regulatory Requirements and Compliance; Medical Cost Utilization; Data Integrity; Cyber Security/Data Breach Protection; Reputation, etc.
Operational – Level Threat Categories	Hazards and Vulnerability Assessment (HVA)	Workplace Security/Safety; Utilities Infrastructure; Severe Weather; Infectious Disease Outbreak; Supply Chain Events, etc.

Business Impact Analysis

The Business Impact Analysis or BIA, is a management-level analysis that quantifies the financial and other losses of an organization's business processes, determines their criticality, and then establishes the acceptable recovery objectives. The results of the BIA provide the basis for developing continuity strategies and associated plans; the analysis' objectives can be summarized as follows:

- Prioritize the availability and recovery order of business processes and information.
- Calculate the cost of downtime to the business.
- Identify and prioritize the critical business functions and key dependencies.
- Link applications to the prioritized business processes.
- Determine and establish consensus on the Recovery Time Objective and the Recovery Point Objective

In essence, BIA should answer two very basic questions:

1. When will you give it (defined as service, functionality, capability, process power, etc.) to me?
2. In what state will you give it to me (defined as complete or incomplete with the degree of completeness defined in terms of data loss)?

The basic evaluative metrics for answering the above two questions are the *Recovery Time Objective* (RTO) and the *Recovery Point Objective* (RPO). The RTO is defined as the point in time when a business disruption will have a significant impact on business operations. Significant impact may be a quantitative measure, qualitative measure or both. The RTO is basically the time by which critical business operations need to be restored. As might be expected, Recovery Time Objectives can vary widely across industries, organizations and business processes – for hospitals and utilities those objectives may be minutes, for financial service firms minutes and hours, while it could be hours and days for some manufacturing firms.

As an example, RTOs in the healthcare insurance industry are often arranged in 'buckets': the first bucket is typically 8-24 hours; the second is usually 24-36 hours, the third 36–48 hours, and so forth. Again, these time windows will vary by organization. Business processes falling within the range of 8 to 24 hours include corporate and emergency communications, call center operations, customer internet accessibility, critical-care health management programs, cash management and investments. Embedded within each RTO range is a component for technology, workspace and business process recovery, thus it is very important that those objective be reviewed and approved by senior management as they serve as the basis for business recovery planning.

The Recover Point Objective, on the other hand, is that point in the past to which recovered systems, applications and data will be restored. Examples of RPOs may include the close of business on the previous day, the start of the day, etc. Like RTOs, RPOs will vary by industry, organization and business process: In the financial services industry one expectation may be the recovery of systems without the loss of data, while in other industries, it may be acceptable to recover to a previous backup period supplemented by data re-entry and reprocessing. One way to address this type of exposure is by having a robust and well running data backup strategy. To that end, both sets of objectives must also be viewed in tandem, as clearly defined RTOs and RPOs will provide objectivity in assessing the compatibility of the required recovery solutions within the existing infrastructure and corporate requirements.

The BIA should also identify the dependencies between business processes. These dependencies can be internal (business process and business areas), technology-related (telephony and web technology) or extend outside the enterprise (suppliers and business partners). Examples of external dependencies include parts suppliers for an airline manufacturer and key ingredient sources for a drug company. The point here is that critical dependencies must be accounted for in the BIA and the recovery planning process.

However, it does not end here. The past few years have seen significant increases in internet-based transactions, growing reliance on the 'extended enterprise' model, just-in-time inventories and far-swung supply chains, all of which can have a pronounced effect on recovery expectations. With all of these factors in play, it is important that a company define and document its critical recovery path and associated recovery sequence and that this be understood by the responsible parties. Though that may sound straightforward, in reality it can become quite complicated, especially when multiple business areas and their often-competing priorities are factored-in.

It is also important to acknowledge the difference between a 'critical' and an 'important' function. Two human resources related processes illustrate this idea: Maintaining the capability to process payrolls during a significant event can certainly be considered a critical function, even if this involves manually recreating payroll records from prior period data. Recovering the employee evaluation information, although important, should not be considered a critical function during a significant event. (Unless, of course, it has ramifications in the support of other critical functions.)

Lastly, it is also worthy of note that 'important' business functions can become 'critical' and vice versa. As a result, maintaining and updating a company's criticality assessment should be a dynamic process.

Business Continuity Strategies

Fortunately, most events that may adversely impact business operations are addressed in the emergency management process, especially if the organization has paid attention to the results of their BIA (business impact analysis) and HVA (hazard and vulnerability assessment) and implemented the appropriate infrastructure and systems controls. Very few instances involve disaster declarations and the activation of recovery plans. However, there are occasions where this is still not enough to offset the impact of a significant event and a company will need to go into a recovery mode. During this phase, the company undertakes the recovery of its most mission- critical business operations. The idea is to get things back up and running as soon as possible, even in a reduced operating mode. To do this most effectively requires a considerable amount of front-end assessment and planning.

The following graphic identifies the general sequencing of the transition from incident management to business recovery:

Figure 7.3
Business Continuity Lifecycle

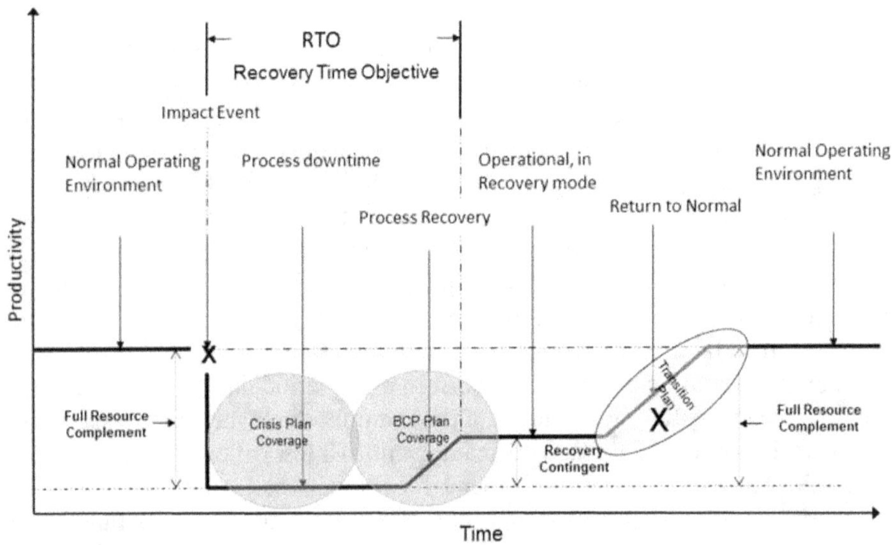

The DRII addresses the development of business continuity strategies as a separate subject area in its Professional Practices. The objective is to leverage the outcome of the BIA and threat assessment to develop and recommend business continuity strategies. The DRII recommends the following five level approach[8]:

- Utilize the data collected during the BIA and Risk Assessment to identify the available continuity and recovery strategies for the business operations that will meet the RTOs and RPOs identified during the BIA process.
- Utilize the data collected during the BIA and Risk Assessment to identify the available continuity and recovery strategies for the

organization's technology that will meet the RTOs and RPOs identified during the BIA process.

- ❖ Consolidate strategies where appropriate to reduce costs and/or complexities.
- ❖ Assess the cost of implementing identified strategies through a cost/benefit analysis.
- ❖ Recommend strategies and obtain approval to implement.

Strategic recovery requirements and alternative options should be evaluated using criteria such as; functionality, cost/benefit analysis, timing considerations and existing mitigation and control measures. This should also include an assessment of internal and external solutions as well technology considerations.

In general, recovery solutions should be capable of supporting the mission critical functions, application and operations; cost effective; flexible; organization-appropriate; capable of supporting business-based recovery time objectives of an organization. Recovery solutions are often categorized into one or more of the following options:

- ❖ Repair and/or rebuild after the event has occurred, with little or no recovery activities.
- ❖ Revert to manual workaround procedures.
- ❖ Initiate reciprocal recovery agreements with other organizations.
- ❖ Utilize the facilities and services of third party BCP providers.
- ❖ Use existing internal space and technology that may be able to partially support a recovery.
- ❖ Develop and activate a dedicated recovery location.
- ❖ Implement a workforce mobility program where employees can work remotely from home.

Like all investment options, business continuity should represent the best value for the money and selecting an appropriate strategy is an essential part of this. The optimum solution may not be a single option but a combination of several options. Some of these recovery options deserve a closer look:

Revert to manual workaround procedures.
Manual options and other workarounds should always be a consideration in the recovery process. However, because of the size and scope of many companies, volumes of transactions, time and service level requirements and technology

considerations manual processing is usually not a primary enterprise-wide option. That is not to say it cannot be part of a business area recovery solution. For example, a significant outage with a company's accounts payable system may be addressed through manual processing including the issuing of checks.

Initiate reciprocal recovery agreements.
On the surface, reciprocal agreements between organizations may seem like a straightforward, cost-effective option but in reality they usually are not. There are just too many variables for reciprocal agreements to be considered as the primary business recovery strategy. Some of these variables include contractual liabilities, equipment and systems incompatibility, insufficient processing capacity, access and usage constraints, confidentiality and security considerations. There are however, some areas where reciprocal agreements may be valid. Companies often enter into these types of agreements for post-evacuation employee assembly areas. One other reciprocal option is across business areas within the same firm, where there is a greater control over the environment and changes can be coordinated.

Use alternate site of business facility.
Use of an alternate site or business facility can take a couple of different forms. It may be an external location at a commercial recovery services provider or it could be designated space within a company-owned facility. Another option is mobile recovery, where the recovery infrastructure and components are established at or near the impacted area through freestanding trailers or mobile recovery units. Commercial recovery locations usually come in three forms:

1. *Hot Sites* - An alternate facility that already has in place the computer hardware, storage devices, telecommunications, data and environmental infrastructure as well as the employee workspace required to immediately recover critical business functions or information systems. Hot sites are often exact duplicates of production sites in terms of process capability and data and may in fact include monitoring capability such that when a production site is lost, the hot site automatically takes over. The RTO for true hot sites often is less than 4 hours as is the RPO.

2. *Warm Sites* - An alternate processing and workspace location that is equipped with some computer hardware and storage devices, as well as communications interfaces, electrical and environmental

conditioning that is only capable of providing a backup operation after additional provisioning: data recovery software or customization is performed. While a warm site may be configured just like the production site that it supports, it typically requires that a restoration process be performed to update this site with the information from the production site that it supports. Warm site recovery RTOs can vary but are typically in the range of 12 to 48 hours.

3. *Cold Sites* - An alternate facility that has in place the environmental infrastructure required to recover critical business functions or information systems, but does not have any pre-installed computer hardware, storage devices, telecommunications equipment, communication lines, employee workspace, etc. These must be provisioned at time of disaster. The provisioning process typically consists of equipment that is 'drop shipped' to this location via prior agreement with an equipment provider. Cold sites are most effective when the RTO can be measured in days (48 hours or two or more days).

Some of the considerations associated with identifying and selecting an alternate recovery site include cost, capacity requirements, occupancy period and geographic location. A few observations about external recovery workspace are in order.

First of all, under some third-party contractual arrangements, companies can take advantage of recovery locations that include employee workspace, pre-imaged PCs, telephone services, network connectivity as well as other amenities. The idea being that impacted employees could be relocated to these recovery seats and resume working with minimal downtime. (Some of the local recovery services providers have facilities that can accommodate several hundred employees.) This concept certainly sounds appealing, but there are certain elements that deserve closer scrutiny. One initial consideration is the cost of a recovery workspace agreement, which can start at several thousand dollars a month and quickly grow higher, depending upon a company's requirements. Another equally important practical consideration is reflected in an idea known as 'seat subscription'. With a finite number of available seats, fluctuating demand, and the goal to be profitable, recovery services providers have formulas for subscribing their seats, and those formulas commonly allow over - subscription. Typically, that translates into a per seat subscription rate of about 5-to-1 up to as many as 15-to-1, which, when coupled with a common service provision of 'first come, first serve' can create considerable recover uncertainties. I should point out that the recovery seat allocation is based on the timing of companies' disaster declarations, which means that during a region wide event, a company may not get access to all of the local seats they reserved. One way to address this is by contracting for 'dedicated' space instead of 'shared' space, an option that is usually very costly. Given that the availability of external recovery workspace can play an important role in a company's recovery strategy, the considerations mentioned above need to be carefully considered during the recovery services vendor assessment process.

Another strategy that some companies utilize is mobile recovery, where the recovery resources are delivered to the corporate location. The basis for this option are pre-configured mobile recovery units, some with data center equipment and others with recovery workspace. Besides hardware, these units often come equipped with generators, satellite uplinks for voice and data connections, peripheral equipment, etc. Some of these units are 48 feet long and can accommodate up to 50 employees. The primary advantage of mobile recovery is that it brings the recovery site to the business in a well-configured and controlled environment. The major disadvantages are cost, unit delivery time (usually 48 hours or longer) and site logistics such as space and permitting. Because of these and other factors, mobile recovery may not be a viable alternative for many companies. Depending upon the location and scenario, mobile recovery can be a real plus for other companies.

An increasingly popular option that falls under the alternate site umbrella is to establish a company's own internal recovery workspace. Of course, this works best for organizations that have multiple facilities located at appropriate distances. Those internal recovery workspaces are typically set up in conference rooms and training spaces, and tend to be supplemented with third party drop-ship equipment arrangements. The advantages of internal recovery workspace include employee familiarity, availability of network connectivity and technical capacity, proximity to corporate resources and amenities, etc. On the downside, implementing the supporting infrastructure can be costly and chances are that the recovery workspace may be impacted by the same event confronting the primary facility (given its relative proximity).

Another fairly recent addition to the business continuity toolkit is the use of wireless technology within office buildings. A number of companies have implemented Wi-Fi within their facilities; providing wireless access to both data and voice networks. As a result, employees can be easily relocated within a building or between buildings during several types of incidents.

Lastly, workforce mobility is gaining popularity as a recovery strategy option. Many organizations used the avian flu threats as justification for developing a more mobile workforce. Through combinations of web-based VPN access and the use of specialty applications such as Citrix, more and more companies are including this in their recovery repertoire. However, the workforce mobility option is not a viable option for all companies (e.g., assembly line worker at an auto manufacturing plant cannot perform their work remotely); its applicability is ultimately dictated by company-specific operational characteristics.

Technology Recovery

Referring back to Table 7.1, we see that technology recovery has been identified as one of the three key components of a Business Continuity Program. Why is that so important? Well, the fact is that almost no business or industry today can survive without its technology infrastructure. Like electrical power and water, it is a critical component of the overall infrastructure.

Interestingly, technology recovery is paradoxical: On the one hand, it is one of the most mature aspects of business recovery (it has been around much longer than business continuity planning) – at the same time, it is often the most overlooked or static part of that process (which is ironic, given the incredible pace of change and innovation that characterizes information technology).

As previously mentioned one common definition for business continuity is a management process that identifies potential impacts that threaten an organization and provides a framework for building resilience. Given that, technology recovery can be defined, for our purposes, as the technological aspect or dimension of business continuity planning.

Traditionally, the task of technology recovery planning was undertaken in order to recover from serious or catastrophic events. In the last few years, however, there has been a paradigm shift in the way organizations approach this aspect of their business continuity planning, which manifested itself in heightened emphasis on day-to-day outages and related issues. This is important because within the information technology environment, the approaches to planning for outages and those for planning for disasters are likely to be different. Outages tend to take place on a localized basis, therefore requiring localized solutions and strategies. In the event of data corruption or deletion, the data can usually be restored using onsite backup copies. The offsite copies of the backup data would normally be available, but it would likely take additional time in order to bring the data onsite. In most cases, if there is a hardware failure, the local vendors will be able to repair or replace the affected equipment within hours. Companies can address IT resilience relating to outages as well as disasters in several different ways, including:

- *Normal Break/Fix*. Respond at the time of an outage to repair with spare parts, service contracts, and other resolution methods.
- *High Availability*. Fault- tolerant, failure- resistant infrastructure supporting continuous processing.
- *Continuous Operations*. Non- disruptive backups and system maintenance coupled with continuous availability of applications.
- *Disaster (Technology) Recovery*. Protection against unplanned outages such as disasters through reliable, predictable recovery.

These recovery strategies need to encompass the four fundamental components of information technology:

- *Servers*. The processing power or heart of the data center or computing environment. While the computing landscape has changed over the years, servers are no more than the computer itself, the mainframe or midrange of the early days. To oversimplify, servers do the work.
- *Storage*. The online or near line disk environment on which information is stored. Historically, storage was server or computer-centric, dedicated to a given computer, but with the birth and growth of Storage Area Networks (SANs), this has changed. Now storage is much more of a 'pool' or series of pools at the site level with no alignment or dedication to a given computer system.
- *Networks*. The arms or tentacles of the information flow; whether it be a Local Area Network (LAN) that is dedicated to a given department of a broader Wide rea Network (WAN) servicing an entire corporation.
- *Facilities (Data Centers)***.** The space, power, cooling required to house and run business systems and other IT infrastructure components. These facilities often include two or more locations; one where the production systems operate and a second where systems are recovered in the case of a disaster to the production

facility. Facilities may be owed, rented, or belong to a vendor for outsourced systems.

Keeping the above in mind, planning for disaster recovery (again, in contrast to planning for addressing outages) deals with the prospect of the primary data center being unavailable for many days, weeks, or even months. One primary goal of a technology recovery plan is to relocate the data center resources to an alternate site in order to restore functionality of the data center to optimum levels. Today it is also very important that an organization's technology recovery strategy include provisions for voice, web-based and email infrastructure and associated systems.

To use a car analogy, it is not enough to put back the engine, drive train, etc., for a car to become operational again, one must also make sure that those 'technical' items needed for operation are available as well. We do not just 'drive a car' with gas, brakes and steering – we operate a system that includes feedback indicators, controls, monitors, etc. Well, the same is true of the computing environment. Without telephone, web or email access, it may not matter that the servers, network and storage are up and fully functional. At the end of the day, it is about presence during a crisis and presence comes largely in the form of telephone, web and email access.

Emerging Technologies and Business Continuity

One of the challenges in developing material for a textbook is ensuring that it stays current. This is especially true where technology is involved and truest where that technology centers on information (i.e., IT). In concluding this chapter, I felt it important to cover four areas that have significant and evolving ramifications for organizational resilience: information security, cloud computing, social media, and internet-connected mobile devices.

Information Security

During this day and age of hacking, worms, viruses, malware, etc., many companies and organizations are under constant threat of cyber-attacks and security breaches. The period spanning from the latter half of 2014 thru the first half of 2015 saw significant data breaches involving Anthem Insurance, Home Depot, JP Morgan Chase as well as the US Government[9]. Each of these breaches involved millions of records, with some going undetected for extended periods of time.

Those and other data breaches were costly experiences for each of the organizations, both in terms of remediation expenses as well reputational impacts. Many organizations and companies have implemented preventive and reactive controls to address the threats to information security. Those measures include establishing a Chief Information Security Officer (CISO) position along with a team and associated roles and responsibilities; developing information security policies and protocols; creating employee training and awareness programs; establishing an incident response and management program, etc. It goes without saying that information security and disaster (technology) recovery should be, colloquially speaking, 'joined at the hip'. A company's disaster recovery and business continuity plans must be flexible enough to address information security threats.

Often the requisite planning takes place within two or more business areas in a company; hence it is essential that there be multiple points of interaction and connectivity. Organizations often address this by establishing cross-functional teams and associated protocols; those with mature business continuity planning mechanisms leverage key elements of their program in developing their data breach response/recovery planning strategies.

---

[9] The 2015 Gemalto and SafeNet, *Breach Level Index,* an industry report.

Cloud Computing

Cloud computing is the next step in the paradigm shift that started in the early 1980's – mainframe to client-server…now to *cloud computing*. It is based on utilizing the internet in order to share resources, software, and data in an on-demand fashion, similar to electricity grid.

Cloud computing is a delivery model for IT services based on the internet. It involves the provision of scalable and often virtualized resources as a service over the Internet. It is a by-product and a consequence of the ease-of-access to remote computing sites provided by the internet. The term 'cloud' is purely a metaphor that was derived from the cloud drawings that were utilized to represent the underlying network when presenting at various events or to prospective clients.

How does cloud computing and business continuity fit together? Cloud computing can be leveraged fairly well in the business continuity planning environment, as many of the recovery site vendors are now offering cloud services in relation to working with clients and prospects. The message often delivered by these service providers is that the cloud-based services can provide substantial data backup capability, server virtualization and fail over, as well as a secondary data center located far enough away from the primary data center. In theory (or at least in promotional literature), all those services can be deployed and delivered in a secure, cost effective manner with quicker recovery times. However, cloud computing is not necessarily the best choice for all applications in a data center environment, which in turn has a direct impact on what companies do with their technology recovery architecture. The goal of planning for disasters is to ensure that end-users have access to recovered applications and data, but just because the remote 'cloud environment' is operational does not mean that users can access it. In addition to access considerations, security may become an issue as well. In short, the strategy to use the cloud for the purposes of business continuity planning and management should be determined by the results of the business impact analysis, balanced by the associated cost, access and security considerations.

Social Media

The relatively recent emergence and rapid proliferation of *social media*, defined here as forms of electronic communication through which users create online communities to share information, made the job of organizational communication managers a lot more difficult. From the standpoint of organizational resilience, the core of social media related threat is the combination of two factors: 1. the speed with which information spreads through social networks, and 2. what I call the 'Hyde Park[10]' effect: unbounded access to mass communication means that gives virtually everyone a platform for expression…Those factors, coupled with an explosive rise of different types of mobile device platforms now poses a reputational challenge for corporations. At any time, organizations can fall victim to blistering attacks, which might or might not be justified but might nonetheless spur customer backlash.

Although the threat posed by social media is real, organizations can also utilize social media as an effective communication tool during a crisis situation. The KPMG/Continuity business continuity management benchmark study[11] found that over half of the companies they surveyed had incorporated social media into either their incident management or continuity plans. The bottom line is that organizations should establish policies and procedures that define proper use of social networks during a crisis, including a list of approved sites and approved spokespersons. Using social networks during crisis to communicate instructions or provide status reports should be limited to personnel qualified to communicate on behalf of the enterprise.

Internet Connected Mobile Devices

There were an estimated 93 million connected devices in 2000, rising to 5 billion in 2010 and 31 billion expected in 2020[12]. It is also anticipated that mobile/smart phones will soon overtake personal computers as the most common internet access device worldwide. Many organizations have increased their presence of externally owned devices (a practice known as bring your own device or BYOD) by employees or suppliers accessing the network for information.

The KPMG/Continuity Insights Benchmark Study indicated that over 40% or reporting organizations had no plans in place to address the use of these personal devices in the workplace. It is understood, that mobile device considerations should be as part of companies' regular operational policies and procedures, as well as their business continuity planning efforts.

---

[10] One of the largest parks in London, UK, and the home to the famous Speaker's Corner, where open-air public speaking and debate are a long-standing tradition.
[11] Continuity Insights and KPMG (2014), *Global BCM Benchmarking Study*.
[12] Hiles, A. (2014), *Business Continuity Management: Global Best Practices,* 4th ed., Rothstein Publishing, p. xxii.

8

Emergency Management

Large scale emergencies, both natural and man-made are the most visible, and in many regards the most frightening organizational threats. Even armed with technological marvels of the modern age we stand helpless in the face of powerful hurricanes, earthquakes or tsunamis. Given the force and scale of those events, it is not surprising. What is, however, surprising, if not inexplicable, is that organizations can be just as helpless when facing governance, corruption and other self-made crises. All considered, it seems reasonable to say that while being overrun by the force of a powerful storm might be understandable, being unprepared for such a storm is not. Furthermore, it is outright inexcusable for an organization to be unprepared for the possibility of a self-made crisis, such as a corruption scandal or a class action lawsuit.

Organizational emergencies take many forms and often – though not always – are unexpected and explosive. However, relatively few emergencies are truly 'new', occurrence-wise. Whether it is a natural disaster or a man-made crisis, it probably happened before, somewhere. Hence while it might not be possible to anticipate every detail, an organization should exhibit a general level of preparedness. Conceptually, that seems logical and straightforward; however, it is not always clear what being 'prepared' means in practice. The goal of this chapter is to answer that very question.

Emergency Classifications and Definitions

Terminology and definitions abound in the world of disaster recovery and business continuity. There are 'events', 'emergencies', 'crises', 'disasters', etc. Depending upon one's focal point, these terms can have different meanings to different entities. From the public perspective, the Federal Emergency Management Agency (FEMA) defines 'disaster' as an event that results in widespread losses to people, the infrastructure, and/or the environment. From the corporate perspective, 'disaster' is the loss or interruption of a critical service or process for a period of time which threatens the ability of the enterprise to fulfill its mission. Both of these definitions are certainly valid and fundamental to business continuity planning. But what about 'outages' and 'incidents' that organizations are confronted with on a more frequent basis? In the business world, there are many examples of how routine outages can individually or cumulatively lead to a disaster.

As practitioners, emergency managers often consider *incidents* as a wide spectrum of events affecting an organization, illustrated in the following diagram:

Figure 8.1
Incident Spectrum

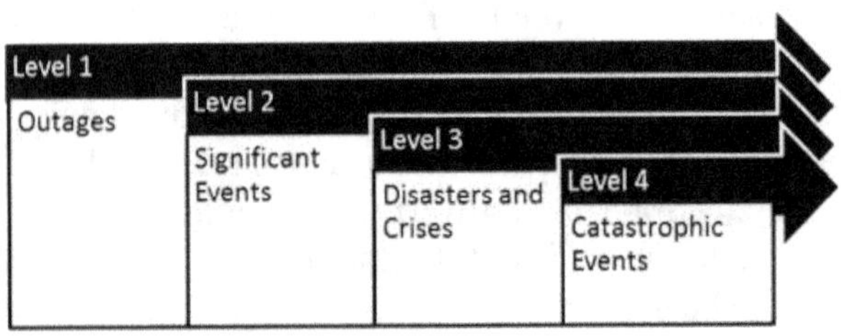

The Incident Spectrum depicted above communicates two important sets of insights: 1. There are four distinct categories of emergencies, and 2. The four emergency categories can be rank-ordered along an organizational impact continuum. Each of the four categories can be characterized as follows:

- *Outages* - Events that result in a temporary interruption or disruption of business operations with minimal impact. An outage is usually minor in scope and handled by routine recovery procedures that are part of the daily operations process. Examples of this are false fire alarms, momentary loss of power at a building, and minor unplanned systems downtime.

- *Significant Events* - Events that result in the temporary loss of a facility or systems resulting in delayed access and/or delayed operations for an extended period. These types of events can be multiple days in duration and could have a moderate to substantial impact on business operations. Examples of this are major snowstorms, extended power outages, loss of water at a building, and a prolonged network access issue.

- *Disasters* and *Crises* - Events that are larger in scale, longer in duration, and with more sustained effects. As used within the TEM framework, 'disasters' are consequences of forces or entities impacting an organization, while 'crises' are consequences of an organization's own actions. Those incidents often involve multiple facilities and/or systems and have a direct impact on 'the ability of the enterprise to fulfill its mission'. Disasters may result from floods, fires, major data loss/security breaches, while crises may result from organizational governance breakdowns, labor disputes, financial exigencies and similar events.

- *Catastrophic Events* - Events that are disaster- or crisis-like in nature, but with a more significant impact on organizational survival (recall Figure 7.1), including a significant potential for organizational failure. Examples of catastrophic events include large-scale natural disasters, systemic financial or governance breakdowns and pandemics.

The above impact categories can also be classified into several different groupings based on origination:

- Acts of nature such as hurricanes, floods, and earthquakes.
- External man-made events such as terrorism, evacuation, and security failures.
- Internal unintentional events such as accidental loss of information, computer failure, power and HVAC outages, and chemical spills.

- Internal intentional events such as workplace violence, strikes, sabotage, and intentional data deletion.
- Legal, regulatory, compliance or governance failures.

It is important to note that there are several ways to classify events, which means that companies ought to consider establishing their own definitions of incidents, along with associated severity levels, and then develop the necessary response structure and plans to address those events. For instance, the 'acts of nature' category listed above may need to be broken down into several more specific sub-categories for an organization that operates physical facilities in diverse geographies, to better reflect threats that are particularly salient in individual locations.

In addition, the numbers of potential events confronting an organization are significant and expanding. It is simply not practical to develop and maintain multiple emergency management structures and individual plans to address every possible event. That is why many industry experts are proponents of a single corporate emergency management structure with the necessary teams and processes in place to address a range of incidents, which addresses the need to be both flexible and scalable.

Public Sector Emergency Preparedness

An important responsibility of the private sector emergency manager or business continuity planner is to become familiar with the public agencies, initiatives and resources. Given that very few business and other non-governmental entities maintain a full spectrum of emergency management response assets, such as appropriately trained and equipped fire and medical emergency response departments, it is likely that those organizations' emergency response will call for assistance from public emergency agencies. Furthermore, developing at least a rudimentary understanding of the public emergency response infrastructure will expose organizational emergency managers and planners to some of the best practices in that field, which they can then apply to their own organizations. Last but certainly not the least reason for private sector emergency managers to develop familiarity with public emergency management agencies is to establish the foundation for a more coordinated effort during an actual incident.

Federal Emergency Management Agency

In 1979, the Federal Emergency Management Agency (FEMA) was established by an executive order, which merged many of the separate disaster-related responsibilities into a single agency. FEMA's mission is to help communities nationwide prepare for, respond to, and recover from natural and manmade disasters. In 2003, FEMA became part of the DHS. Headquartered in Washington, DC, FEMA has ten regional offices located throughout the United States.

State and Local Emergency Management Agencies

The ten regional FEMA offices work in partnership with the emergency management agencies established in each state. As examples, California has the California Emergency Agency, Florida has the Florida Division of Emergency Management, and Massachusetts has the Massachusetts Emergency Agency or MEMA. MEMA is responsible for coordinating federal, state, local, voluntary, and private resources during emergencies and disasters in Massachusetts. Many cities and towns also maintain an emergency management presence. For example, Boston has the Mayor's Office of Emergency Management, which oversees the City's homeland security and emergency management programs.

Incident Command System

First utilized in the 1970s, the Incident Command System (ICS) is a standardized, on-scene, all-hazards emergency management approach that:

- Allows for the integration of facilities, equipment, personnel, procedures, and communications operating within a common organizational structure.
- Enables a coordinated response among various jurisdictions and functional agencies, both public and private.
- Establishes common processes for planning and managing resources.
- Encompasses a full spectrum of emergencies and is applicable to small as well as large and complex incidents.

ICS represents organizational 'best practices' and it has become the standard for emergency management across the country. One of the most important and noteworthy attributes of the System is that it is a scalable framework, and, as a result, is able to fit just about any situation due to its ability to expand and contract to fit the situation(s) at hand. Many private sector business continuity planners incorporate elements of ICS into their emergency management programs.

The Department of Homeland Security

Before the establishment of the Department of Homeland Security (DHS), more than forty (40) federal agencies were responsible for homeland security activities[1]. The Homeland Security Act of 2002 created the DHS to re-organize multiple government entities into a single department. That was not a small task: The Department has about 240,000 employees and annual budget of about $40 billion; furthermore, over 80,000 different governmental jurisdictions at the federal, state and local level have homeland security responsibilities[2]. In contrast to FEMA and ICS which are focused on natural

---

[1] It is a little-known, and often surprising fact that there are more than 500 separate federal agencies; the vast majority were created and operate under the executive or legislative branches of the US Government, but there are a few that operate under the judicial branch as well.

[2] Department of Homeland Security, www.dhs.gov

disasters, the Department of Homeland Security's primary focus is on physical and cyber security threats. More specifically, the five core homeland security missions are to:

- Prevent terrorism and enhance security
- Secure and manage borders
- Enforce and administer immigration laws
- Safeguard and secure cyberspace
- Ensure resilience to disasters

The National Incident Management System

In 2004, Homeland Security Presidential Directive 5, *Management of Domestic Incidents,* directed the DHS to develop and administer the National Incident Management System (NIMS) and the National Response Plan (NRP). The Directive also required all federal government agencies to adopt NIMS as part of the NRP, but the latter was replaced by the National Response Framework (NRF), which took effect in March of 2008. The NRF works in tandem with NIMS – the former provides the structure, roles, and mechanisms for national-level policy and best practices for managing incidents, while the latter establishes the template for the management of incidents.

NIMS provides a consistent nationwide template to enable governmental agencies, non-governmental organizations, and the private sector to work together to prevent, protect against, respond to, recover from, and mitigate the effects of incidents, regardless of cause, size, location, or complexity. As such, it outlines a comprehensive, nationwide, systematic approach to incident management.

Public – Private Sector Emergency Management Integration

More than any of the other aspects of organizational resilience, emergency management calls for close integration between an organization and the appropriate local, state and federal authorities for a number of reasons, not the least of which is that, as noted earlier, most business organizations tend to rely on public emergency response infrastructure. The vast majority of business organizations do not operate their own fire or medical emergency departments, thus it is critical that an organization's emergency response plans expressly contemplate those needs and dependencies. Summarized below are some of the high-level considerations characterizing the needed public—private sector integration.

Coordination with External Agencies

DRII Professional Practices[3] Subject Area 10—Coordination with External Agencies—recognizes the importance of establishing policies and procedures for coordinating continuity and restoration activities with the external agencies. For an organizational emergency response / business continuity planner, this should include a combination of the following steps:

- Determine the relevant external agencies and their roles and responsibilities.
- Identify representatives in these agencies and establish open dialogue.
- Maintain current contact information and establish communication protocols.
- Develop and document joint response roles and escalation procedures.
- Align elements of the corporate incident response plans with those of the relevant external agencies.
- Participate in joint exercises.

For many companies, coordination with external agencies has not been an easy activity due, in part, to the public sector's perceived lack of willingness to participate. One of the ways that the private-public sector relationship is being enhanced is through various joint initiatives.

---

[3] DRI International (2012), *Professional Practices for Business Continuity Planners.*

Public – Private Sector Initiatives

The private sector is responsible for much of the critical infrastructure and resources in the United States and thus becomes a key partner in federal, state, and local incident management activities. Public-private partnerships have been recognized by several presidential directives and standards as a necessary element of emergency preparedness and response.

The National Response Framework discussed earlier includes a private sector coordination support annex which describes the policies, responsibilities, and concept of operations for federal incident management activities involving the private sector during incidents requiring a coordinated federal response. In this context, the annex further describes the activities necessary to ensure effective coordination and integration with the private sector. As a result, since the enactment of the NRF more public-private sector initiatives have been taking place. Examples of these include:

- *Corporate Emergency Access System (CEAS)*—CEAS is a credentialing program which allows pre-designated critical business employees access to restricted areas following a disaster or serious emergency using a secure identification card recognized by the police. CEAS program activations have taken place during the Boston Marathon bombings, an underground steam pipe explosion in Manhattan and during a Baltimore blizzard. Depending upon the situation, CEAS-credentialed employees could potentially operate vehicles on the roads and gain access to a company's facilities to keep or get things running.

- *Health and Homeland Alert Network (HHAN)*—HHAN provides secure web-based communication and other information sharing capabilities to public and private sector user groups. HHAN disseminates notifications via email, the web, and telephonic alerts. Recent communications have covered snowstorms, floods, Amber alerts, and train accidents.

- *Government Emergency Telecommunications Service (GETS)*—GETS is a government-directed emergency phone service provided by the National Communications System. GETS provides emergency access and priority processing in the local and long distance segments of the public telephone network. It is intended to be used in an emergency when the public telephone network is congested and the probability of completing a call over normal or other alternate telecommunication means has significantly decreased.

The Corporate Emergency Management Model

Conventional emergency management usually entails responding to an event and dealing with the impacts on people and resources affected by the event. Many of the early approaches towards emergency management placed some emphasis on pre-event planning and post-event recovery management, with a smaller emphasis on reducing exposure to these events.

Emergency managers now place greater emphasis on reducing exposures, improving preparedness and on managing recovery, resulting in a balance between pre-incident, during-incident and post-incident management. This has often been identified as the 'Four R' approach to emergency management: Reduction, Readiness, Response and Recovery[4]. There are three transition points that exist within the emergency management domain: from pre-incident to incident response; from incident onset to incident impact management; from impact management to recovery management. During these transition points there are sets of activities that will need to be addressed. In pre-incident management, the focus for the first set of activities is on prevention and preparedness. The second set of activities consists of two parts: 1. confronting the emerging situation before significant damage arises, and 2. managing the impact of the event on the organization and employees, so that the damage sustained is minimal. The third set of activities involves transferring the focus from dealing with the incident and its impacts to recovering from those impacts.

Each of these transition points may require different employees and skill sets to plan and perform the activities. This is an important concept that needs to be factored into the response and recovery team dynamic. For example, during an evacuation, leadership is typically in the hands of a security or safety function rather than with the traditional organizational management. This means that the CEO, CFO, etc., are being told what to do by employees many levels below them in the corporate organization chart; the 'leaders as followers' is certainly an interesting if not very challenging dynamic.

In building the corporate model, we will consider emergency management as an integrated process consisting of mitigation and

---

[4] Heath, R. (2008), 'A Crisis Management Perspective of Business Continuity', in Hiles, A. editor, *The Definitive Handbook of Business Continuity Management,* 2nd ed., Wiley, New York, NY.

preparedness, incident response, and ongoing emergency management. Taken as a whole, it is best described in terms of it key attributes and components.

Key Program Attributes

What makes an effective corporate emergency management program? Using the accumulated wisdom of the combination of experience and best documented practices, the following attributes emerge:

- Active support and participation from senior management
- Commitment of resources and associated funding
- A centralized command and control structure with established decision-making capability and accountability
- Well-defined teams, roles and responsibilities
- Actionable plans and associated protocols
- Integration with public authorities and the extended enterprise
- An understanding of the importance of the human element
- Continuous training and testing

From a theoretical perspective, the above are all necessary to sustain an effective program. However, because of competing priorities, organizational risk tolerance levels, organizational politics and related issues, program implementation can often be a difficult undertaking. In short, the reality of organizational and interpersonal dynamics often renders 'good ideas' infeasible in practice. Also, without active support from senior management and the commitment of necessary resources, a company's emergency management program has little chance to be effective. The potential impediments notwithstanding, the above should at least be viewed as aspirational goals.

The C3 Structure

Some organizations have a single emergency management team while others have multiple teams and layers. While the latter is recommended by the ICS framework, what is 'best' for an organization depends on a number of factors, such as decision-making speed (rapid decisioning may not lend itself to a complex team structure) or cross-event requirement invariance. A possible solution to those and other potential ambiguities is offered by the Command, Control, and Communication (C3) Model. Conceived as a hybrid, the C3

Model has a relatively simple structure that ensures the flexibility, as well as the capability to address a range of incidents; its structure is summarized in Figure 8.2.

Figure 8.2
Corporate C3 Process

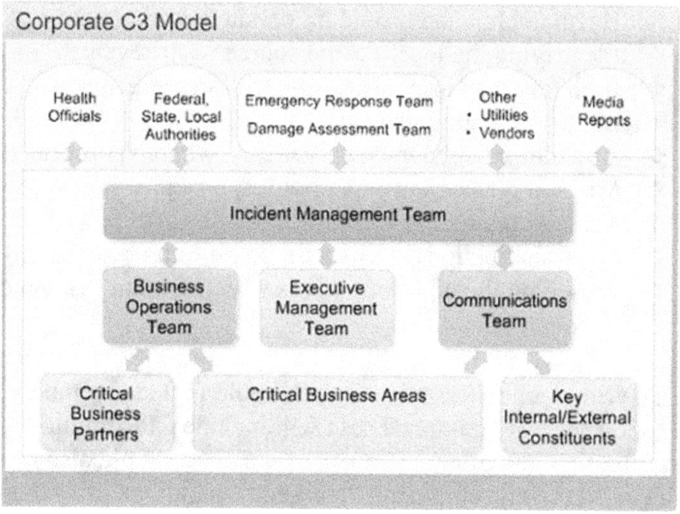

Our model is based in part on the Incident Command System (ICS) and consists of six core teams: Emergency Response, Damage Assessment, Incident Management, Executive Management, Business Operations, and Communications. The model is also based on another important factor – depending upon the event, the transfer of emergency response and management into recovery mode may happen almost simultaneously. As a result, emergency management plans and procedures must be integrated with technology recovery and business continuity plans and activities. The same can be said for the team members involved with emergency management, technology recovery, and business continuity. It makes sense to have selected members of the emergency management teams also involved with the recovery operations. The objectives, roles and responsibilities, and make-up of each of the teams in our model can be summarized as follows:

Emergency Response Team

As a company's first responders, the Emergency Response Team has primary responsibility for addressing the safety and well-being of the organization's employees. The team members' responsibilities include:

- Contacting the local emergency services (e.g., fire, police, EMS, Hazmat, etc.) and providing on-site coordination;
- Identifying the location and source of the event;
- Initiating response measures such as emergency shut-downs, and use of fire extinguishers;
- Attending to medical emergencies, where appropriate;
- Managing hazardous material response;
- Managing building evacuations;
- Coordinating the activities of the building safety wardens;
- Providing the other C3 Teams with an initial assessment of the incident.

The Emergency Response Team should include members with certain skill sets and specialty training. These will include CPR training and administering first aid. Some members of the team should also be trained in the use of fire suppression equipment, emergency shutdown procedures, and evacuations. The Emergency Response Team should include representatives from Facilities, Human Resources, Security & Safety, and Information Technology. Since it is essential to maintain adequate ‘bench strength,’ the Emergency Response Team should be made up of least three ‘deep’. That is, each primary team member should have a designated secondary and tertiary back up.

It is essential that the Emergency Response Team be the first group out of the gate and that the focus be as indicated above. Extending into other areas such as damage assessment and business recovery without determining personnel welfare and whereabouts opens the firm up to serious damage, liability and disdain in the court of public opinion.

Damage Assessment Team

Similarly to the above-discussed emergency first responders, the Damage Assessment Team requires specific, and often technical, knowledge to arrive at sound, initial damage estimates. More specifically, the Assessment Team is typically responsible for the following:

- ❖ Providing ongoing damage assessments of the physical structure, facility infrastructure and systems, and IT infrastructure and systems;
- ❖ Determining if employees' health or safety would be at risk in using all or part of the existing premises;
- ❖ Estimating the usability and time to recover critical infrastructure and systems;
- ❖ Maintaining security provisions including access restriction to impacted areas;
- ❖ Identifying methods for protecting onsite equipment, materials, and documents;
- ❖ Coordinating the activities of the appropriate utilities, subcontractors and vendors;
- ❖ Assisting in the salvage and restoration processes;
- ❖ Providing periodic status updates, corrective action plans, and associated periods to the Incident Management Team and the Executive Management Team, as needed.

In many organizations, the Damage Assessment and Emergency Response Teams are closely aligned and may in fact be part of one team. Because its focus is on facilities and systems stabilization, the Damage Assessment Team should include representatives from Facilities, Information Technology, and Risk Management.

Incident Management Team

This team is responsible for directing a Company's response and recovery efforts through coordination with all of the C3 teams. Primary responsibilities of this team include:

- ❖ Coordinating preparation across the organization;
- ❖ Developing an incident monitoring and reporting process, including incident escalation procedures;
- ❖ Activating the command centers and the conference lines;
- ❖ Interfacing with regulatory bodies and agencies;
- ❖ Monitoring outside agencies for information;

- Collecting information from the Emergency Response and Damage Assessment Teams and assessing the impacts;
- Ensuring that the Executive Management Team is briefed and updated on all related activities;
- Recommending to the Executive Management Team the appropriate corporate response strategies and related policies to enact;
- Managing requests for administrative support, procurement, funding, internal resources, or external assistance;
- Addressing legal, insurance, and financial issues and requirements;
- Attending to human resource matters and activating employee assistance programs;
- Representing the organization with the families of any dead or injured employees;
- Overseeing the execution and integration of all facets of response and recovery.

In many cases, the Incident Commander will come from the Incident Management Team. As a result, this team should be comprised of experienced, more senior level decision makers. As an example, three members of the team could be the heads of IT Operations, Facilities, and Human Resources. Depending upon the type of incident involved, any one of these three individuals could become the Incident Commander. Team members should also include the leads from each of the other C3 teams, as well as representatives from critical business areas and supporting functions. Another important member of the incident management team is the head of Business Continuity.

Executive Management Team

The Executive Management Team serves as the primary decision-making body prior to and during a significant event. This team is responsible for the following:

- Reviewing the damage assessment analyses and the recommendations from the Incident Management Team;
- Declaring a disaster, if appropriate;
- Authorizing the appropriate corporate response strategies and related policies to enact;

- ❖ Approving changes to corporate standards and policies;
- ❖ Reviewing and approving communications.

The membership of the Executive Management Team will vary among companies and industries. This team will often consist of the COO, CFO, CIO, and Chief Human Resources Officer. Some companies will include the CEO, while others will not, choosing instead to create a team that reports into and guides the CEO. The latter choice is usually driven by the belief that the CEO may need to focus on media presentations, customer/business partner relations, employee morale, etc.

Business Operations Team

The Business Operations Team is comprised of business area leaders who are responsible for the following:

- ❖ Determining how the event has impacted their respective operations;
- ❖ Informing the Incident Management Team of the business operations status;
- ❖ Activating and managing their business area contingency plans;
- ❖ Coordinating business area response and recovery efforts with those of their essential business partners and vendors.

Members of the Business Operations Team should come from the critical, Tier 1 business areas along with key support functions, which typically include Information Technology, Human Resources and Finance. What constitutes a Tier 1 technical business area is, to a large degree, dependent on a company's core value creation activities. For instance, organizations that are involved in manufacturing, energy or transportation would likely deem engineering and logistics to be a part of their Tier 1, but that would generally not be the case for financial services firms.

Communications Team

The Communications Team is responsible for all internal and external communications during an event, including:

- Assessing individual constituents' communication needs;
- Developing a formal crisis communication program including holding statements, plans, and scripts;
- Coordinating and executing consistent messaging for all groups including employees, customers, business partners, and others;
- Interfacing with the media;
- Assisting the Incident Management Team in their interactions with federal, state and local agencies;
- Communicating with the family members of victims.

Members of the Communications Team will come from Corporate Communications, Media Relations and business areas that may have an external communications component such as Sales, Marketing and Human Resources.

Leadership and Decision-Making during an Emergency

An important consideration that, implicitly, cuts across the C3 Model's logic is that of decisioning and leadership during an emergency. Even the best thought out, most thorough plans and protocols cannot account for all possible contingencies – as attested to by any experienced emergency manager, there simply are always going to be decisions that have to be made, on-the-spot, in the course of an emergency. In view of that, it is important to examine some of the critical success factors that define effective management of an incident; to pinpoint those factors, however, we first have to delineate a set of generalizable emergency characteristics. To that end, Dennis Hamilton, the President of the Crisis Response Planning Corporation has compiled an informative series on in-crisis decision making, in which he identified the following elements that are typically present during an emergency:

- An unpredictable situation due to an evolving threat or event;
- Stress, confusion, fear and anxiety amongst all stakeholders;
- Little or no time in which to respond;
- Missing or uncertain information on which to base decisions;
- Ineffectual interference of well-intentioned executives;
- Inactivity on the part of internal and external stakeholders due to the unknown;
- Rumors and speculation.

When the threat to employees and the lack of available resources is added into the above mix, the pressure on the key decision makers grows exponentially. To counter the negative effect of these elements, Hamilton believes the following four major success factors are essential:

1. Having the right team to respond to and manage an event
2. Applying an in crisis "majority rules" decision making process
3. Providing an unconditional "authority to act" to your team
4. Communicating to stakeholders in threatening and time critical situations.

While I agree with Hamilton's assessment, I recommend including two additional factors: 1. availability of adequate resources, and 2. compassionate response. Those, together with Hamilton's key success factors are discussed in the next section.

The C3 Team Skills and Dynamics

Recall the previously discussed composition of the various C3 teams. Members of these teams must have the skills and temperament to make decisions under extremely stressful circumstances. This skill set should include the ability to accomplish the following:

- ❖ Make quick and effective decisions;
- ❖ Focus 100% of their concentration on managing the incident;
- ❖ Prioritize and manage multiple tasks concurrently;
- ❖ Maintain empathy and rationality under pressure;
- ❖ Delegate and assign appropriate tasks to others best suited to assist;
- ❖ Effectively communicate with a variety of groups.

The above are largely personal characteristics that are deemed important to an effective functioning of individual C3 teams – in addition to those individual traits, to function effectively teams also need to foster a number of (emergency management related) performance enhancing dynamics, which is discussed next.

Majority Rules

It is critical for C3 teams to embrace and practice the 'majority rules' decision-making process, as stress caused by a disaster or catastrophic event will have a significant impact on all parties. No one is immune regardless of their position, age, experience, etc., and people deal with this stress differently. In a crisis situation, most every employee has the following four priorities:

1. Their own personal safety;
2. The safety and well-being of their families;
3. The safety of close friends and fellow employees;
4. Their employer and their in-crisis roles.

Taking the above into account, an organization should not rely on the decision-making authority or capability of a single individual as this may become a single point of failure. A large number of action steps will be required during an emergency, performed by multiple groups and influenced by a large number of people – the challenge is to quickly and accurately determine which decisions and actions must be focused upon. Many organizations utilize 'majority rules' decision-making process because it:

- Provides a safeguard against emotionally driven or politically motivated actions on the part of individuals;
- Ensures compliance with the priorities of emergency response and management;
- Eliminates the unpredictability of actions caused by individual stress and trauma;
- Draws on the knowledge and experience of many, versus the possible limited reasoning capability of one individual.

Authority to Act

When an organization is impacted or threatened by an event that could result in serious economic consequences or loss of life, critically important decisions have to be made in short time periods. There may be little time for debate and no time to work your way through the corporate hierarchy for approval. The executive management teams must have unconditional authority to take the actions necessary to protect employees and property. This means that:

- ❖ Team members have collectively accepted this responsibility and are accordingly charged with that obligation. This 'authority to act' must be formally approved by senior management.
- ❖ While the authority to act can be a legally obligating commitment on the part of the organization, there should be no qualifying conditions, prerequisites or exceptions.
- ❖ The authority to act is given to the team or teams and not to the individuals on the teams.

At the same time, the 'authority to act' should be restricted to decisions where employees' well-being is currently impacted or is imminently threatened by an event. While it is important to arm the executive management team with the appropriate authority, it is also important to bound that authority to actions that directly relate to a particular emergency.

Effective Communications

It is obvious that being able to effectively communicate is an essential critical success factor. In practice, that compels an emergency-impacted organization to identify its primary stakeholders and then to be timely, accurate and forthcoming with the information shared with those stakeholders. Other elements of effective crisis (or more generally, emergency) communications include:

- ❖ Providing time-sensitive information to ensure the safety and well-being of employees;
- ❖ Providing management with information necessary to make strategic and tactical operational decisions;
- ❖ Providing threat and event status information relevant to internal and external stakeholders;
- ❖ Managing rumors and perceptions and the application of assumptions as facts;
- ❖ Satisfying regulatory or mandated reporting requirements.

Successful implementation of core communication elements must be placed in the proper context: An organization may have to communicate with hundreds or thousands of stakeholders during a significant event; multiple communication methods may have to be used to ensure contact; and stakeholders may have to be reached within minutes or very few hours. It is worth noting that, as discussed in the previous chapter, some of the advances in popular communication technologies may hinder a company's ability to effectively communicate. Text messaging, Twitter and mobile phone cameras all make communication of an incident almost instantaneous and possibly uncontrolled. Both the insiders (i.e., employees) as well as bystanders have the ability to transmit photos or videos to third parties or the media while an event is taking place, which may be beneficial or detrimental.

Adequate Resources and Funding

When an incident occurs, having the right resources available at the right place can mean the difference between success and failure. Some of the more critical resources include the following: access to funds, especially cash; communications management for the flood of incoming information requests; transportation to and/or away from the crisis area; legal and insurance advice and services; moral and emotional support; media management and an effective command center. It needs to be acknowledged that during an emergency, the impacted organization will incur additional expenses, over and above the cost of response and recovery. Some of the expenses include employee assistance programs, travel expenses including lodging, employee overtime, replacement of lost, damaged or destroyed property for employees, as well as additional compensation for those who were injured.

Compassionate Response

During an emergency, employees need to know that their company cares about them. This means that the emergency management must have the necessary people skills and be able to demonstrate that they understand the personal difficulties that may have arisen due to the incident. A widely held belief among disaster recovery practitioners is that proactive management of the ‘human side’ of a traumatic incident, or more specifically, putting employees and other constituents before the ‘business side’ (e.g., facilities, technology, etc.) will lead to a quicker recovery. Among the ‘human variables’ that may be associated with a significant event are the following:

- Daycare and schools in the area may be closed or may be early-releasing children;
- Roads and utilities may be impaired;

- Family members may be trying to reach each other with limited modes of available communication;
- Elderly family members may be in need of assistance from working family members;
- People may be displaced from their homes;
- Healthcare and service agencies may be overwhelmed.

It is common for organizations to respond to an emergency by focusing on financial and technical matters, while paying less attention to its most significant asset – the employees. In some cases, the workplace environment may be returned to a level of stability before the home and personal environments are restored. In a rush to recover facilities and other operating assets it is easy to overlook the less visible damage that might have been inflicted on the workforce. Hence the importance of the 'human side' – organizations need to incorporate meaningful employee assistance provisions as part of their emergency management programs, inclusive of grief counseling and post incident employee/family assistance.

Actionable and Easy to Understand

As mentioned previously, there are many different types of incidents and emergency scenarios that a company may face. Should we consider developing separate plans for each of these incidents? The quick answer is a resounding 'No'. Not only would those plans be of limited operational value – they would be very difficult to maintain. Given a singular Command, Control and Communication structure, organizations would be well advised to institute a single master emergency management plan that is:

- Impact based and designed to cover a wide range of incidents, including worst case scenarios;
- Actionable and easy to understand, something that can be easily utilized by the backup C3 team members;
- Specific with respect to the incident escalation process and associated protocols;
- Supported by more detailed operating procedures and checklists;
- Integrated with the company's business continuity and disaster (technology) recovery plans.

It is important that the emergency management plans be integrated with the business continuity and disaster (technology) recovery plans. In fact, these emergency management plans should logically lead you into the other recovery plans. However, the 'actionable and easy to understand' plan concept is often a difficult one to execute. What should an emergency management plan contain and how detailed should it be? There is no easy answer to this question, especially when one considers the need to balance the requirement for detail with the need for quick and effective decision- making. Not surprisingly, the key challenge is to find the right balance between too much and not enough information. Detailed operating procedures and reference material are certainly important but they should not impede the response process. Emergency management plans need to be structured in a way to separate executable procedures from supportive information. Addressing those considerations is a four-layered planning approach that organizations with mature emergency management capabilities rely on:

> *First Layer – Corporate Emergency Management – C3 Teams.*
> This is the emergency management plan designed for the various C3 team members and their backups. This relatively succinct (10–15 pages) plan summarizes the processes and protocols necessary to effectively respond to and manage a wide range of events.
>
> *Second Layer – Emergency Management Operating Procedures.*
> Although not part of the corporate C3 plan, these supporting documents comprise an essential part of the emergency management process. This documentation would include information on: building evacuation and assembly plans, property records, building and data center layouts, generator/UPS systems, utilities feeds and emergency system shut-down, HAZMAT procedures, emergency agency contact information, key vendor/contractor contact information, etc.
>
> *Third Layer – Emergency Management Checklists.*
> Emergency management checklists are often prepared to tie the first two plan layers together. These checklists should be developed for each of the emergency management teams at a sufficient enough level to describe the action step, responsible owner and relative timeline for each of the activities. During incidents, these checklists can become very important response tools because of their scope and ease of use. Requirements of the public authorities also need to be incorporated into each layer of the emergency management plans, where

appropriate, inclusive of the applicable federal, state and local regulations governing employee safety. It should be noted that during certain types of incidents, actions of an organizational emergency management structure may be restricted by the public response agency.

Fourth Layer – Employee Focused Apps and Documents.
The effectiveness of the emergency response plans and documentation often depends, among other things, upon employee commitment, training and awareness. Many companies prepare hard copy emergency guidebooks for their employees to reference; other ones take it a step further by developing scenario-based response apps for personal mobile devices. So instead of fumbling through a guidebook which may or may not be readily accessible, all that employees have to do to gain access to the appropriate action steps, contact information and the like is to find the right icons on their smartphones.

Specialty Plans

Earlier, we emphasized the need to develop and maintain emergency management plans that are relatively simple, impact based and actionable. For many organizations this can mean one master plan and layers of supporting documentation (e.g., operating procedures and checklists). There are however instances where the 'one plan fits all' philosophy may not be appropriate – for instance, some types incidents, because of their unique nature and/or potential consequences may warrant separate plans.

Two types of incidents that fall into that category are violence in the workplace and an outbreak of an infectious disease. Both of these incidents involve specific prevention and containment measures best left to the specially trained responders. In those types of events, the Incident Commander may very well come from an external entity such as the fire or police department or HAZMAT. Should that be the case, the organizational emergency management process would likely become subordinate to that of the external entity in command.

Testing and Awareness

Having good written plans is one thing, making sure that they are operational is another. Enough cannot be said about the importance of regular plan testing and validation. Testing can take place in several different formats ranging from component testing, tabletop exercises, and structured walkthroughs, to complete end-to-end systems tests. The process of responding to a live incident and the lessons learned from that experience also constitute a form of testing. Involving senior management in these tests is another way of demonstrating their commitment and visibility.

Emergency preparedness and response testing will likely result in changes to plans and possibly re-testing, depending upon the severity of the issues uncovered. That is one reason why the testing process has to be coordinated with the plan maintenance program.

The second important element is program and plan awareness. This can be accomplished through several mechanisms such as intranet websites, employee orientation programs, specific awareness campaigns, company news articles and training classes. Many companies experienced this first-hand in their efforts to prevent and control internal outbreaks of the H1N1 virus.

Change Management

The Practice of Change Management

Philosophical and socio-cultural inquiry into the nature of 'change' dates back to ancient Greece, and possibly beyond. However, as a practical consideration focused on organizational self-adaptation and responsiveness, it is a relatively new discipline with roots reaching back to 1950s and W. Edwards Deming's work on quality control. It is even 'younger' when looked at as a formally recognized area of business practice, where what is known today as 'change management' began to take shape starting in the 1980s. In fact, the discipline's relative 'newness' is underscored by the fact that there are only two national/international change management professional organizations, and the older of the two was founded in 2005.

Another important consideration is that, as far as I can tell, the Threat Exposure Management framework described in this book is the first attempt at including change management in the scope 'risk', or what is broadly characterized within the TEM framework detailed in this book as *threat abatement*. Hence whereas the focus of the earlier discussed professional associations devoted to risk management or organizational resilience is explicitly on deepening the knowledge and furthering the practice of those disciplines as means of responding to internal and external threats, the change management associations listed below are focused on the effectiveness and the efficacy of organizational change as such.

Industry Associations:

The Change Management Institute (CMI): Established in 2005, the Institute aims to promote and develop the profession of change management through education, networking, and development of standards and recognition of excellence.

Association of Change Management Professionals (ACMP): Founded in 2011, the Association currently has about 2,000 members spanning educational institutions, business organizations and consultancies; its stated goal is to advance the theory and practice of change management and serve as a networking platform for its members.

9

Planned Organizational Change

Change is ubiquitous in virtually all aspects of commercial activities. When considered from a broad philosophical perspective, it can be seen as an inescapable consequence of the dynamism of natural and socio-economic ecosystems. What has been termed *continuous complex change* can thus be characterized as inevitable, and at times even imperceptible. Looked at from that perspective, continuous change can be seen as a force shaping organizational learning, often manifesting itself in small increments.

Not all change, however, takes the form of continuous ad hoc adaptations – organizations also undertake discrete and deliberate change initiatives, often with profound consequences. For example, a business firm may opt to amend its governance structure or operational processes to better suit its needs or goals. In a more general sense, whether it is strategic restructuring or operational process reengineering, the resulting alteration is a manifestation of *self-imposed episodic change*, also known as *planned change.*

Self-initiated change events are usually motivated by organizational betterment; however, upsetting of organizational equilibrium can be disruptive, at times it can even lead to adverse consequences. While in principle the potential downsides of change initiatives are implicitly acknowledged by change management frameworks, those conceptualization nonetheless lack meaningful means of assessing the potential for, and responding to threats posed by a combination of failure to reach the desired 'future state' and the disruption of organizational status quo. Similarly, the widely used enterprise risk management (ERM) frameworks – ISO 31000 and COSO – fail to expressly address risks associated with planned organizational change initiatives, which runs counter to their stated goal of managing the totality of organizational risks. Hence it is the purpose of this research to compel a more explicit treatment of threats arising out of self-imposed organizational change by contributing how dangers posed by those initiatives are conceptualized and measured.

Understanding Organizational Change

Heraclitus, a pre-Socratic Greek philosopher, is believed to be one of the first thinkers to formally acknowledge the ubiquity of change, as captured in his doctrine of universal flux and its derivative claim that 'change is the only constant in life'. However, it was the late 19th century's wave of great socio-cultural changes, coupled with the rise of rationality and the embrace of the scientific method that spurred wider interest in the nature and the process of change. It was within that context that the leading social thinkers of the era, including Herbert Spencer, began to conceptualize *social change* as an evolutionary process, much like the biological ones described by Charles Darwin (in fact, it was Spencer who coined the term 'natural selection', often erroneously attributed to Darwin).

Building on the conceptual foundation of the concept of social change, Kurt Lewin introduced the notion of *planned change,* which since became one of the foundations of the field of organizational development. Seeking deeper understanding of the mechanics of social change, Lewin developed field theory, which posits that mapping out the totality and complexity of the 'field' (the environment) is key to making sense of the manner in which an 'entity' (an individual or an organization) interacts with its environment. Ultimately, he was able to capture the essence of change in a simple 3-step model of 'unfreeze, change and refreeze'. Although researchers today tend to dismiss his model as overly simplistic and outdated, it drew attention to the two distinct aspects of self-imposed organizational change: 1. interactions between the individual and the organization, and 2. interactions between the organization and its ecosystem. Recognizing and expressly addressing the distinctiveness between those two dimensions of organizational change is critical as the former addresses the process of change, while the latter sheds light on factors that precipitate episodic self-imposed organizational change.

Another important, though less direct contribution to the theory and practice of intentional organizational change was W. Edwards Deming's work on statistical quality control. Although not overtly focused on organizational change, Deming's 4-stage, plan-do-check-act virtuous process, deeply rooted in the scientific method, drew attention to the importance of methodological rigor and the need to develop objective measure of the efficacy of the process of change.

Further contributing to better understanding of the mechanics of change were the more recent inquiries focused on complex systems, and the idea of *multifaceted change*. The emerging evidence suggests that change in complex systems cannot be adequately understood when examined through the prism of one-way causal process, as used in studies of technological innovation-precipitated economic dislocation; instead, such change should be studied in terms of process, interrelationships, and rhythms of mutually interactive systems. Within the confines of organizational self-change, those insights suggest the need to look beyond the determinism of the scientific method, and emphasize conditions over causes.

Another important consideration is that, at their core, business and other organizations are essentially groups of individuals joined together in pursued of shared goals, thus organizational change is ultimately personal and as such cannot be fully understood without expressly taking into account the human dimension. Empirical evidence from social psychology and organizational behavior lends credence to that assertion by pointing out that when one's self-interest is threatened by organizational change, that individual is likely to resist change. More specifically, research evidence suggests that organizational commitment, or the degree of an individual's dedication to the organization, is of particular importance to developing a deeper understanding of the human dimension of organizational self-change.

Impact of Commitment

Organizational commitment is a multidimensional summary construct, comprised of three distinct elements: 1. compliance, or willingness to conform to organizational rules and policies and reward structures, 2. identification, or the attachment one feels to being socially affiliated with the organization, and 3. internalization, or the degree to which an individual is willing to adapt organizational values. Evidence points to meaningful positive relationship between one's organizational compliance, identification and internalization, and one's openness to change. The strength of organizational commitment is in turn a function of individual personality traits, and organizational dynamics. Some personality traits, such as respect for authority, tend to be ingrained in each person and thus more change-resistant; other traits, such as identification, are usually more situational or aspirational – in general, individuals tend to identify more readily with groups that convey achievement, selectivity, or bear other marks of distinction. Also worth noting is the impact of the degree of congruence between the values brought about by change and one's own beliefs and attitudes; more specifically, a person's resistance to change tends to heighten when aspects of change conflict with that person's innermost feelings, which are usually hard to discern and even more difficult to alter.

At a group level, attainment of envisioned benefits of change also depends on successfully navigating through two core sets of organizational dynamics: transformational, and transactional. The former are those that require new behaviors resulting from internal or external pressures, such as leadership, strategy or organizational culture changes, while the latter encompass a host of psychological and organizational factors that directly affect motivation and performance, such as organizational structure, reward system or management practices. Transformational dynamics are exemplified by adoption of a new, more structured workflow management system, which often entails a fundamental re-setting of how work is done throughout the organization; transactional dynamics, on the other hand, can be exemplified by organizational restructurings, which often result in numerous reporting changes and re-alignments. Both can take considerable time to unfold, thus the importance of thoughtful planning cannot be overstated.

Benefit Maximization

Consider Figure 9.1 depicting a graphic summary of the now-familiar TEM framework. There is a major distinction between organizational change and the other two broad threat abatement functions (risk management and organizational resilience): While the goal of both risk management and organizational resilience efforts is to protect organizational assets, the goal of change management is to grow those assets. Hence the former can be seen as 'defensive' mechanisms the success of which is ultimately measured in terms of damage minimization; the latter, on the other hand, can be seen as a 'constructive' mechanism measured in terms of benefit maximization.

Figure 9.1
TEM Framework

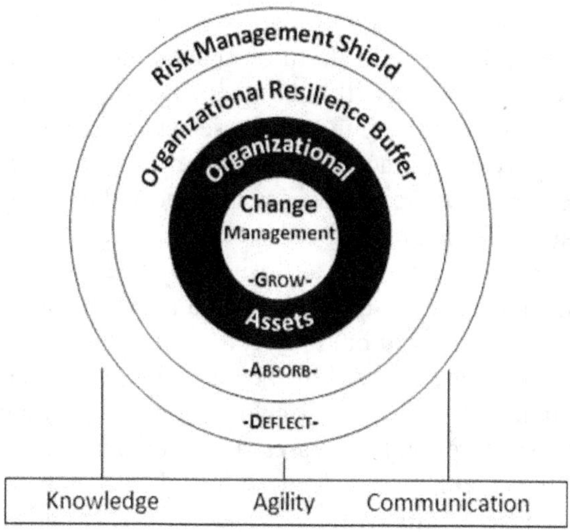

The ensuing sections of this chapter expressly address the self-selected or planned character of organizational change, the approaches that have been proposed to manage the process of organizational transformations, and the general approach proposed here for identifying, estimating and responding to specific change-precipitated threats. However, while the discussion of the various planned change related considerations is focused on change management as a distinct area, it is important to keep in mind that, as depicted in Figure 9.1 above, it should ultimately be seen as a part of the larger endeavor of systematically assessing and managing the totality of organizational exposures to all external as well as internal threats.

Managing Organizational Change

No change is truly value-free. Organizational alterations often touch upon individuals' self-interest thus many – if not most – change initiatives have their proponents and opponents. In more general terms, uncertainty regarding the impact of change on self will likely shape how impacted individuals react to change. As can be expected, those who see change to be personally beneficial are likely to embrace it, while those who do not are likely to oppose. Behavior wise, emotional responses can be expected to influence not only how individuals handle change related tasks, but also what information regarding the process of change they retain, as posited by the cognitive-emotional model.

Further adding to the difficulty of managing organizational change is that adaptive responses occur not only at the individual, but also the group level, where the former captures how people experience change, while the latter draws attention to the impact of change on group dynamics, organizational structures and processes. The challenge emanating from that response duality is that no single leadership style is ideally suited to managing the totality of a change initiative. More specifically, organizational leaders who are more effective at task-oriented behaviors are more likely to focus on activities associated with the implementation of change, while leaders who are more effective at person-oriented behaviors are more likely to emphasize on communication-related activities.

Change Management Frameworks

To reach its stated goals, the strategy of planned organizational change ought to be carefully mapped out, and change-enabling tactics should be controlled and directed. That entails anticipating requirements and obstacles, and designing means to fulfill needs and overcome obstacles, all while staying focused on successful transition from the current to future state. Given the earlier discussed complexities stemming from the combination of personality traits and group dynamics, change planning and management framework can be highly beneficial. Over the past several decades, multiple planned organizational change conceptualizations have been proposed, some quite similar and others offering drastically different perspectives.

Formal typologies of change management can be traced back to the pioneering work of Kurt Lewin in the 1940s, in which he attempted to capture the individual and group mechanics governing the process of organizational change. Viewing organizations as highly resistant to change, Lewin theorized that to be successful – i.e., to reach the desired state and to endure – the organization-initiated change must begin by first disrupting the current equilibrium, to be then followed by the introduction of a new state, and lastly the creation of a new equilibrium. He captured that reasoning in a 3-step process of unfreeze—change—refreeze, modeled on the thermodynamic process of breaking down, changing, and re-constituting of matter, as exemplified by changing the shape of a block of ice. Process wise, the 'unfreeze' step focuses on clearly stating and communicating the need for change and preparing the organization for breaking down the existing states; the 'change' step resolves change-related uncertainty (by communicating details of the new state), and the 'refreeze' stage solidifies the new state. Intuitive and simple, the 3-step process has been the staple of theoretical research and practice for several decades following its introduction, but its use waned as researchers began to view it as overly simplistic and only applicable to relatively small-scale change initiatives.

Building on Lewin's work and hoping to overcome its main shortcomings, Judson (1991) proposed an alternative conceptualization which views self-imposed organizational change as being comprised of five distinct phases: analyzing and planning the change, communicating the change, gaining acceptance of new behaviors, changing from the status quo to a desired state, and consolidating and institutionalizing the new state. Although more granular than Lewin's 3-step model, Judson's framework was also criticized as too simplistic, vague and difficult to operationalize. Not surprisingly, change management conceptualizations that followed offered considerably more operational details – among the better known of those are the Kotter's (1995) eight-steps, and Galpin's (1996) nine-wedges (so named due to being graphically depicted as nine wedges forming a wheel) model.

The point of departure in Kotter's model is establishing a sense of urgency by relating external environmental realities to actual and potential crises and opportunities facing an organization, followed by forming a powerful coalition of individuals who embrace the need for change and who can rally others. Next, carefully chosen change agents are empowered to act on the vision by amending structures, systems, policies and procedures in ways that will facilitate implementation, followed by planning for, achieving and publicizing short-term wins with the goal of building momentum for continued change. Next, improvements are consolidated and other structures, systems, procedures and policies, to the degree to which those are not consistent with the new vision, are also amended. Lastly, the new approaches are institutionalized by publicizing the connection between the change effort and organizational success.

Galpin sees the process of organizational change as being a bit more complex – his model divides the continuum of organizational change into nine parts, starting with establishing the need to change, followed by developing and disseminating a vision of a planned change, diagnosing and analyzing the current situation, leading to generating and detailing recommendations. Once compiled, the recommendations are pilot-tested and, assuming satisfactory results prepared for rollout and rolled out; the final stage in Galpin's model is focused on measuring, reinforcing and refining the newly introduced alterations.

An altogether different view of self-imposed organizational change management process has been put forth by Amenakis, Harris and Field (1999) who proposed an even more involved two-phase, multi-consideration model. The goal of the first general phase is to minimize any resistance to change by creating individual-level readiness for change, while the second phase aims to facilitate adaption and institutionalization of desired change. The authors see the effectiveness of change adaption efforts as being a function of five distinct factors: discrepancy, which is the perception of envisioned change as being necessary, self-efficacy, which reflects organizational capacity to change, personal valence, which is the recognition of personal relevance of change, (organizational) leadership support, and appropriateness, which speaks to the conviction that the contemplated change is right for the organization.

It should be noted that the original Lewin's 3-step process, as well as its conceptual descendants that followed treat the process of managing organizational change as primarily a group, socio-psychological phenomenon – not all researchers, however, view change in that manner. For instance, Tichy and Devanna (1990) see the transformational role of the change leader as the nexus of organizational change; using a 3-act theatre metaphor they depict the process of change as the leader 'acting out' the changing roles of recognizing the need for change (act 1), creating the vision of a new state (act 2), and institutionalizing change (act 3). Taking a still different approach, Hannan and Freeman (1989) and Aldrich (1999) likened organizational change to the evolutionary biology model of variation—selection—retention, itself a generalization of Darwin's (1859) theory of evolution. Interestingly, both approaches bear some clear similarities to Lewin's 3-step process insofar as all see the process of change as proceeding through conceptually alike stages of upending the current status quo, presenting an alternative, and solidifying the resultant new status quo; as such, those approaches are subject to the same shortcoming of being overly simplistic and operationally vague.

Whereas the above outlined change conceptualizations approach organizational change from either social or biological perspective, the transtheoretical model proposed by Prochaska and colleagues (1992) seeks to integrate the totality of biopsychosocial processes (hence the name 'transtheoretical') governing intentional behavioral change into a single framework. The model postulates that change-compelled behavioral modifications follow a series of discernable stages of pre-contemplation (no change readiness), contemplation (emergence of change readiness), preparation (ready for change), action (change), and maintenance (post-change reinforcement); it also posits that while the amount of time required to move through individual stages tends to vary across individuals, the actions required to move to the next stage do not vary.

Building on the cumulative wisdom of the above outlined work, Hiatt (2006) proposed the ADKAR model, an expressly practice focused change management framework offering parsimonious, yet action directing specificity-rich means of guiding purposeful organizational alterations. The ADKAR (short for *A*wareness, *D*esire, *K*nowledge, *A*bility and *R*einforcement) framework is based on the original Lewin's premise that change usually meets resistance and thus the focal point of change management efforts should be to overcome that resistance. The model posits that resistance can be lessened by developing cognizance of the need for change (awareness), instilling a felt need to participate in the planned change (desire), developing sound understanding of how to change (knowledge), enabling the acquisition of new skills and behaviors called for by the planned change (ability), and lastly taking well planned actions geared toward making the change 'stick' (reinforcement).

Regardless of philosophical or operational differences, the above change management frameworks implicitly recognize that organizations are more than sums of their constituents, which underscores the importance of the human dimension of change, as well as organizational processes, structures and systems. However, the prevailing change management rationale fails to recognize that the organizational choice to disturb the current state of its group dynamics as well as organizational processes, structure and systems may leave the organization worse off than it was prior to initiating change. In the language of risk assessment, self-initiated change can be characterized as upside risk, as it has the potential to either advance or regress organizational well-being, yet the widely used enterprise risk management conceptualizations do not expressly take into account self-imposed organizational change.

Planned Organizational Change as a Source of Risk

A widely cited industry estimate places the organizational self-change failure rate at roughly 70%[1]; setting aside any potential measurement validity related considerations (e.g., operationalization of 'success' and 'failure'), there are reasons to believe that change is a source of risk, which underscores the need for sound risk assessment. There are two general approaches to categorizing organizational change: by intensity, and by subject. The former yields broad meta-types, such as 'developmental', 'transitional', and 'transformational' (continuous improvement of the current state, discontinuous alterations of the current states, and replacement of the current with the new state, respectively). The latter usually yields more narrowly scoped groupings, as exemplified by the six-type categorization schema of strategy, structure, process, people, culture and assets. Although both approaches have distinct advantages and can yield valuable insights, the subject-of-change focused categorization is more definitionally granular and operationalization friendly, thus better aligned with the stated goals of threat assessment.

The strategy for managing planned organizational change has also been a subject of competing conceptualizations. Higgs and Rowland (2005) view the process of managing organizational change as complex but predictable, and assert that the key determinants of how organizational change should be managed are the perception of the complexity of change, and the extent to which it is believed that change can be effected on uniform bases. Van de Ven and Poole (1995), on the other hand look at change through the lens of natural process of variation, selection, and retention, advocating focusing on the unit and the mode of change as the key to resolving inevitable conflicts arising out of competition for scares resources, that tends to accompany organizational change. Embracing a yet different perspective, Dunphy and Stace (1988) see clearly delineated scope of change as being of central importance in framing an effective change management strategy, which, depending on the breadth of scope of the envisioned change, can take the form of a more adaptive variant, such as incremental or transformative change strategy.

---

1 This estimate is derived from several applied research studies including a recent (2013) study by Towers Watson consultancy which found that only about 30% of change management initiatives were successful over the long term, which is in line with an earlier (2010) McKinsey's survey of business executives which also concluded that about 30% of change program were successful in the long term, while the 2008 IBM study estimated that nearly 60% of projects aimed at achieving business change did not fully meet their objectives.

A synthesis of the divergent approaches to categorizing types of organizational change suggests two distinct sets of meta-categories: One characterizing the 'how', and the other one the 'what' of change. The former – the 'how' of change – can be conceptualized as being comprised of three distinct dimensions: complexity of change, unit of change, and scope of change, abbreviated as CUS. The latter, or the 'what' of change', can be conceptualized as being comprised of six distinct facets: culture, assets, process, people, strategy, and structure, abbreviated as CAPPSS. Furthermore, the CUS dimension characterizes every instance of organizational change, which is to say that all planned change initiatives are described in terms of the requisite behavioral and related modifications (complexity), the elementary entities that are to change (unit), and the span or scale of the desired alterations (scope). On the other hand, the CAPPSS dimension delineates specific focal points of change, thus as few as one or as many as all six can be impacted by a given initiative. For instance, a simple reorganization might only entail re-drafting of organizational structure, while a more expansive one might entail changing of not only the organizational structure, but also its culture, processes (how work is done), strategy, and more. The generalized relationship between the two meta-categories is graphically depicted in Figure 9.2 shown below.

Figure 9.2
Generalized CUS – CAPPSS Relationship

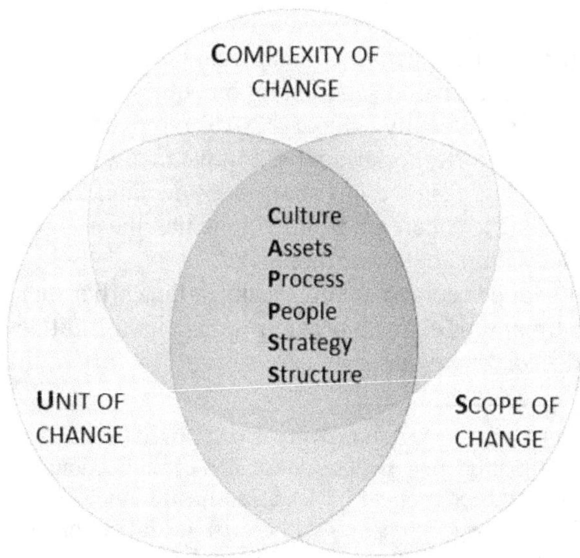

Within the broad confines of enterprise risk management (ERM), assessment of organizational threats entails capturing within-threat-category as well as cross-threat-categories factors, which is commonly accomplished using a process comprised of several distinct steps[2]. Accepting that management of organizational change falls within the broader scope of ERM, and it constitutes a single category of threats, assessment of planned self-change emanating threats should follow the general logic of ERM risk assessment, but its scope should be adjusted accordingly. Thus while assessment of enterprise-wide risks needs to encompass both the within-threat-category and the cross-threat-category exposures, assessment of only the planned change-emanating risks should only encompass the within-threat category risks. Consequently, the commonly used five-step enterprise-wide risk assessment framework of identification, estimation, mapping, response, and capitalization should be reduced into the three-step process of identification, estimation, and response.

Threat Identification

One of the more common and visible types of organizational change is reorganization. It is a fairly broad category of organizational alterations encompassing changes such as reshaping of organizational control structures (e.g., moving from a product- to geography-centric model), financial reward mechanisms (e.g., tying a larger part of compensation to performance) or processes (e.g., deploying a comprehensive management system). When considered from the perspective of risk management, even best thought out reorganizations can deliver disappointing outcomes. For instance, Yelp, a business review site, recently (January, 2015) removed geography from the way it assigned territories to sales reps, a move that was aimed at increasing efficiency but instead resulted in a sharp sales decline, followed by a precipitous share price decrease (following which the company reverted to its previous model within about two months).

Yelp's failed reorganization speaks to the earlier mentioned 70% failure rate estimate for planned organizational change initiatives – it could be characterized as *outcome threat,* which is the possibility of the change initiative

---

[2] Perhaps the most widely used framework is comprised of five distinct steps of identification, estimation, mapping, response, and capitalization; however, a broader 7-step process has also been proposed: Risk assessment framework implementation, delineation of risk managers' responsibilities, risk identification, threat estimation, risk response, risk incidence recording, risk profile update.

producing adverse outcomes. Each initiative, however, also faces the possibility of process failure, defined here as the inability of the organization to successfully transition from the 'current' to 'future' state. As discussed earlier, planned organizational transformations must overcome resistance stemming from individual self-interest and group dynamics, thus the resultant *process threat* is endemic to all planned change initiatives.

From the standpoint of risk management, each of the two threat dimensions pose different risk identification challenges. Outcome threats are ultimately an expression of uncertainty of anticipated benefits of the future state, while process threats represent the possibility that the means and mechanisms deployed to bring about the future state will not produce the desired outcome. Identification of the former is tantamount to delineating all possible change outcomes. In the above Yelp example it would entail anticipating the sales drop as one of the possible consequences of the change that has been instituted, which could be approached deductively or by drawing inferences from reviews of similar initiatives deployed by similar organizations.

Identifying of specific process threats is considerably more involved, particularly for complex organizational change initiatives that take significant amounts of time to achieve, and that encompass numerous alterations. To yield a sufficiently exhaustive set of potential risks, the process threat identification needs to be rooted in a normative typology enumerating distinct elements of the process. The CUS-CAPPSS conceptualization of the 'what' and 'how' dimensions of organizational change depicted in Figure 9.2 can be used as the starting point in the development of such a normative framework.

The CUS-CAPPSS conceptualization suggests that organizational change related threats could emerge in the context of 'focus of change' and 'aspect of change' dyads. For example, introduction of a discontinuously different organizational structure could be seen as very complex, thus giving rise to the possibility of failure of the change initiative. The resultant general threat, complexity of the new structure, can be further distilled by individual-specific (i.e., self-interest) and group-wide potential change inhibitors. The general 'complexity of the new structure' threat can be broken down into more narrowly defined person-specific and group-wide risks.

Focusing first on person-specific factors, individuals tend to resist change primarily because no change is truly value-free, thus it can pose a threat to one's well-being, which often manifests itself in cynicism toward proposed change. Those relatively abstract person-specific change inhibitors can be operationalized using the earlier discussed ADKAR model of organizational change management, which offers parsimonious yet complete assessment of the core resistance-to-change root causes. More specifically, the following five operationally specific but generalizable ADKAR model-derived factors suggest potential threats emanating from person-specific resistance to organizational self-change:

1. Absent or insufficient *awareness* of the need for change;
2. Insufficient *desire* to fully participate in the planned change;
3. Insufficient *knowledge* of how to change one's behaviors and/or skills;
4. Perceived lack of *ability* to acquire new skills and behaviors;
5. Insufficient *reinforcement* of why, what and how to change (to make the change stick).

The somewhat harder to delineate are the group-wide potential change inhibitors, as those encompass a broad array of interpersonal interactions, as well as organizational processes and structures. Building on the cumulative wisdom of past research efforts captured in the 'aspects of change' summarization, several distinct root causes can be delineated: change rationalization, clearly stated future state, the scope of what is expected to change, the specifics of the desired future state, and an implementation roadmap. Those root causes in turn suggest the following group-wide inhibitors:

1. No compelling *change rationale*;
2. Lack of clear *future state vision*;
3. *Scope of change* ambiguity;
4. Uncertainty regarding *specifics of the future state*;
5. No clear *implementation roadmap*.

Threat Estimation

A 'typical' risk estimation problem focuses on assessing the probability and the impact adverse events, such as accidents or floods. Although many such events, exemplified by natural catastrophes such as hurricanes and manmade crises such as accounting scandals, are difficult to anticipate and thus estimate, as distinct events occurring at a point in time they nonetheless present clear estimation targets. In contrast to that, planned organizational change manifests itself as a basket of activities spread over a period of time that, in total, do not exhibit the distinctiveness of risk events. In addition, process and outcome failures alike may not be immediately visible. More specifically, whereas the occurrence of an accident is immediately obvious, discerning that a change initiative has stalled (process threat) or did not produce the anticipated benefits (outcome threat) can be comparatively difficult, which further underscores the difference between risk as a perilous event and risk as the possibility of process or outcome failure. It thus follows that while the distinctiveness of the occurrence and consequence of peril-type risks can be aggregated into empirical distributions, ultimately giving rise to mathematically sound estimates of probability of occurrence and magnitude of impact, that is not the case for threats associated with planned change, which lack the discrete point-in-time characteristics.

Instead, planned organizational change initiatives can be expressed as a process of mutually dependent successive stages, where the threat of failure of the overall initiative is expressed as the cumulative possibility of failure of individual process stages. Conceptualized in that manner, the threat of initiative-wide failure can be expected to decrease as successive stages are completed, as graphically illustrated in Figure 9.3.

Figure 9.3

Generalized Initiative-Level Threat of Failure

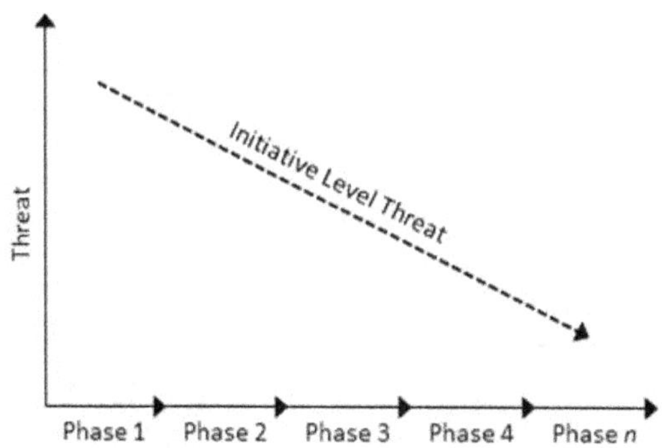

The generalized idea depicted above is an oversimplification, but it reflects the rationale imbedded in change management conceptualizations discussed earlier. Recalling the five individual level inhibitors of organizational change derived from the ADKAR model, organizational constituents, most notably its employees, becoming *aware* of the need for change (represented by Phase 1 in Figure 9.3) can be construed as a necessary precondition for the development of *desire* to fully participate in the planned change (Phase 2), which, if successful, should then lead to openness to acquiring the necessary *knowledge* (Phase 3), the successful completion of which should in turn can be expected to compel an individual to develop the change-mandated *abilities* (Phase 4), finally paving the way for *reinforcement* related activities (Phase 5). As each successive stage is successfully completed, the chances of failure of the entire organizational change initiative decrease. The same reasoning applies to the five group-wide inhibitors of change, where clearly spelled out change rationale followed by well-articulated vision of the future state, scope of change, specifics of the future state, and the implementation roadmap can also be conceptualized as largely sequential phases; thus as each stage is completed, the organizational dimension-attributed threat of initiative level failure decreases. The two dimensions of organizational self-change can be assumed to be largely independent of each other, as evidence suggests that individual-level imperatives and group dynamics are driven by diverging considerations.

From the standpoint of threat assessment, the initiative-level possibility of failure can be conceptualized as a decreasing function of person-specific and group-wide dimensions of organizational change, as graphically illustrated below.

Figure 9.4

Change Initiative Threat Assessment

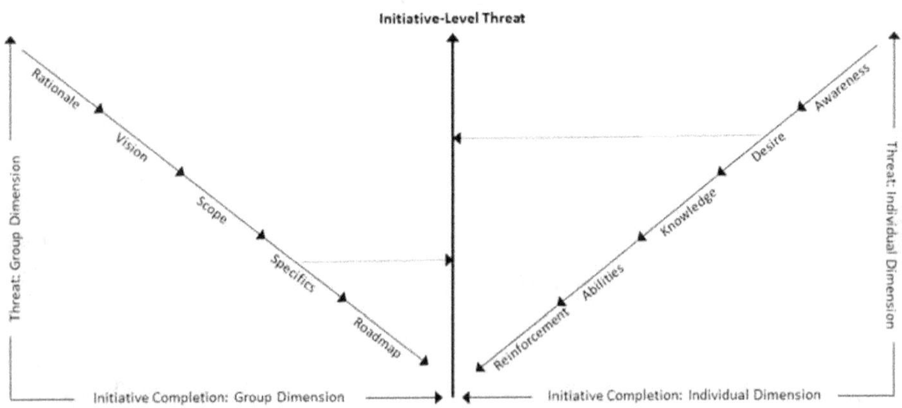

Independence of the two dimensions of organizational change, depicted above as two separate sets of Cartesian coordinates, suggests that the pace of transformation can vary, as shown by the two horizontal dotted lines. It follows that the initiative-level threat can be approximated by slower of the two completion rates, which in Figure 9.4 is the second stage (Desire). The greater the progress along both dimensions, the lower the overall risk of the change initiative failure, which initially is represented by the 'benchmark', derived from the average failure rate for similar initiatives. Putting it all together, the initiative level completion threat can be approximated as follows:

$$\text{Initiative Failure Threat} = \left(\frac{Max(PNC_g, PNC_i)}{PT_{lag}}\right) \times Benchmark_{mn}$$

where,

PNC_g = phases not yet completed – group;
PNC_i = phases not yet completed – individual;
PT_{lag} = total number of stages in the lagging dimension;
$Benchmark_{mn}$ = long-term failure rate for initiative *m* implemented in sector *n*;

As noted earlier, the above Initiative Failure Threat operationalization expresses the risk posed by an organizational self-change initiative as a function of the rate of completion of the slower paced of the group and individual dimensions of change (numerator), and the total number of change stages in the 'lagging' dimension (denominator). Stated differently, even if one of the two dimensions of change was fully completed, the initiative-wide threat would still be a function of the degree of incompletion of the other dimension.

Application and interpretation wise, the initial failure threat operationalization is comprised of two distinct parts: the assessment of the change initiative's completion rate, and a reference benchmark. The former, which assumes the value of '1' or 100% at the onset (denoting that none of the stages have yet been completed) is meant to communicate the potentiality of threat, which is the degree to which the current status of the initiative of interest creates a potential for the expected threat to materialize. The 'reference benchmark' contributes an a priori generalized expected initiative failure rate, which represents the long-term average failure rate of peer organizations implementing similar initiatives.

To illustrate the mechanics of the proposed self-change threat of failure estimation approach, let us assume that, on average, 30% of organizational restructuring efforts in a particular industry ultimately fail to deliver sought after benefits. Starting with that general benchmark as the initial threat estimate, an organization choosing to embark on a restructuring project could reasonably assume that it faces an estimated chance of failure of roughly 30%

at the onset of the project[3]. Subsequently, the initial 30% failure estimate would gradually diminish as the overall initiative completion rate begins to increase. When 4 out of 5 phases remain to be completed, that estimate could be reduced to 30% * 0.8 (4÷5), or 24%; when only a maximum of 3 phases remain, the threat estimate is further reduced to 18% (3÷5 *30%), and so on; once all phases of the initiative have been completed the initiative wide threat becomes 0% (e.g., 0÷5 *30%).

Stage-Level Threats

The next logical threat estimation step is to address the possibility of failure at the level of individual stages comprising the overall change initiative, but numerous challenges stand in the way. To better understand those impediments it is helpful to recall the two components of the 'initiative failure threat' operationalization discussed earlier: change initiative's completion rate, and the reference benchmark. Reducing the scope of estimation from initiative-wide to a stage-specific requires corresponding changes in the computational approach, which in turn calls for appropriate analogs. On the surface that would appear to be quite simple, but serious difficulties emerge upon closer examination.

To start with, analyzing the process of self-imposed organizational change at a more disaggregate level leads to confounding of generalizable (i.e., not unique to an organization or a situation) and non-generalizable, or situation-and-organization-specific factors, which ultimately obfuscates the applicability of external benchmarking. That is because even seemingly very similar organizations, most notably those that offer comparable mixes of products and/or services and directly compete with one another, are often distinguished by noticeably different organizational management styles and organizational cultures, and possibly even somewhat different operational systems and technological infrastructures. As a result, trying to implement a similar type of change may give rise to materially different sets of challenges across the otherwise similar organizations, ultimately greatly degrading the validity of cross-organization stage-of-change-initiative comparisons. Moreover, the definition of what constitutes 'failure' (or 'success', for that matter) is not universal, nor is its operationalization. The expected definitional and operational invariance is likely to be particularly pronounced in the context of the individual-level dimension of organizational self-change, given the

3 30%*1, where '1' is the initial (since 5 out of the total of 5 phases are yet to be completed) potentiality of the 30% threat of failure materializing.

inherent difficulty of objectively measuring emotional states of individuals. This challenge is well illustrated by the 'Desire' phase of the 5-step process depicted in Figure 9.4, which encapsulates individuals' emotional commitment to fully participate in the intended change. When attempting to assess that particular aspect of individual-level change readiness, organizations often utilize noticeably different data capture mechanisms – for instance, one organization might elect to survey all change-affected employees using a 6-point Likert scale, while another organization may rely on managers' assessment of employees' desire to participate in the planned change, and yet another one might choose to utilize qualitative techniques, such as focus groups. In the end, a group of similar organizations trying to enact comparable types of changes is likely to utilize substantially different measurement approaches, making any stage-of-the-change-initiative based side-by-side comparisons difficult, if not outright impossible.

Lastly, timing differences could also lead to skewed comparisons – change takes time, but how much? Even if the just discussed measurement differences were controlled for (by means of using the same method across organizations), the choice of 'when' to measure could have a material impact on findings. All considered, the nature of self-imposed organizational change may effectively impose 'granularity limits' on the assessment of threat of failure, effectively limiting it to the initiative level of analysis.

Threat Response

The ultimate goal of organizational risk management is twofold: Firstly, it is to prevent the occurrence of those adverse events that can be avoided, and secondly to minimize the impact of those that cannot be avoided. Once identified and assessed, each distinct risk calls for a planned response, which can take the form of one or more of the following: avoidance, or refraining from risk event precipitating activities, reduction, or lessening the risk's chance of occurrence, transfer, or contractual reassignment of economic loss responsibility, and acceptance, or acknowledgement of the risk and assumption of responsibility for its consequences. The avoid-reduce-transfer-accept typology offers an excellent summation of broad strategies for responding to episodic risks – it is, however, poorly suited to the task of managing threats emanating from planned organizational change. There are two reasons for that: First, the typology sees risks as perilous events to be dodged which, as discussed earlier is conceptually and operationally different from threats posed by planned change. Second, threat avoidance is not a viable response mechanism because doing so would effectively mean foregoing the planned change; similarly, threat transfer is also not viable due to lack of clear event triggers that are typically called for by insurance and other risk transfer arrangements.

Recalling that the principal goal of managing organizational self-change, which is to assure successful transformation of organizational culture, assets, people, processes, strategies and/or structure, appropriate threat response mechanism should thus be built around the general notion of 'change process support'. An outline of the proposed threat response framework is graphically shown in Figure 9.5.

Figure 9.5
Organizational Self-Change Threat Response Framework

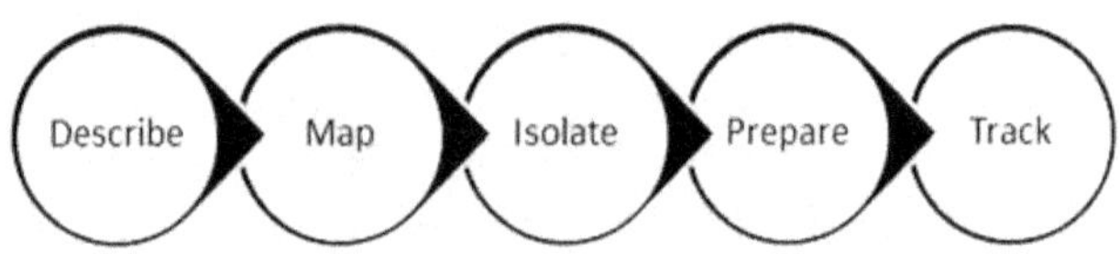

The point of departure in the 5-step process outlined above – *describe* – entails developing a comprehensive and detailed understanding of the envisioned change process, to be followed by carefully *mapping* out all process step specific requirements and dependencies. The next step is to *isolate* all actors who both impact and are impacted by the envisioned change (i.e., can potentially inhibit the desired change), followed by *preparing* a plan to overcome the anticipated change resistance. The last step in the process – *tracking* – is focused on systematic gathering and communication of change process progress information.

Implicit in the above threat response framework is that perception of those conducting the assessment can shape the organizational *control outlook*, which is a combination of how threat related information is processed, and what response posture it precipitates. The more subjective the evaluation, the greater the chance of a bias resulting from cross-individual differences in perception of intangible outcomes. Although perceptual biases can have numerous root causes, one's cultural background, or the totality of socially transmitted norms and behaviors, frequently emerges as the leading contributor. As suggested by the cultural theory, which offers a framework for understanding the impact of cultural differences on, among others, managers' control posture, there are four major, culture-shaped control outlook prototypes: individualists, hierarchists, egalitarians, and fatalists.

Individualists' decisions are generally unconstrained by the demands of the organization at large; as change managers they tend to feel empowered to take steps necessary to mitigate any observed threats, which is in stark contrast to chain of command focused hierarchists, who tend to await explicit directives. Egalitarians, on the other hand, favor more democratic decision-making, thus are inclined to build consensus regarding appropriateness of threat response related courses of action. The last of the four culture-shaped control outlook types, the fatalists, are characterized by 'there is little that can be done' mindset, hence tend to be inclined to simply accept the consequences of identified threats. Although very broad generalizations, the culture inspired prototypes are nonetheless suggestive of potentially meaningful impact of individual-level differences on organizational threat response posture.

***

The overview of organizational threat abatement would not be complete without addressing *organizational compliance,* especially in light of the steadily expanding regulatory oversight. The increasing frequency and severity of financial and other man-made crises precipitated, in a fairly predictable manner, tightening or revising of currently existing regimes (e.g., the EU's Solvency II regulatory framework) and the introduction of new, often sweeping oversight provisions (e.g., US's Dodd-Frank Wall Street Reform and Consumer Protection Act). In addition, the very notion of what constitutes 'compliance', in terms of organizational behaviors, and what is the burden of proof to show evidence of proactive rule enforcement have been targets of numerous legislative, judicial and regulatory steps. In short, the conventional view of compliance as a set of 'check the box' activities ought to be reconsidered, which is the focus of the next section.

Meeting Mandates

Compliance: Black and White or Shades of Gray?

Overtly, 'compliance' sounds quite straightforward: A particular regulation calls for specific actions or lays out specific prohibitions which in turn leads to an easy to understand and implement 'if-then' decision rule. And indeed, there are numerous instances when that is precisely the case, as exemplified by clear insider trading or workplace discrimination rules; in those cases, noncompliance is tantamount to violations of 'black letter law.' There are, however, instances where regulatory mandates and the resultant organizational liability are not quite that easy to discern…In a sense, that almost sounds contradictory – shouldn't 'compliance' only attach to clear, unambiguous rules? To a large degree, the answer to this question depends on the very definition of 'compliance'.

The 'standard' or general definition of *compliance* states that is the act or the result of conforming to a rule, such as a policy, standard or law. When considered from a narrower perspective of business regulations, the meaning of compliance becomes more aspirational as encompasses organizational efforts to ensure that they are aware of and take steps to act in accordance with relevant laws and regulations. In that context, compliance is a product of two somewhat distinct endeavors: 1. developing awareness of all applicable laws and regulations, and 2. behaving in accordance with those laws and regulations. Considering that the US Congress alone enacts, on average, more than 300 legislative acts per year and all US federal agencies with rulemaking powers create an estimate 10,000 new rules during the same timeframe, being aware of those that matter and staying current are far from simple…In addition, as a common law country, where legal precedents and doctrines are continuously evolving as results of new judicial rulings, the awareness of all applicable laws and regulations has to also encompass common law (in addition to the earlier mentioned statutory law), which further compounds the difficulty of staying informed and staying current. Behaving in accordance with applicable laws and regulations is not a simple matter, either…Whereas some commandments and prohibitions are clearly stated, others may require reading 'between the lines', especially when dealing with rules that only tangentially address an area of interest, especially is that area is ill-defined to begin with...

Organizational resilience is one of those 'ill-defined' aspects of business. It is still in the process of self-coagulation as the originally distinct fields of continuity planning, disaster recovery and emergency management are beginning to coalesce together. Not surprisingly, compliance is both extremely important and equally hard to clearly define.

10

Regulatory Compliance

The most fundamental distinction of the Threat Exposure Management (TEM) framework detailed in this book is that it views 'threat' as the degree of an organization's exposure to adverse developments, rather than focusing on those developments as such. This heightens the importance of thorough and sound organization-specific threat profiling which, in operational terms, conveys the aggregate measure of the totality of potential adverse developments confronting an organization. In addition, the TEM framework's scope reaches far beyond the enterprise risk management (ERM) view of risk discussed in Chapter 4 by including the historically distinct areas of business continuity planning, emergency, and change management. More specifically, the TEM framework posits that the end goal of managing the totality of an organization's exposures is to make positive contribution to organizational competitiveness, ultimately increasing the economic value of an organization. This is a very important philosophical shift in how an organization views the role of its broadly defined function of threat abatement: Formerly focused on expense minimization, those efforts are now a part of the organizational value creation process. Lastly, also heightens the importance of the frequently overlooked dimension of compliance with applicable laws and regulations.

The Legal Underpinnings of Compliance

Key to understanding the ideas imbedded in the notion of legal and regulatory compliance that is an important part of managerial accountability of managers of public[1] North American business organizations are several business law concepts of liability, intent, duty of care and the business judgment rule. Each is briefly discussed next.

Liability and Business Conduct

Broadly defined, *liability* encompasses any action that puts an individual or a group at a disadvantage or creates a hindrance; in a somewhat narrower context of business activities, liability is an expression of a legally binding obligation, or a responsibility. Perhaps the most obvious example of business liability is debt, as exemplified by corporate bonds, a commonly used mechanism that allows business organizations (and other entities) to borrow money in the marketplace. In that sense, corporate bonds represent an obligation, or a liability, on the part of the borrower to repay the principal plus the applicable interest at an agreed upon time.

Thus, commercial liability can take many forms, including a wide array of financial obligations, such as debt or accounts payable, negligence, as exemplified by faulty product design resulting in harm, and prohibited behaviors, such as insider trading. Obviously, some liabilities are merely a part of the normal course of business (e.g., borrowing), while others can be unexpected and adverse (e.g., violations of securities laws). However, all commercial liabilities share three basic commonalities: First, they arise out of business conduct of individuals; second, they are legally binding; and third, they encompass both intentional and unintended actions.

Although corporations, as well as some other types of business organizations (such as limited liability companies) are ascribed with a legally distinct status, actions of organizations are ultimately actions of individuals representing organizations. Those actions can have wide-ranging legal, political, ethical and moral consequences: For instance, some may be ethically

[1] The definition of 'public' vs. 'private' business organization varies between North America and other, most notably European Union (EU) jurisdictions: in the US and Canada, a 'public' company is one whose stock is traded on a public stock exchange, whereas in the EU that company would be considered 'private'(a 'public' EU company is one that is owned/controlled by a governmental body).

or morally questionable, such as decisions to maintain business ties with organizations that promote social inequality; still others may be outright illegal, such as directly engaging in unfair labor practices or withholding (from shareholders) company performance related information. It is important to note that while all such behaviors can have adverse consequences (i.e., can be a source of risk), only illegal activities can be a source of liability, a distinction that is at the heart of the risk-liability relationship.

Furthermore, liability related business conduct of organizational managers should be considered in the context of a continuum ranging from 'acceptable' (no liability) to 'unacceptable' (potential liability). At the most rudimentary level, acceptable business conduct encompasses behaviors that do not violate any of the applicable laws or regulations, while unacceptable conduct encompasses any and all behaviors that breach one or more of the applicable regulations or laws. Of course, it is intuitively obvious that some transgressions might be worse than others, which means that executive conduct-related business liability can range considerably in terms of the severity of its consequences.

It is worth noting, however, that the scope of business conduct extends beyond statutorily mandated reporting requirements, when considered in the context of distinct organizational stakeholder groups. More specifically, there are somewhat distinct behavioral norms framing interactions of directors and officers with different external and internal constituent groups that may be affected by actions and decisions of the organization's executive leadership.

Legally Binding

Building on the ideas encapsulated in the discussion of business conduct of individuals with the goal of drawing a clear line of demarcation between (executive) risk and liability demands distinguishing between potentially damaging, i.e., risky, and prohibited or prescribed behaviors. To fall within the latter category, and thus to be a source of liability, an executive action has to fall within a category of behaviors described by applicable laws, or regulations derived from underlying laws. In other words, executive liability is a direct consequence of legal non-compliance. It is worth noting that it can stem from general obligations emanating from applicable laws or a specific agreement spelled out in a written contract; it can also take the form of violations of implicit, i.e., unwritten arrangements.

The enforcement of legally binding obligations of organizational management lies at the heart of interactions between the organization and its distinct stakeholder groups (discussed in more detail later in this chapter). In general, any organizational stakeholder who can establish 'legal standing' within the confines of a distinct set of legally binding organizational actions can initiate the enforcement of those obligations. Establishing of legal standing requires that the stakeholder demonstrates sufficient connection to the actions of organizational decision makers, typically a straightforward task in the content of commercial relationships[2]. As will be discussed later, shareholders have legal standing when pursuing matters pertaining to their investments (company stock); employees have legal standing when pursuing employment related matters; customers have legal standing when pursuing product liability claims.

Intent

The US securities laws require all of the approximately 5,000 business organizations traded on US stock exchanges to submit (to the Securities and Exchange Commission, SEC) quarterly and annual detailed financial reports. Subsequent to those filings, about 1,000 corrections, known as 'restatements' are filed each year to rectify mistakes that were made in the original fillings, ranging from minor typographical errors to fairly significant corrections of key performance outcomes, such as sales or profitability. Some of those mistakes are inadvertent clerical errors, while others are indicative of troubling governance breakdowns, as was the case with now-defunct Enron' and WorldCom's massive revenue and expense revisions[3]. In the latter of the two scenarios, it became clear (through a legal process that landed some of the key executives of both companies in prison) that the original SEC filings were fraudulent, which points to what is legally known as the *intent to deceive.* An intentional behavior, it is characterized by the deceiver knowing that the information s/he is spreading is false or that the withholding of the information would constitute a fraudulent action.

In the field of social psychology there are several theoretical constructs that aim to explain intentional behaviors, or why one chooses to take a

---

[2] This is known as the *locus standi* principle in U.S jurisprudence; a failure to make a compelling locus standi argument will effectively terminate the stakeholder's enforcement actions.

[3] Forced to restate $3.8 billion of improperly accounted for expenses WorldCom filed for Chapter 11 bankruptcy protection in 2002; with $107 billion in assets, that was the largest bankruptcy in the US history (the reorganized company is now a subsidiary of Verizon Communications).

particular course of action. The best known of these is the theory of reasoned action proposed by Fishbein and Ajzen in 1975[4] and its earlier predecessor, the expectancy-value theory[5]. These theoretical frameworks posit that reasoned actions are direct results of the interplay among three distinct constructs of behavioral intentions, attitudes and subjective norms. Hence, actions of organizational decision makers tend to be shaped by a combination of their attitudes toward the action of interest and their subjective norms, which in turn are their beliefs and attitudes regarding the focal behavior.

On the other hand, unintended actions, as the name implies, are outcomes that were not deliberate, or stated differently, not a calculated behavioral aftereffect. The consequences of unintended actions could be foreseen or unforeseen, but in order to give rise to liability they need to be likely or logical consequences of the action. It is understood that it can be quite difficult to establish whether or not a particular outcome is a likely or a logical consequence of the action of interest, but nonetheless, this type of proof effectively forms the boundary of business liability.

Duty of Care vs. Business Judgment Rule

There are two important, contrasting legal concepts that frame the extent of managerial liability: On the one hand, organizational managers are bound by the *duty of care,* which compels them to act in the best interest of the corporation and its shareholders. On the other hand, however, they are protected by the relatively wide-reaching provisions of the *business judgment rule,* which affords them a considerable amount of decisioning immunity. More specifically, the business judgment rule stipulates that, so long as managers act in 'good faith' (i.e., do not engage in intentional deceit or similar activities) and their decisions reflect their 'best efforts' to enhance the well-being of companies and their owners, they cannot be held legally liable for unfavorable outcomes, such as an acquisition that leads to disastrous consequences.

In practice, acting in good faith and the applicability of the business judgment rule reflect the use of relative, rather than absolute standards, as

---

[4] Fishbein M. and Ajzen I. (1975), *Belief, Attitude, Intention and Behavior: An Introduction to Theory and Research*, Addison-Wesley, Reading, MA.

[5] Fishbein M. (1963), 'An Investigation of Relationships between Beliefs about an Object and Attitudes toward that Object,' *Human Relations* vol. 16, 233-240.

illustrated by the landmark Walt Disney Company derivative litigation case[6]. The reliance on relative rather than absolute appropriateness tests means that as much as a severance package worth $140 million could be scarcely defended as reasonable in the eyes of most onlookers (an absolute standard), in a relative context it was not unprecedented and thus deemed 'reasonable'…). This is an important point, particularly when considered in the context of the business judgment rule as it suggests that in a context of organizational decisioning, a 'reasonable' choice is one for which a relevant precedent exists.

Duty of Care

As noted earlier, the duty of care placed upon organizational managers demands that their decisions are made with the best interest of the corporation and its shareholders in mind. Operationally, this entails two somewhat distinct considerations: 1. the duty to act, and 2. the just discussed decision making due diligence.

The *duty to act* compels directors and officers to be actively involved in the affairs of the business. It amounts to saying, 'It is unacceptable to be a figurehead passively watching the company-impacting events unfold, or not paying attention at all, for that matter; indeed, it is incumbent upon the organization's leadership to actively engage in activities aimed at helping to positively affect the well-being of the organization.' The power and the trust placed in the hands of the broadly defined executive leadership by the corporation's shareholders do not come with an option to act – they come with a requirement to act.

An important consideration associated with the duty to act is *decisioning due diligence.* As much as passively watching the fate of the

---

[6] Under 'derivative litigation' shareholders pursue legal action against organizational managers (specifically, a company's directors and officers) on behalf of the company itself (for more details, see Banasiewicz, A., 2015, *Cracking the Code of Executive Risk,* Routledge, New York, NY). The Walt Disney Company Derivative Litigation (C.A. No. 15452, Del. Ch. Aug. 9, 2005) revolved around whether or not the Board of Directors breached their fiduciary duties by approving former President Michael Ovitz's compensation/severance package (worth an estimated $140 million) which was awarded to him as a part his controversial termination without cause after less than 2 years on the job. (Disappointingly, the Delaware Court of Chancery which heard the case, concluded that even though the terms of Mr. Ovitz's severance seemed outlandish, the Board nonetheless demonstrated an adequate amount of due diligence, in the form of outside expert opinions and evaluations to relieve the Board of any liability).

organization play itself out is a violation of executive responsibilities, making decisions without thoughtfully considering the available and applicable information may also be a violation of executive duties. In other words, the duty to act should not be interpreted as making random decisions for random reasons, but rather making thoughtful decisions for well-considered reasons. This is not to say that it demands clairvoyance – it simply calls upon organizational managers to carefully weigh what might be known at the decision time.

When either the duty to act or the decisioning due diligence are not soundly discharged, organizational managers may be charged with *dereliction of duty*, which is failure to perform the responsibilities of their office. From the standpoint of the TEM threat abatement framework there are two distinct sets of consequences that may follow: 1. Managers may be subject to monetary, or even criminal penalties, and 2. The value the organization may decline.

Business Judgment Rule

In theory, a business organization is free to pursue any strategic alternative, so long as it is not in conflict with any of the applicable laws, rules, or regulations. In practice, however, strategic choices of organizations are constrained by a long list of both internal as well as external factors. The internal constraints include core competencies (or more precisely, absence of competencies), the availability of economic resources and prior commitments, to name just a few. External constraints include actual or anticipated actions of competitors, prevailing market characteristics and expectations regarding the future (demand, actions of competitors, regulatory developments, etc.). Hence the universe of feasible strategic alternatives is, to a large degree, determined outside the actions of directors of organizations.

Still, within the realm of the available options, executive decision makers have the freedom to pursue the alternatives that – according to their judgment – will yield the best possible outcomes for the organization and its shareholders, which is the essence of the business judgment rule. Arguably, there is no other executive decision making context where this rule has quite as profound an impact as it does here.

Industrial history is full of examples of poor strategic choices leading to demise or near-demise of organizations. Consider the once prosperous – even dominant – retailers, such as Marshall Field's, Circuit City, Service Merchandise, Filene's; banks, such as Washington Mutual, Lehman Brothers or Bear Stearns; or manufacturing organizations, such as American Motor

Company (AMC), Polaroid or Cambridge Sound. For reasons as varied as their products, these companies' strategic choices turned out to be quite a bit less 'inspired' than those made by the competitors. It was not earthquakes, floods, securities class actions or even labor disputes that drove these once-thriving businesses to extinction – it was poorly conceived strategies.

What does all of that have to do with business judgment rule? Strategic planning is one of the most visible and consequential manifestations of executive decision-making and the business judgment rule is intended to encourage an active participation in the affairs of the company. Going back to the now-extinct business organizations mentioned above – which of the following is a more reasonable conclusion? 1. Taken as a group (a fraternity of dubious distinction), were the directors and officers of the now-defunct organizations significantly less capable than their peers, or leaders of peer organizations still thriving today? or, 2. Were the now-extinct organizations' boards significantly less engaged in the running of those companies? It is difficult to imagine managing bodies of otherwise similar organizations being set apart by a sizable competency differential; on the other hand, it is quite a bit easier to envision one board of directors being considerably more active and engaged (in the running of the company) than another one. In fact, the assessment of *corporate governance* commonly includes overt activity indicators, such as the annual number of board meetings, which point to a noticeable amount of variability across organizations, so much so that it is worthwhile to take a close look.

Organizational Resilience as a Mandate

There are numerous reasons business organizations choose to invest in the development and ongoing maintenance of a sound resilience infrastructure. First and foremost, it is simply reckless to not have a contingency (i.e., a business continuity) plan in place in the event of a natural or a man-made catastrophe. In fact, it could be argued that it violates the earlier discussed duty of care. Moreover, according to research by the American Management Association, about 50% of businesses that experience a major disaster without a disaster recovery plan in place never re-open. Hence proactive business continuity planning and emergency preparedness efforts should be as much a part of an organization's threat abatement efforts as insurance procurement. A second, more reactive reason is to fulfill any applicable external requirements. Those usually include laws and regulatory mandates (henceforth jointly referred to as 'regulations'), as well as voluntary 'subscriptions' to standards.

The first of the two external reasons to develop sound organizational resilience means and processes, governmental *regulations*, are mandatory rules imposed (typically) by regulatory agencies; failure to adhere to their provisions typically results in an economic penalty or an operational sanction. Broadly categorized, regulations can either be general (i.e., equally applicable to all industries), or industry-specific. When considered from an organizational resilience standpoint, some industries play such a fundamental role in the overall commercial ecosystem that a prolonged operational outage would likely impair the wellbeing of the entire system[7]. Those commerce-critical industries typically include Banking and Finance, Healthcare, Transportation, Energy, and Communications; in developed economies, such as those of North America or Western Europe, numerous laws have been enacted with the goal of ensuring continuity of operation of those critical industries. Lastly, although the bulk of regulations are country-specific in scope, i.e., have been created by individual countries' legislative bodies and/or regulatory agencies, the rapid pace of globalization gave rise to a smaller but growing set of transnational regulations, best illustrated by the Basel Capital Accord developed by the Basel Committee on Banking Supervision[8].

---

[7] Consider the Great Recession of 2007/2008 discussed in Chapter 1: Systemic failures that crippled the financial sector led to a credit crunch, which in turn led to a sharp decline in commercial activities, which ultimately precipitated deep global recession.
[8] A committee of banking supervisory authorities that was established by the central bank governors of the Group of Ten countries in 1974; its core objective is to provide a mechanism for improvement of the quality of banking supervision worldwide.

The second of the two external reasons to develop sound organizational resilience means and processes embodies the desire to maintain competitive parity through adherence to *standards*. Best exemplified by ISO[9] certifications, which offer universally recognized acknowledgment of attainment of 'best in class' levels of quality, reliability or performance in a wide range of industrial areas, including business continuity and disaster recovery (i.e., organizational resilience). As noted earlier, the attainment of standards is, from a legal perspective, voluntary, which means that choosing to not do so will not precipitate fines or other governmental sanctions (of course, it may hinder the non-certified firm's competitiveness ultimately resulting in economic damage far worse than regulatory fines). Although the best-known standards, particularly those developed by ISO, are global, each country maintains a varying number of own standards, thus similarly to regulations discussed earlier, standards can be international or domestic.

The above considerations can be summarized along three distinct (i.e., independent) dimensions of regulations – standards (dimension 1); general – industry (dimension 2) and international – localized (dimension 3), as graphically depicted in Figure 10.1. The resultant 8-category categorization schema can then be used to give a more meaningful overview of the otherwise overwhelming array of organizational resilience related general and industry-specific regulations and standards. The eight categories are as follows:

1. General localized regulations
2. General localized standards
3. General international regulations
4. General international standards
5. Industry localized regulations
6. Industry localized standards
7. Industry international regulations
8. Industry international standards

[9] International Organization for Standardization, ISO, is an independent, non-governmental international organization dedicated to the promulgation of standards; its membership is comprised of 162 notional standards bodies.

Figure 10.1
Typology of Organizational Resilience Rules

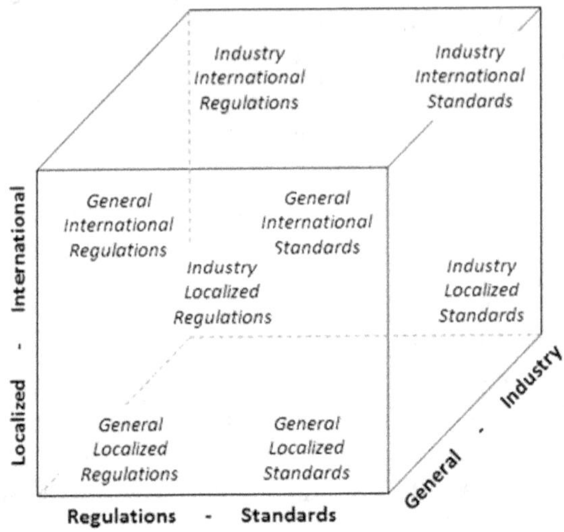

Before delving into each of the eight categories listed above, it is important to note that organizational resilience managers are not expected to have an attorney-like command of the law. However, they are encumbered with the responsibility of understanding the pertinent details of existing regulatory guidelines, along with the legal consequences of their company's failure to implement an effective resilience plan. It is also important to note that although no specific laws state categorically that companies must have a business continuity or a disaster recovery plan, there is a body of legal precedents which can be used to hold companies responsible to those affected by a company's inability to cope with a disaster. Two precedents are particularly noteworthy:

- The FJS Electronics vs. Fidelity Bank case.
  One of the better known such precedents is drawn from the case of FJS Electronics v. Fidelity Bank. In this 1981 case, FJS Electronics sued Fidelity Bank over a failure to stop payment on a check. Although the failure to stop payment of the check was procedural in nature, the court nonetheless ruled that Fidelity Bank assumed the risk that the system would fail to stop a check, and the court further ruled that the bank's failure to install a more flexible, error-tolerant system inevitably led to problems. This case shows that the use of a computer system in business does not change an

organization's duty of reasonable care in its daily operations; organizations can breach that duty by not diligently pursuing the development of a business continuity or a disaster recovery plan.

- The Hooper Doctrine.
  Dating back to the 1932 TJ Hooper vs. Northern Barge Corp. case, this legal doctrine can be used when courts are looking to determine a company's liability. This doctrine establishes that even though many companies do not have a disaster recovery plan, there are 'precautions so imperative that even their universal disregard does not excuse their omission.' Simply put, a company cannot use, as a defense, the fact that there are no specific requirements to have a business continuity or a disaster recovery plan and that many other companies do not have one.

In a more general sense, in the US the legal imperative to invest in the establishment of sound organizational resilience processes and mechanisms emanates from five distinct groupings of legal statutes:

1. *Contingency Planning Statutes*. Apply to the development of plans to ensure the recoverability of critical systems; examples include the Federal Financial Institutions Examination Council's guidelines.
2. *Liability Statutes*. Establish levels of liability under the 'Prudent Man Laws' for directors and officers of a corporation; examples include the Securities Act of 1933 and the Sarbanes-Oxley Act of 2002.
3. *Life / Safety Statutes*. Set out specific ordinances for ensuring the protection of employees in the workplace; examples include National Fire Protection Association and Occupational Safety & Health Administration rules.
4. *Risk Reduction Statutes*. Stipulate areas of risk management required to reduce and/or mitigate the effects of a disaster; examples include Section 404 of the Sarbanes-Oxley Act and Office of the Comptroller's Circular 235.
5. *Vital Records Management Statutes*. Specifications for the retention and disposition of corporate electronic and hardcopy records; example include the IRS Records Retention requirements.

General Localized Regulations

The first of the eight categories delineated in Figure 10.1, this grouping encompasses country-specific (i.e., 'localized') regulations aimed at all commercial entities (i.e., 'general'). According to the Business Continuity Institute, about 40 countries have at least one discernable law or regulatory provision aimed at some aspect of organizational resilience, such as business continuity, disaster recovery or emergency management; given that, our focus here will be just on US legislative and regulatory provisions. Those are as follows:

- *Foreign Corrupt Practices Act.* Directors and officers of business organizations can be held liable for 'failure to enact standards of care', should they fail to document their assessment that led them to conclude that it was not necessary to develop a contingency plan.
- *Health Insurance Portability and Accountability Act (HIPPA).* Calls for a contingency plan to be instituted as a part of data backup plan; also calls for emergency mode operation plan, testing and revision procedures and data criticality analysis.
- *Privacy Act.* Requires management to safeguard and to keep the information accurate and current to protect the individual.
- *Sarbanes-Oxley Act.* Requires auditors to increase scrutiny of all areas of internal control, including security and business continuity controls.
- *Computer Fraud and Abuse Act.* Makes it a federal offense to produce, buy, sell or transfer credit card or other access devices that are counterfeit, forged, lost or stolen.
- *Patriot Act.* Lays out requirements regarding records protection and availability, in the context of disaster recovery and business continuity.

General Localized Standards

Similarly to 'general localized regulations' discussed above, it is not possible to summarize all country-specific, organizational resilience related standards, thus the focus of the ensuing analysis will be just on US standards (some of which might have been adapted by other countries). Of most interest are the following:

- *National Fire Protection Association's Standard on Disaster / Emergency Management and Business Continuity Programs*. It establishes a common set of criteria for all hazards, disaster / emergency management and business continuity programs; it also provides the fundamental criteria to develop, implement, assess, and maintain the program for prevention, mitigation, preparedness, response, continuity and recovery.
- *ASIS American National Standard.* It provides organizations with a comprehensive management framework to anticipate, prevent (if possible), prepare for and respond to a disruptive incident. Additionally, it provides generic criteria to establish, check, maintain and improve a management system to enhance prevention, preparedness, mitigation, response, continuity and recovery from an emergency, crisis or disaster.
- *American National Standards Institute (ANSI) Standard.* It sets the requirement for establishment of a Vital Records Program; it clarifies what a Vital Records Program should encompass, and sets forth requirements for identifying and protecting vital records, assessing and analyzing their vulnerability, and determining the impact of their loss on an organization.
- *National Fire Protection Association's Standard on Stored Electrical Energy Emergency and Standby Power Systems*. Outlines performance requirements for stored electric energy systems providing an alternate source of electrical power in buildings and facilities during an interruption of normal power source.
- *National Fire Protection Association's Emergency Services Incident Management Systems Standard.* Defines and describes the essential elements of an incident management system that promotes coordination among responding agencies.
- *National Fire Protection Association's Standard on Protection of Records*. Details a process for protecting business records, archives and record centers.

In addition to the formal standards outlined above, numerous federal governmental and non-governmental trade organizations also developed a number of 'good practices' focused on different aspects of organizational resilience. Not surprisingly, the Federal Emergency Management Agency developed several sets of such recommendations, including guidance for business managers to respond to, and recover from disasters, or a step-by-step approach to emergency planning, response and recovery. Other examples of resilience related 'good practices' include the National Institute's of Standards and Technology delineation of fundamental planning principles for developing an effective contingency capability; the National Institute's for Information Technology Systems guidelines for selecting and specifying security controls for information systems; the Institute's of Internal Auditors business continuity management practice guide.

General International Regulations

This is the least developed of the eight organizational resilience segments, but considering the seemingly inevitable deepening of globalization, it is reasonable to expect the emergence of more and more specific international business resilience related accords. The United Nations Office for Disaster Risk Reduction, which was established in 1999 as a part of UN's Secretariat (the governing body of United Nations), is a natural nexus for the promulgation of future regulations. The bulk of future regulatory development is expected to grow out of the Sendai Framework for Disaster Risk Reduction 2015-2030, which was adopted by UN Member States in 2015 at the Third UN World Conference on Disaster Risk Reduction in Sendai, Japan. The Sendai Framework is a 15-year, voluntary, non-binding agreement which recognizes that each member state has the primary role to reduce disaster risk but that responsibility should be shared with other stakeholders including the private sector. In its current form, the Framework spells out four priorities for action:

> *Priority 1. Understanding disaster risk.*
> Disaster risk management should be based on an understanding of disaster risk in all its dimensions of vulnerability, capacity, exposure of persons and assets, hazard characteristics and the environment. Such knowledge can be used for risk assessment, prevention, mitigation, preparedness and response.
>
> *Priority 2. Strengthening disaster risk governance to manage disaster risk.*
> Disaster risk governance at the national, regional and global levels is very important for prevention, mitigation, preparedness, response, recovery, and rehabilitation. It fosters collaboration and partnership.

Priority 3. Investing in disaster risk reduction for resilience.
Public and private investment in disaster risk prevention and reduction through structural and non-structural measures are essential to enhance the economic, social, health and cultural resilience of persons, communities, countries and their assets, as well as the environment.

Priority 4. Enhancing disaster preparedness for effective response and to 'Build Back Better' in recovery, rehabilitation and reconstruction.
The growth of disaster risk means there is a need to strengthen disaster preparedness for response, take action in anticipation of events, and ensure capacities are in place for effective response and recovery at all levels. The recovery, rehabilitation and reconstruction phase is a critical opportunity to build back better, including through integrating disaster risk reduction into development measures.

Another noteworthy source of international organizational resilience related rules is the European Commission's Program for Critical Infrastructure Protection, which applies to the currently 27-member strong European Union[10]. The legislation covers the identification of important assets, risk analysis based on major threats scenarios and the vulnerability of each asset, and the identification, selection and prioritization of counter-measures and procedures.

General International Standards

While the above-discussed international resilience related regulations are still in their infancy, there are numerous international resilience standards that have already been developed and deployed. Given its scope and mission as the world's 'standard bearer', it is not surprising that the bulk of international resilience standards were developed by the International Organization for Standardization (ISO). Among the more widely known and used are:

- *ISO 22300 Societal Security Standard.* The is the 'parent' standard for business continuity management; it offers a broad set of rules which serve as a foundation for more narrowly scoped standards addressing specific domains within this broad area.

[10] European Union's membership is fluid – when it was first formed, the Union only had 6 members (France, Germany, Italy, Belgium, The Netherlands and Luxemburg); currently Turkey and Croatia are official candidates and negotiations are underway with Bosnia-Herzegovina, Serbia, Montenegro, Albania and Macedonia.

- *ISO 22301 Societal Security – Business Continuity Management Systems – Requirements Standard.* It details emergency / security, as well as technology recovery processes.
- *ISO 22313 Societal Security – Business Continuity Management Systems – Guidance*. Provides guidelines for establishing incident response and continuity programs.
- *ISO 22311 Societal Security – Video Surveillance Standard.* Specifies common file format that can be extracted from video-surveillance contents collection systems by an exchangeable data storage media or through a network.
- *ISO 22320 Societal Security – Emergency Management Requirements for Incidence Response Standard.* Details specific steps and processes aimed at facilitating effective emergency response.
- *ISO 22351 Societal Security – Emergency Management Message Structure Standard.* Details the recommended structure of effective exchange of information.
- *ISO 22397 Societal Security – Public-Private Partnerships Guidelines*. Provides guidelines for establishing partnering agreements among organizations to manage multiple relationships for events affecting security.
- *ISO 22398 Societal Security – Guidelines for Exercising and Testing*. Details standards for an organization to plan, conduct and improve its emergency testing provisions.
- *ISO 22399 Societal Security – Guidelines for Incidence Management and Operational Continuity Management*. Developed to allow organizations to establish their own management systems for operational continuity and incident preparedness.
- *ISO/IEC[11] 27031Guidelines for Information and Communication Technology Readiness for Business Continuity*. Describes the concepts and principles of information and communication technology (ITC) readiness for business continuity, and provides a framework of methods and processes all aspects of ITC readiness to ensure business continuity.
- *ISO/IEC 27001 Management Systems Standards for Information Security*. Provides information security management system guidelines for business continuity.

---

[11] International Electrotechnical Commission.

- *ISO/IEC 24762 Guidelines for Information and Communications Technology Disaster Recovery Services*. Addresses the provision of information and communications technology disaster recovery services as part of business continuity management.
- *ISO/IEC 27036 Management Systems Standard for Information Security*. Provides an overview of the guidance intended to assist organizations in securing their information and information systems within the context of supplier relationships.
- *ISO 31000 Risk Management Standard.* Offers a high-level principles and generic guidelines for establishing, deploying and ongoing maintenance of enterprise risk management.

In addition to the standards outlined above, ISO, IEC and other organizations developed a number of 'good practices' geared toward offering additional resilience related help. For example, the Business Continuity Institute developed a global business continuity management (BCM) lifecycle as a step toward practitioners, consultants and regulators developing a common frame of reference; similarly, the Disaster Recovery Institute International developed the '10 professional practices for business continuity professionals'; the American Institute of Certified Public Accountants developed a set of standards (SAS No. 70) to help auditors conduct more robust assessment of organizations' disaster preparedness.

Industry Localized Regulations

As noted in the context of general localized and regulations, at least 40 different countries developed at least some of their own regulations addressing different aspects of organizational resilience. Although the number and the specificity of legislative and regulatory frameworks vary considerably across that group of nations, in general, organizational resilience focused, industry-specific regulations tend to be focused on a handful of sectors that are believed to be of fundamental importance to commercial well-being of nations. Those are: Banking and Finance, Healthcare, Transportation, Energy, and Communications. Reducing the scope of the analysis to just the United States, the vast majority of US, industry-specific regulations are focused on a single industry – Banking and Finance; in fact, our research revealed only a single non-financial institutions focused regulation (shown at the end of the list). The key regulations that fall within this domain are summarized below.

- *Consumer Credit Protection Act.* A broad legislative act, it provides a basic framework establishing the right, liabilities and responsibilities of participants in electronic fund transfer systems.
- *Expedited Funds Availability Act.* Requires federally chartered financial institutions to have a demonstrable business continuity plan to ensure prompt availability of funds.
- *Fair Credit Reporting Act.* With the goal of ensuring that credit information is accurate and up-to-date, the Act also addresses the importance of internal controls and continuity.
- *Federal Deposit Insurance Corporation Improvement Act.* Requires all FDIC insured depository institutions with total assets of $500 million or more to certify that their internal control systems function properly.
- *Gramm-Leach-Bliley Act.* Addresses standards for developing and implementing administrative, technical and physical safeguards to protect the security, confidentiality and integrity of customer information.
- *Securities Exchange Act.* Spells out civil and criminal liability of directors and officers of business organizations for failure to protect information.
- *National Association of Securities Dealers Rule 108.* It compels each member to create and maintain a written business continuity plan identifying procedures for responding to an emergency or a significant business disruption.
- *National Association of Securities Dealers Rule 3500.* Mandates business continuity plan containing alternative communications among customers, employees and the organization, assessment of operational and financial impact, and the identification of mission critical systems.
- *National Association of Securities Dealers Rule 3520.* Requires NASD members to designate two emergency contact persons that NASD may contact in the emergency, and to provide NASD with that information.
- *Federal Financial Institutions Examination Council FIL 67-97.* Spells out the responsibility of a company's board of directors for ensuring that a comprehensive business resumption and contingency plan has been implemented.

- *National Future Association's Compliance Rule 2*-38. It requires all members to establish and maintain a written business continuity and disaster recovery plan.
- *Federal Financial Institutions Examination Council Policy SP-5.* Mandates corporate-wide contingency planning, including the development of recovery alternatives for distributed processing and service bureau processing.
- *Financial Industry Regulatory Authority Rule 4370.* Requires firms to create and maintain business continuity plans appropriate to the scale and the scope of their businesses, and to provide the Authority with emergency contact information.
- *New York Stock Exchange Rule 446.* It requires members to develop and maintain a written business continuity and contingency plan establishing procedures to be followed in the event of an emergency or a disruption.

Non-Banking and Finance regulations

- *Telecommunications Act.* As further developed by the Federal Communications Commission's Network Reliability and Interoperability Council, the Act spells out best practices for business continuity and disaster recovery in the telecommunications industry.
- *Federal Energy Regulatory Commission RM01-12-00.* Mandates disaster recovery plans for electric utility providers (excludes certain rural providers).
- *North American Electric Reliability Council's Security Guidelines for the Electricity Sector.* Provides general business continuity and disaster recovery guidelines aimed at reducing the likelihood of prolonged interruptions and prompt resumption of operations when interruptions occur.

Given the plethora of federal regulations that address one or more aspects of organizational resilience, it is advisable, from the compliance point of view, to become familiar with the general business continuity management guidelines within International Organization for Standardization (ISO) publication 17799 as a guide for satisfying most federal- and state-mandated BCP requirements. In addition, it is further recommended to review resilience related publications made available by the US National Institute of Standards and Technology

(NIST) for generally accepted principles and practices in the area of business continuity planning, paying particular attention to NIST's Information Technology Laboratory (ITL) publications.

Industry Localized Standards

In a manner similar to above outlined industry-specific localized regulations, localized US standards tend to emphasize primarily the Banking and Finance sector; however, Communications and Energy industries have also been targets for organizational resilience standard development. In view of that, the ensuing overview will first focus on the Banking and Finance related standards, followed by Communication standards.

US Banking and Finance Organizational Resilience Standards

- *American National Standards Institute and ASIS International Maturity Model of Organizational Resilience.* It offers guidance for the implementation of six-stage organizational resilience with the goal of creating a holistic environment for resilience management.
- *Federal Financial Institutions Examination Council Handbook.* Specifies that directors and managers are accountable for organization-wide contingency planning and for 'timely resumption of operations in the event of a disaster.'
- *PCI Security Standards Council's Data Security Standard.* Detail data security and recovery standards for disaster recovery, backup data sites.
- *Office of the Comptroller of the Currency Third Part Relationship Standard.* Provides operational guidance to national banks to managing the risk arising out of their business relationships with third parties.
- *Department of Homeland Security Private Sector Preparedness Standard.* It details the requirements for receiving DHS emergency management preparedness certification.
- *ASIS SPC.1 Standard.* Guides the establishment of robust organizational resilience programs.

- *Cellular Telecommunications and Internet Association's BCM Standard and Certification.* Offers guidelines for establishing industry-specific continuity capabilities.
- *Federal Electric Reliability Council's Security Standards for Electric Market Participants.* Mandates that every company operating a critical electric resource shall have contingency plans that define roles, responsibilities and actions for protecting the rest of the electric grid and market from the failure of its own critical resources.
- *Federal Drug Administration's Guidance on Computerized Systems in Clinical Trials.* Call for written contingency procedures, including backup and recovery of electronic records.

In addition to the above outlined standards, there are a number of industry-specific 'good practices' that have also been developed, the bulk of which, once again, are aimed at the Banking and Finance sector. The general tenor of those published examples is to provide banks and other financial institutions with more tangible guidance for mapping out, deployment and testing of business continuity, emergency management and disaster recovery programs. Examples of 'good practices' include the Office of the Comptroller of the Currency publications OCC 2003-18, OCC 99-9 and OCC 97-23 as well as the OCC Handbook.

Industry International Regulations

The focus of industry-specific international regulations mirrors that of industry-specific localized regulations by emphasizing, primarily the Banking and Finance sector. There are two specific sets of regulations addressing organizational resilience that are currently in use:

- *High Level Principles for Business Continuity jointly developed by the Basel Committee on Banking Supervision, International Organization of Securities Commissions and International Association of Insurance Supervisors.* The regulation details a comprehensive business continuity planning process and the responsibility for the development and ongoing function is explicitly assigned to a company's board of directors and its executive management.

- *Basel Capital Accord (II and III).* Further refines the business continuity and disaster recovery processes with the goal of strengthening banks' resilience to internal and external threats.

Industry International Standards

As the 'go-to' source of internationally recognized standards, the International Organization for Standardization (ISO) defines 'standard' as 'a document that provides requirements, specifications, guidelines or characteristics that can be used consistently to ensure that materials, products, processes and services are fit for their purpose.' Of the more than 20,000 standards developed and published by ISO, several address the issues of organizational resilience planning and management in the context of specific industries; more specifically:

- *ISO 16949.* Applicable to any supplier to automotive original equipment manufacturer, it calls for the preparation of contingency plans to satisfy customer requirements in the event of an emergency or a disruption.
- *ISO 17799.* Addresses information security in the context of business continuity planning for IT organizations.
- *ISO 14001.* Spells out emergency preparedness and response for organizations in the environmental management sector, or those whose operations directly affect the environment.
- *ISO 9001.* Addresses record retention and data availability requirements for organizations holding the 'quality management' certification.

***

As noted in the beginning of this chapter, compliance is a very dynamic part of the overall organizational threat abatement efforts outlined in this book. The combined forces of new legislative acts, regulatory decrees and judicial rulings are constantly reshaping norms and liabilities, thus the above discussion should be treated as merely a primer to organizational resilience related compliance.

In Closing

The Threat Exposure Management (TEM) framework described in this book represents an effort to develop a more holistic view of the diversity of threats confronting business and other organizations. The Framework is built on a premise that, from the standpoint of an organization, there is no compelling reason to treat the historically distinct functions of 'risk management', 'resilience' and 'change management' as stand-alone endeavors. To be sure, there are notable differences among the types of threats that are focal to each of those disciplines, but does it really matter if an unexpected financial jolt is due to a storm, supply chain problems, security breakdown or a shareholder class action? From the business point of view, the goal of broadly defined organizational threat abatement is to minimize adverse financial impact of any and all threats. Doing so in an economically sound manner requires a combination of knowledge (of sources, root causes, characteristics, and possible remedies), communication (cross-organization skill set and up-and-down organizational decisioning chain) and agility, which can only be attained in the context of a single management framework. The TEM framework was developed to serve as roadmap for organizations wishing to transform the historically *cost minimization* focused risk, disaster and change management endeavors into *benefit maximizing* management of the totality of threats confronting them.

I would like to further emphasize the potential value of approaching organizational threat abatement efforts from the standpoint of benefit maximization. In the realm of business, it is hard to think of an organization that does not have direct or indirect competitors and to whom gaining and maintaining competitive advantage is anything other than critical. In principle, the same is true of non-business organizations, which compete for resources, share of mind, voice or influence. Squeezed by the ever-expanding globalization, organizations are finding it increasingly difficult to compete – not surprisingly, they are constantly on a lookout for new sources of advantage. Yet the 'out-of-sight, out-of-mind' areas of risk, resilience and change management are rarely looked at as potential sources of competitive advantage, which is remarkably myopic. That is simply hard to understand as being in business entails a combination of economic and other resource deployment and uncertainty, which just about guarantees the possibility of adverse developments…A firm that can minimize its exposure to internal and external threats to its economic wellbeing will find its next source of competitive advantage.

Index

D

E

F

G

H

I

S

T

U

V

W

Bibliography

Aldrich, H. (1999), *Organizations Evolving,* Sage Publications, London, UK.

Armenakis, A., S. Harris & H. Field (1999), 'Paradigms in Organizational Change: Change Agents and Change Target Perspectives', in *Handbook of Organizational Behavior,* R. Golembiewski (ed.), Marcel Dekker, New York, NY.

Banasiewicz, A. D. (2016), *Cracking the Code of Executive Threat.* Routledge, New York, NY.

Banasiewicz, A. D. (2011), *Risk Profiling of Organizations,* Erudite Analytics, Bristol, RI.

Battilana, J., M. Gillmartin, M. Sengul, A. C. Pache & J. A. Alexander (2010), 'Leadership Competencies for Implementing Planned Organizational Change', *The Leadership Quarterly,* vol. 21, 422-438.

Benoit, W. L. (2004), 'Image Restoration Discourse and Crisis Communication', in D. P.. Millar and R. L. Heath (eds.), *Responding to Crisis: A Rhetorical Approach to Crisis Communication,* 263-280, Lawrence Erlbaum, Mahwah, NJ.

Berlo, D. K. (1960), *The Process of Communication,* Holt, Rinehart & Winston, New York, NY.

Black, F. & M. S. Scholes (1973), 'The Pricing of Options and Corporate Liabilities', *Journal of Political Economy*, 81(3), 637-654.

Bowman, E.H, (1980), 'A Risk/Return Paradox for Strategic Management,' *Sloan Management Review*, vol. 21, 17-31.

Bowman, E.H, (1982), 'Risk Seeking by Troubled Firms,' *Sloan Management Review*, vol. 23, 33-42.

Churchland, P. S. & T. J. Sejnowski (1992), *The Computational Brain*, MIT Press.

Continuity Insights & KPMG (2014), *Global BCM Benchmarking Study.*

Coombs, T. W. (2007), 'Protecting Organization Reputations During a Crisis: The Development & Application of Situational Crisis Communication Theory' *Corporate Reputation Review*, vol.10(3), 163-176.

Darwin, C. (1859), *On the Origins of Species by Means of Natural Selection,* J. Murray, London, UK.

Davenport, T. H. (2006), 'Competing on Analytics', *Harvard Business Review,* January, 98-107.

DRI International (2012), *Professional Practices for Business Continuity Planners.*

Duckert, G. H. (2011), *Practical Enterprise Risk Management: A Business Process Approach,* Wiley, Hoboken, NJ.

Dunphy, D. C. & Stace, D. A. (1988), 'Transformational and Coercive Strategies for Planned Organizational Change: Beyond the OD Model', *Organization Studies*, vol. 9(3) pp. 317–334.

Fishbein M. (1963), 'An Investigation of Relationships between Beliefs about an Object and Attitudes toward that Object,' *Human Relations* vol. 16, 233-240.

Fishbein M. & Ajzen I. (1975), *Belief, Attitude, Intention and Behavior: An Introduction to Theory and Research*, Addison-Wesley, Reading, MA.

Galpin, T. (1996), *The Human Side of Change: A Practical Guide to Organizational Redesign,* Jossey-Bass, San Francisco, CA.

Hannan, M. T. & Freeman, J. (1988), *Organizational Ecology,* Harvard University Press, Cambridge, MA.

Heath, R. (2008), 'A Crisis Management Perspective of Business Continuity', in Hiles, A. editor, *The Definitive Handbook of Business Continuity Management,* 2nd ed., Wiley, New York, NY.

Hiatt, J. M. (2006), *ADKAR: A Model of Change in Business, Government and Our Community,* Prosci Research, Loveland, CO.

Higgs, M. & Rowland, D. (2005), 'All Changes Great and Small: Exploring Approaches to Change and Its Leadership', *Journal of Change Management*, vol. 5(2) pp. 121-151.

Hiles, A. (2014), *Business Continuity Management: Global Best Practices,* 4th edition, Rothstein Publishing.

Horizon Scan (2014), *Business Continuity Institute British Standards Institute.*

Hubbard, D. (2007), *How to Measure Anything: Finding the Value of Intangibles in Business*, John Wiley & Sons, Hoboken, NJ, pg. 46.

International Monetary Fund (2009), *World Economic Outlook* database.

Jeffrey, R. C. (1992), *Probability and the Art of Judgment.* Cambridge University Press, New York, NY, 54-55.

Judson, A. (1991), *Changing Behavior in Organizations: Minimizing Resistance to Change,* Basil Blackwell, Cambridge, MA.

Kahneman, D. (2011), *Thinking, Fast and Slow,* Farrar, Strauss and Giroux, New York, NY.

Kolmogorov, A. N., *Foundations of the Theory of Probability*, 1950.

Kotter, J. (1995), 'Leading Change: Why Transformation Efforts Fail', *Harvard Business Review,* 73(2), 59-67.

Lam, J. (2014), *Enterprise Risk Management: From Incentives to Controls,* 2nd ed., Wiley, Hoboken, NJ.

Lewin, K. (1943), 'Psychological Ecology', in Cartwright, D. (ed.), *Field Theory in Social Science,* Social Science Paperbacks, London, UK.

Lewin, K. (1947), 'Group Decisions and Social Change', in Newcomb and Hartley (eds.), *Readings in Social Psychology,* Henry Holt, New York, NY.

Liu, B. F., Austin, L., & Jin, Y. (2011), 'How Publics Respond to Crisis Communication Strategies: The Interplay of Information Form and Source', *Public Relations Review*, vol. 37(4), 345-353.

Marchetti, A. M. (2012), *Enterprise Risk Management: Best Practices from Assessment to Ongoing Compliance,* Wiley, Hoboken, NJ.

Markowitz, H. (1952), 'Portfolio Selection', *Journal of Finance*, 7 (1), 77-91.

Pierre Simon de Leplace (1812), *Analytical Theory of Probability.*

Pivotal IT (2012), *10 Backup and Disaster Recovery Statistics You Must Know.*

Prochaska, J. O., DiClemente, C. C. & Norcross, J. C. (1992), 'In Search of How People Change: Applications to the Addictive Behaviors', *American Psychologist,* vol. 47, pp. 1102-1114.

Quinn, J.B., P. Anderson, & S. Finkelstein (1996), 'Managing Professional Intellect: Making the Most of the Best*', Harvard Business Review*, March-April, 71-80.

R. A. Fisher (1925), *Statistical Methods for Research Workers*, 1st edition.

Rosenblum, B. & F. Kuttner (2008), *Quantum Enigma, Physics Encounters Consciousness.*, Oxford University Press, New York, NY.

Rowan, F. (1996), 'The High Stakes of Risk Communication', *Preventive Medicine,* vol. 25(1), 26-29.

Shannon, C. E. & W. Weaver (1949), *The Mathematical Theory of Communication,* University of Illinois Press, Urbana, IL.

Sharpe, W. F. (1964), 'Capital Asset Prices: A Theory of Market Equilibrium under Conditions of Risk', *Journal Finance*, 19 (3), 425-442.

Slywotzky, A. J. & J. Drzik (2005), 'Countering the Biggest Risk of All', *Harvard Business Review*, April, 78-88.

The 2015 Gemalto and SafeNet, *Breach Level Index,* an industry report.

Tichy, N. & Devanna, M. A. (1990), *The Transformational Leader,* 2nd ed., Wiley, New York, NY.

Thompson, M., R. Ellis & A. Wildavsky (1990), *Cultural Theory*, Westview Press, San Francisco, CA.

Van de Ven A. H. & Poole, M. S. (1995), 'Explaining Development and Change in Organizations', *Academy of Management Review*, vol. 20(3), pp. 510-540.

List of Figures & Tables

Professional Organizations

American Society for Healthcare Risk Management (ASHRM)
Association of Change Management Professionals (ACMP)
Business Continuity Institute (BCI)
DRI International (DRII)
Global Association of Risk Professionals (GARP)
Institute of Risk Management (IRM)
International Association of Emergency Managers (IAEM)
International Consortium for Organizational Resilience (ICOR)
Private Risk Management Association (PRMA)
Professional Risk Managers' International Association (PRMIA)
Public Risk Management Association (PRIMA)
Risk and Insurance Management Society (RIMS)
Society of Actuaries (SOA)
Society for Risk Analysis (SRA)
Society of Risk Management Consultants (SRMC)
The Change Management Institute (CMI)
The Risk Management Association (RMA)
University Risk Management and Insurance Association (URMIA)

www.ingramcontent.com/pod-product-compliance
Lightning Source LLC
LaVergne TN
LVHW022154200926
848481LV00006B/1743
* 9 7 8 0 9 8 1 5 6 9 0 6 2 *